Parallel Complexity Theory

Ian Parberry
Whitmore Laboratory
Pennsylvania State University, USA

Parallel Complexity Theory

Pitman, London

John Wiley & Sons, Inc., New York, Toronto

MATH.-STAT.

02609757

PITMAN PUBLISHING
128 Long Acre, London WC2E 9AN

© Ian Parberry 1987

First published 1987

Available in the Western Hemisphere from
John Wiley & Sons, Inc.
605 Third Avenue, New York, NY 10158

ISSN 0268-7534

British Library Cataloguing in Publication Data
Parberry, Ian
    Parallel complexity theory.—(Research
    notes in theoretical computer science,
    ISSN 0268-7534).
    1. Parallel programming (Computer science)
    I. Title   II. Series
    004'.35   QA76.6

    ISBN 0-273-08783-5

Library of Congress Cataloging in Publication Data

Parberry, Ian.
    Parallel complexity theory/Ian Parberry.
        p. cm.—(Research notes in theoretical computer science.
    ISSN 0268-7534)
        Bibliography: p.
        Includes index.
        ISBN 0-470-20931-3 (Wiley) : 22.95 (est.)
        1. Computational complexity.   2. Parallel processing (Electronic
    computers)   I. Title.   II. Series.
    QA267.P37   1987   004'.35–dc19

Reproduced and printed by photolithography
in Great Britain by Biddles Ltd, Guildford

Foreword

Research in theoretical computer science has experienced tremendous growth both in the depth to which older theories have been pursued and also in the number of new problem areas that have arisen. While theoretical computer science is mathematical in nature, its goals include the development of an understanding of the nature of computation as well as the solution of specific problems that arise in the practice of computing.

The purpose of this series of monographs is to make available to the professional community expositions of topics that play an important role in theoretical computer science or that provide bridges with other aspects of computer science and with aspects of mathematics. The scope of the series may be considered to be that represented by the leading journals in the field. The editors intend that the scope will expand as the field grows and welcome submissions from all of those interested in theoretical computer science.

Ronald V. Book
Main Editor

Contents

Preface

Parallel complexity theory, the study of resource-bounded parallel computation, is surely one of the fastest-growing areas of theoretical Computer Science. In the light of this, it would be foolish to attempt an encyclopedic coverage of the field. However, it is the belief of the author that its foundations are becoming increasingly clear and well-defined. This Monograph is an attempt to present these foundations in a unified and coherent manner.

The material contained herein is aimed at advanced Graduate students or researchers in theoretical Computer Science who wish to gain an insight into parallel complexity theory. It is assumed that the reader has (in addition to a certain level of mathematical maturity) a general knowledge of Computer Science, and familiarity with automata theory, formal languages, complexity theory and analysis of algorithms. The interested reader may wish to augment his or her knowledge with books by Goldschlager and Lister [47], Hopcroft and Ullman [57], Garey and Johnson [39] and Aho, Hopcroft and Ullman [3].

This Monograph contains some of results that the author feels are fundamental, important, or exceptionally beautiful. The reader is free to make his or her own judgements. Lack of space and the current dynamic nature of the field prevent coverage of much recent material. In particular, results that are probabilistic in nature (both probabilistic proofs and results that concern probabilistic computations) have in general been avoided. This Monograph could not hope to do justice to so large and complicated a topic in the limited space available. There are sufficient results in probabilistic complexity theory to warrant a book devoted entirely to that subject.

The main part of this Monograph consists of twelve chapters. Chapter 1, the Introduction, sets the scene for the remainder of the work by elucidating our aims and motivation. Chapter 2 examines some early work in the field including sorting networks, permutation networks and the parallel prefix problem. Chapters 3 and 4 develop a parallel machine model that we will use throughout the remainder of the Monograph. Chapter 5 examines the parallel computation thesis, which is an attempt to characterize time-bounded parallel computation in terms of space-bounded sequential computation. In Chapter 6 we explore the computational power of our machine model by providing upper and lower-bounds for some problems of interest. Chapter 7 contains some elementary results concerning a restricted variant of our machine model. Chapter 8 deals with the asymptotically optimal sorting network of Ajtai, Komlós and Szemerédi [5,6]. The results of Chapters 7 and 8 will be used in Chapter 9 to provide a restricted network which is universal for the general model with a modest increase in resources. Chapter 9 also considers the extended parallel computation thesis, an attempt to characterize time and hardware-bounded parallel computation. Chapter 10 is devoted to a more detailed discussion of universal parallel machines, whilst Chapter 11 covers unbounded fan-in parallelism and provides a new parallel computation thesis which operates in that framework. Finally, Chapter 12 is the Conclusion, which attempts to summarize and put into perspective the results of the previous ten chapters.

This Monograph has grown, under the encouragement of Ron Book, from the author's Doctoral Dissertation [91], which was supervised by M. S. Paterson. The preliminary notes were used for a Graduate-level course on parallel complexity theory at the Pennsylvania State University in 1986 and 1987. Students were required to complete homework problems plus a fairly substantial project (one of the choices for the latter being a summary of one of the papers from recent conference proceedings). With this in mind, some problems are provided at the end of most chapters. Naturally, some chapters are a more fruitful source of problems than others. None of the problems are particularly difficult, the most intransigent requiring the work of perhaps a few hours. No indication of difficulty is provided, since such qualitative judgements are usually unreliable. In the interests of fostering originality, no solutions are given. An attempt has been made to lead the reader to the threshold of the solution during the relevant chapter. If solutions have appeared elsewhere in print, they are either difficult to obtain or are substantially more complicated or more general than necessary. Students requiring inspiration will no doubt consult them despite these difficulties.

Many people have directly or indirectly contributed to the ideas contained in this Monograph. The author is particularly indebted to Les Goldschlager, Friedhelm Meyer auf der Heide, Mike Paterson, Nick Pippenger, Walter Ruzzo, Georg Schnitger, Janos Simon and Hans-Ulrich Simon for numerous discussions, either in-person or by correspondence. The author is also grateful to students, particularly Joe Niederberger and Eric Mettala, who have offered helpful suggestions and pointed out minor errors in the manuscript. The author would particularly like to thank an anonymous referee, whose careful reading of, and thoughtful comments on a rough draft of this manuscript were greatly appreciated.

Ian Parberry,
University Park,
Pennsylvania, U.S.A.
May, 1987.

To my parents
and
to Virginia,

for putting up with me during
the two most difficult periods of my life:
growing up and writing this book, respectively.

1 Introduction

As recently as 1980, Schwàrtz [112] complained of an apparent lack of theoretical results concerning the computational complexity of parallel or concurrent algorithms.

> "In the serial case, the design of algorithms has come to be illuminated by a growing body of theoretical knowledge concerning the ultimate limits of algorithm performance.... Until a like body of theoretical knowledge has been developed for highly concurrent algorithms, we will have little basis for judging the extent to which a given concurrent approach can be improved."

Two of the most important and fundamental papers in the field of parallel complexity theory (those of Goldschlager [41,45], and Pippenger [102]) had already appeared by the time Schwartz's paper reached publication. Since then, the flow of results has increased from a trickle to a steady stream, and is now threatening to become a flood. Today, parallel complexity theory must be ranked as one of the fastest-growing fields of theoretical Computer Science.

A theoretical treatment of parallel computation is an attempt to formalize the intuitive concept of a "parallel computer" based on practical experience or reasonable expectations. Amongst the questions which should be addressed by such a formal exposition are the following:

- What do we mean by parallel computation?
- What constitutes a good model of a parallel computer?
- What are the resources of interest, and how should they be defined?
- How should we express parallel algorithms?
- What kind of problems lend themselves to a fast solution on a parallel computer?
- What resources do we need to solve a given interesting problem in parallel?

The latter question appears to be the most popular, judging by sheer volume of contributions (for example, consult [105,127] and the references contained therein). In contrast, relatively little attention has been paid to the first four questions, which has resulted in a proliferation of parallel machine models in the current literature. Even the most popular model, the shared-memory machine (consisting of a collection of RAMs communicating via a shared memory, see, for example, [33,45]) has many variants.

Intuitively, a parallel machine should consist of a collection of processors which in some way co-operate in order to compute a result. Obviously there are many ways of formalizing this intuition. Compare the SIMDAG of Goldschlager [45] to the model of Galil and Paul [38]. The processors of the former are RAMs; the latter allow processors which range from RAMs to finite-state machines. Lev, Pippenger and Valiant [74] use RACs. Goldschlager has almost identical processors which are all started simultaneously at the start of the computation, and communicate via a shared memory. Galil and Paul have "similar" processors which start up at run-time, and communicate via direct processor-to-processor links. Some of the more obvious variations on these models include the instruction-set (for example, should multiplication be allowed?), and memory access conflicts (should multiple attempts to write to a shared memory location be allowed as in [45], or should even multiple reads be disallowed, as in [74,118]?). Some of these differences are cosmetic in nature, while others are more crucial.

We will choose a model which consists of a network of interconnected RAMs; each RAM can in one step perform an internal computation, or read from or write to a register belonging to one of its neighbours. We believe that the network paradigm is fundamental to the understanding of parallel computation. One attraction is the fact that it possesses a certain theoretical elegance. The network model has the advantage of encompassing a number of popular machine models, for example, a shared-memory machine (see Section 4.2) is just a network where all processors can communicate with a single distinguished processor and no other, and that distinguished processor remains idle throughout the computation. The number of extant papers which use the shared-memory model attest to its ease of programming, and its usefulness as a tool for proving and communicating theoretical results. It is widely accepted, however, that the shared-memory model is not a viable architecture. By placing restrictions on our network model, it is possible to define a practical variant in a natural and elegant fashion.

The aim of this Monograph, then, is to shed some light on the nature of parallel computation. We shall do this by presenting a unified theory of parallel computation based on a network model. We shall demonstrate its utility by providing some fairly concise and elegant proofs of results from the current literature (which will occasionally lead to improved resource bounds or more general theorems). We will also attempt to provide answers to the questions posed at the start of this Introduction.

It should be noted that this is a *theoretical* treatment of parallel computation, and as such is based upon a number of assumptions which are widely accepted amongst workers in the field of parallel complexity theory. Although our model is synchronous (in the sense that the instruction-cycles of the processors are synchronized), we will see in Section 4.3 that this is not an important restriction. Synchronous models are far easier to deal with than asynchronous ones. We assume that inter-processor communications can take place within a single instruction-cycle. In the real world, this assumption is unlikely to be true for large numbers of processors; a complexity theory based on this observation will differ quite radically from ours [111]. However, we feel fairly safe in making the assumption for networks consisting of a small number (say in the millions) of fairly large processors (about the size of a microprocessor), even though it is unlikely to hold for, say, individual gates in a VLSI chip.

Finally, the reader should note that throughout this work, all logarithms are to base 2, N denotes the set of non-negative integers, Z the set of integers, and R the set of real numbers. If $c \in N$, $d \in Z$, then d *mod* c is defined to be the unique integer $a \in N$ such that $0 \leq a < c$ and there exists $b \in Z$ such that $a + bc = d$. For those unfamiliar with the "order" notation, we provide the following reminder. Let $f, g: N \rightarrow R^+$ (where R^+ denotes the set of positive real numbers). We say that:

1. $f(n) = O(g(n))$ if there exists $c \in R^+$, $n_0 \in N$ such that for all $n \geq n_0$, $f(n) \leq c\, g(n)$.

2. $f(n) = \Omega(g(n))$ if there exists $c \in R^+$, $n_0 \in N$ such that for all $n \geq n_0$, $f(n) \geq c\, g(n)$.

3. $f(n) = \Theta(g(n))$ if $f(n) = O(g(n))$ and $f(n) = \Omega(g(n))$.

4. $f(n) = o(g(n))$ if $\lim_{n \to \infty} \dfrac{f(n)}{g(n)} = 0$.

2 Combinational Circuits

Early research in parallel complexity theory focussed on combinational circuits, that is, circuits without feedback loops. In this model, we are given as "basic units" a collection of gates which can compute certain useful functions on a fixed number of inputs in one time-unit. Our aim is to construct a circuit which is efficient in both parallel time and hardware to compute a desirable function on n inputs. We are allowed to wire the gates together in an arbitrary manner without feedback loops. We use the *depth* and *size* of the circuit as a measure of parallel time and hardware respectively. The *depth* of a combinational circuit is the maximum number of gates on a path from an input to an output. The *size* is the number of gates used.

The first problem that we will tackle is that of sorting n values. The "basic units", called *comparators,* are gates which can sort two inputs. The circuits are further constrained in a manner more fully described in Section 2.1. In that section we also prove some useful preliminary results on sorting networks. In Section 2.2 we meet sorting networks based on Batcher's odd-even merge and bitonic sorting networks, with depth $O(\log^2 n)$ and size $O(n \log^2 n)$. Section 2.3 investigates a slightly easier problem, that of performing fixed permutations using basic units called *switches.* We meet Waksman's permutation network, which has logarithmic depth and log-linear size. Finally, Section 2.4 presents the parallel prefix circuit of Fischer and Ladner, of logarithmic depth and linear size.

2.1. Sorting Networks

One of the early investigations into parallel complexity theory concerned a variant of the sorting problem, dubbed the *Bose-Nelson sorting problem* by Floyd and Knuth [31], after Bose and Nelson [17]. We are given a basic unit of hardware called a *comparator.* A comparator takes two integers as input, and outputs them in ascending order. A *comparator network* is a circuit built from comparators according to the following constraints.

4

1. The values to be sorted are treated as atomic units. They may neither be divided nor duplicated.

2. The values travel in n *channels,* which we will represent in our diagrams as vertical lines. The inputs will be presented at the top of the network, and will appear in some permuted order at the bottom.

3. The network is divided vertically into a finite number of *levels,* which are numbered consecutively, starting at 0. The 0th level consists of the inputs. Each of the subsequent levels contains one or more comparators. Each comparator is placed on two channels. At most one comparator is placed on any channel at any particular level. We will depict a comparator using a horizontal line between the two channels, with heavy dots emphasizing the connection-points (see Figure 2.1.1).

We will number the channels 1 through n, in ascending order from left to right. We will say that channel i *carries value v at level j* on input $x_1,...,x_n$ if either

(i) $j = 0$ and $x_i = v$, or

(ii) $j > 0$, there is no comparator on channel i at level j, and channel i carries value v at level j-1, or

(iii) $j > 0$, there is a comparator between channels i and k at level j, $k < i$, channel i carries value v_i at level j-1, channel k carries value v_k at level j-1, and $v = \max(v_i,v_k)$, or

(iv) $j > 0$, there is a comparator between channels i and k at level j, $k > i$, channel i carries value v_i at level j-1, channel k carries value v_k at level j-1, and $v = \min(v_i,v_k)$.

The output of the network consists of the n values carried by the channels at the final level, in left-to-right order. If they are always in ascending order from left-to-right, the network is called a *sorting network.*

Figure 2.1.1 A comparator.

Each level of a comparator network consists of a set of independent comparisons which may be performed in parallel. The number of levels is thus a reasonable measure of parallel time. We will call this the *depth* of the network. We are also interested in the *size* of the network, that is, the number of comparators used. For example, consider the following algorithm for sorting four values. In parallel, compare the first value with the second, and the third with the fourth. This is the first level of the network. Clearly the minimum of the two minima is the smallest of the four values, and the maximum of the two maxima is the largest. This is the second level of the network. However, at that point we know nothing of the relative order of the remaining two values. The third level of the network compares them. This gives us the depth-3, size-5 sorting network in Figure 2.1.2.

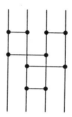

Figure 2.1.2 A sorting network with 4 inputs, of size 5 and depth 3.

We have chosen to build our network using comparators which send the smallest value to the left, and the largest to the right. Let us call these *min-max* comparators, as opposed to *max-min* comparators, which send the largest to the left and the smallest to the right. We have not lost anything by restricting ourselves to min-max comparators:

Theorem 2.1.1 (Floyd-Knuth) For every sorting network built from a mixture of max-min and min-max comparators there is a sorting network with the same size and depth built purely from min-max comparators.

Proof. Suppose C is a sorting network built from min-max and max-min comparators, of depth d and size s. Suppose we represent each comparator as a 3-tuple $<a,b,c>$, where a denotes its level number, and b and c the channels on which its min-output and max-output emerge respectively. Note that a min-max comparator will have $b < c$, while a max-min comparator will have $b > c$.

Let Π be a permutation of the set $\{1,...,n\}$, that is, $\Pi:\{1,...,n\}\rightarrow\{1,...,n\}$ and is one-to-one and onto. Let (i,j) denote the permutation Π such that $\Pi(i) = j$, $\Pi(j) = i$ and $\Pi(k) = k$ for $k \neq i,j$. Define the product of two permutations $\Pi = \Pi_1\Pi_2$ by $\Pi(i) = \Pi_1(\Pi_2(i))$ for $i\in\{1,...,n\}$. Define a Π-*sorter* to be a comparator network whose outputs are in sorted order after application of Π to the channels below the final level. Thus, in this new terminology, a sorting network is an I-sorter, where I denotes the identity permutation.

We will represent a comparator network as a list of 3-tuples, each of which represents a comparator. We will insist that the list is in ascending order on the first index, that is, comparators on the lowest-numbered levels appear first. Let $C = <C_1,C_2,...,C_s>$, where $C_i = <a_i,b_i,c_i>$ for $1 \leq i < s$, and $a_i \leq a_{i+1}$ for $1 \leq i < s$. Consider the following algorithm:

> $L:=C$
> $\Pi:=I$
> **for** $i:=1$ **to** s **do**
>   **if** $b_i > c_i$ **then**
>   **for** $j:=i$ **to** s **do**
>   Consider $L_j = <a_j,b_j,c_j>$
>   **if** $b_j = b_i$ **then** $b_j:=c_i$
>   **else if** $b_j = c_i$ **then** $b_j:=b_i$
>   **if** $c_j = b_i$ **then** $c_j:=c_i$
>   **else if** $c_j = c_i$ **then** $c_j:=b_i$
> $\Pi:=\Pi\ (b_i,c_i)$

Claim 1. After the ith iteration of the outer for-loop, L is a Π-sorter, for $0 \leq i \leq s$.

Proof. The result follows by induction on i. The hypothesis is true for $i = 0$, since immediately before the first iteration, $L = C$, and is thus an I-sorter. Now suppose that the hypothesis is true after the $(i-1)^{st}$ iteration. There are two cases to consider.

Case 1. $b_i < c_i$. No change is made to either L or Π, so L remains a Π-sorter by the induction hypothesis.

Case 2. $b_i > c_i$. The effect of the algorithm is to "swap" channels b_i and c_i "below" level i. Thus by the induction hypothesis, the outputs are Π-sorted, since Π is modified to swap the outputs on those channels back into sorted order.

□

Claim 2. After the ith iteration of the outer for-loop, $\{L_1,...,L_i\}$ are all min-max comparators.

Proof. The proof follows easily by induction on i. □

Claim 3. On termination of the algorithm, $\Pi = I$.

Proof. When the algorithm has terminated, L is a Π-sorter for some Π (by Claim 1) built from min-max comparators (by Claim 2). Suppose we give L a sequence of integers which are already sorted in ascending order. Since L is built from min-max comparators, no swapping is done; the values stay on their respective channels. Thus the values are still in ascending order when they reach the outputs. Furthermore, they are still sorted after application of Π, which implies $\Pi = I$. □

Thus by Claims 1, 2 and 3, on termination of the algorithm, L is a sorting network built from min-max comparators. It is easy to prove by induction that L has depth d and size s. □

An obvious method for proving that an n-input comparator network sorts is to try all n! different permutations of n distinct numbers as inputs to the network. However, slightly fewer trials suffice. The following Theorem is attributed to Bouricius by Knuth [65].

Theorem 2.1.2 (The Zero-One Principle). An n-input comparator network is a sorting network iff it sorts all sequences of n zeros and ones.

Proof. Clearly if a comparator network sorts, then it will correctly sort all sequences of zeros and ones. Conversely, suppose we have a comparison network which sorts all sequences of zeros and ones. Suppose $\alpha \in \mathbf{R}$ is a constant. Define $h_\alpha : \mathbf{Z} \to \mathbf{Z}$ as follows:

$$h_\alpha(x) = \begin{cases} 1 & \text{if } x \geq \alpha \\ 0 & \text{otherwise} \end{cases}$$

Claim. For $j \geq 0$, if for inputs $x_1, x_2, ..., x_n$ a channel carries the value β at level j, then for inputs $h_\alpha(x_1), h_\alpha(x_2), ..., h_\alpha(x_n)$ it carries the value $h_\alpha(\beta)$ at level j.

Proof. The result follows by induction on j. The hypothesis is trivially true for $j = 0$. Now suppose $j > 0$. Consider channel i, which has value β at level j on input $x_1, ..., x_n$. We will write $v(i,j) = \beta$. We will also write $v_\alpha(i,j)$ for the value that channel i carries at level j on input $h_\alpha(x_1), ..., h_\alpha(x_n)$. If there is no

8

comparator on channel i at level j, then $v_\alpha(i,j) = h_\alpha(\beta)$ by the induction hypothesis. Suppose there is a comparator between channels i and k at level j. There are two cases to consider.

Case 1. i < k. Suppose $v(i,j{-}1) = \beta_i$, $v(k,j{-}1) = \beta_k$. Then $\beta = \min(\beta_i,\beta_k)$. Thus:

$$v_\alpha(i) = \min(v_\alpha(i,j{-}1),v_\alpha(k,j{-}1))$$

$$= \min(h_\alpha(\beta_i),h_\alpha(\beta_k)) \qquad \text{(by the induction hypothesis)}$$

$$= h_\alpha(\min(\beta_i,\beta_k)) \qquad \text{(by the definition of } h_\alpha)$$

$$= h_\alpha(\beta)$$

Case 2. k < i. Similar to Case 1, replacing "min" by "max". □

Suppose we have an n-input comparator network C which sorts all sequences of zeros and ones. Suppose we give it inputs $x_1,...,x_n$. Let the outputs, in left-to-right order, be $y_1,...,y_n$. For a contradiction, suppose that they are not in ascending order, in particular that $y_i > y_{i+1}$ for some $1 \le i < n$. By the above Claim, when C is given the inputs $h_\alpha(x_1),...,h_\alpha(x_n)$, its outputs are, in left-to-right order, $h_\alpha(y_1),...,h_\alpha(y_n)$. Choose $\alpha = (y_i+y_{i+1})/2$. Then $h_\alpha(y_i) = 1$ and $h_\alpha(y_{i+1}) = 0$, which contradicts the fact that C sorts all sequences of zeros and ones. Therefore $y_1,...,y_n$ must be in sorted order, and so C is a sorting network. □

2.2. Batcher's Sorting Networks

The sorting networks in this section are due to Batcher [10]. Since we are mainly interested in the *asymptotic* depth and size complexity of sorting networks, it is sufficient to consider sorting n inputs where n is a power of 2 (since if we wish to sort an arbitrary number of values, we can add enough large "dummy" elements to fill out n to a power of 2; this increases the number of inputs, and hence the size and depth, by at most a small constant multiple). This has the added benefit of simplifying the proofs. More detailed proofs for general n can be found in Knuth [65]. Let p be a power of 2. Consider the following recursive description of a network to merge two sorted sequences $a = <a_1,...,a_p>$ and $b = <b_1,...,b_p>$. If $p = 1$ then the network consists of a single comparator. If p > 1 then recursively merge the odd-numbered elements of a with the odd-numbered elements of b, merge the even-numbered elements of a with the even-numbered elements of b, then insert a final level of comparators between channel 2i and channel 2i+1, $1 \leq i < n/2$. Figure 2.2.1 shows the construction of M_p, a comparator network to merge two sorted p-sequences, from two copies of $M_{p/2}$ according to this description. The network thus obtained is called the *odd-even merging network*.

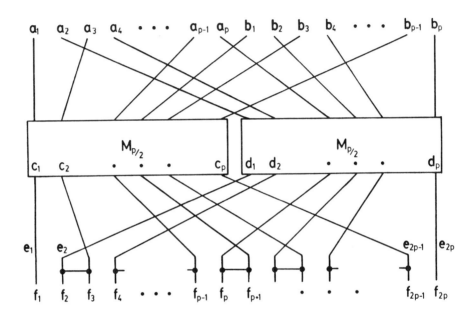

Figure 2.2.1 Batcher's odd-even merging network.

Theorem 2.2.1 M_p will merge two sorted sequences of length p.
Proof. The proof will follow by induction on p. The hypothesis is clearly true for $p = 1$. Now suppose that the two recursive sub-networks merge correctly. We will make use of the fact that the Zero-One Principle holds for merging networks (see Exercise 2.1). Let $a = <a_1,...,a_p>$ and $b = <b_1,...,b_p>$ denote the two sorted input sequences, $c = <c_1,...,c_p>$ denote the output from the left-hand ("odd") recursive sub-network, $d = <d_1,...,d_p>$ denote the output from the right-hand ("even") recursive sub-network, $e = <e_1,...,e_{2p}>$ denote the sequence of values immediately before the final level of comparators, and $f = <f_1,...,f_{2p}>$ denote the output, in left-to-right order (see Figure 2.2.1).

10

Suppose that a consists of g zeros followed by p-g ones, and that b consists of h zeros followed by p-h ones. Then, by the induction hypothesis, c consists of $\lceil g/2 \rceil + \lceil h/2 \rceil$ zeros followed by p- $\lceil g/2 \rceil$ - $\lceil h/2 \rceil$ ones, and d consists of $\lfloor g/2 \rfloor + \lfloor h/2 \rfloor$ zeros followed by p- $\lfloor g/2 \rfloor$ - $\lfloor h/2 \rfloor$ ones. Thus c has either the same number, one more, or two more zeros than d. Therefore, noting that $e = <c_1,d_1,c_2,d_2,...,c_p,d_p>$, there are three cases to consider:

Case 1. c has the same number of zeros as d. If $g = h = 0$ then the output is sorted. Otherwise e is of the form $e = <0,0,...0,1,0,1,1,...,1>$, more specifically, $e_i = 0$ for $1 \le i \le g+h-1$, $e_{g+h} = 1$, $e_{g+h+1} = 0$ and $e_i = 1$ for $g+h+1 < i \le n$. Since g=h, g+h is even, and therefore there is a comparator between e_{g+h} and e_{g+h+1} in the final level. This ensures that f is in sorted order.

Case 2. c has one more zero than d. Then e is already sorted, which implies that f is sorted.

Case 3. c has two more zeros than d. Then, as in Case 2, e is already sorted, which implies that f is sorted.

In each case, the final output is sorted. Therefore, the merger correctly merges all sequences of zeros and ones, which by the Zero-One Principle implies that it merges all sequences of integers. □

Let d(p) be the depth, and s(p) the size of an odd-even merging network which merges two sorted sequences of length p. Then $d(1) = 1$, and for $p > 1$, $d(p) = d(p/2)+1$. By induction on p, $d(p) = \log p + 1$. Also, $s(1) = 1$, and for $p > 1$, $s(p) = 2s(p/2)+p-1$. By induction on p, $s(p) = p \log p + 1$.

The following is the recursive description of an n-input sorting network, called the *odd-even sorting network*. If $n = 1$, then the network is empty. If $n > 1$, sort the first half of the values recursively, sort the second half of the values recursively, and then merge the two sorted sequences using an odd-even merging network. Figure 2.2.2 shows the construction of S_n, a network for sorting n inputs, from two copies of $S_{n/2}$ and one copy of $M_{n/2}$ according to this description.

The correctness of the odd-even sorting network is easily proved by induction. Let D(p) be the depth, and S(p) the size of an odd-even sorting network with n inputs. Then $D(1) = 0$ and for $n > 1$,

$$D(n) = D(n/2)+d(n/2)$$

$$= D(n/2)+\log n.$$

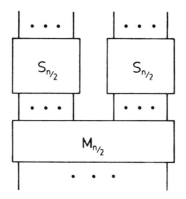

Figure 2.2.2 Batcher's odd-even sorting network.

Therefore, by induction,

$$D(n) = \frac{1}{2}(\log n)(\log n + 1).$$

Also, $S(1) = 0$ and for $n > 1$,

$$S(n) = 2\,S(n/2) + s(n/2)$$

$$= 2\,S(n/2) + \frac{n}{2}\,(\log n - 1) + 1.$$

Therefore, by induction,

$$S(n) = \frac{n}{4}(\log n)(\log n - 1) + n - 1.$$

Figure 2.2.3 shows an odd-even sorting network with 32 inputs, of depth 15 and size 191. The recursive structure of this network is immediately apparent.

Thus we see that it is possible to sort n inputs in depth $O(\log^2 n)$ and size $O(n \log^2 n)$, with very small constant multiples in the resource bounds (certainly less than 1 for large enough n, even when n is not a power of 2). Recently, Ajtai, Komlós and Szemerédi [5,6] demonstrated that depth $O(\log n)$ and size $O(n \log n)$ is possible. This new network (which we will describe in more detail in Chapter 8) is of great interest theoretically because it is asymptotically optimal in both size and depth (see Exercise 2.2). However, since the constant multiples in the depth and size bounds are so large, the odd-even sorting network outperforms it

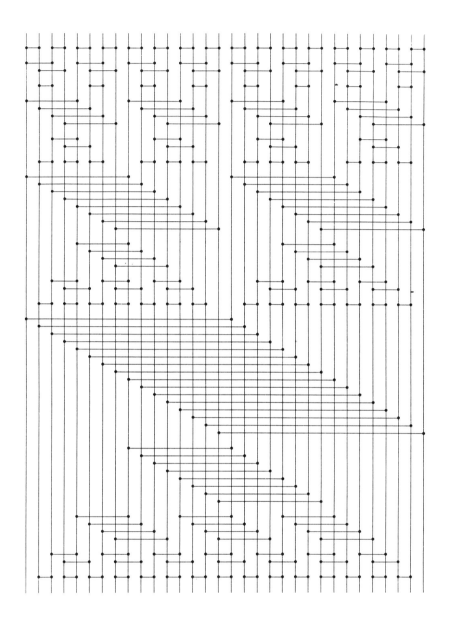

Figure 2.2.3 An odd-even sorting network with 32 inputs.

for all practical values of n.

In [10] Batcher presents a second sorting network which is based, not upon merging, but upon a principle which he calls *bitonic sorting*. To simplify the presentation, we will demonstrate the construction when the number of values to be sorted is a power of 2. Let p be a power of 2. A *bitonic* sequence of length p is a sequence of p integers, the first q of which are non-decreasing, and the last p-q of which are non-increasing (or vice-versa), for some $0 \le q \le p$. The following is a recursive method for sorting a bitonic sequence. If $p = 1$, the network is empty. Suppose $p > 1$, and the input is a bitonic sequence $a = <a_1,...,a_p>$. Compare a_i with $a_{i+p/2}$, for $1 \le i \le p/2$. Separate the min-outputs and the max-outputs from these comparators, and recursively sort each group. The result is a sorted sequence. Figure 2.2.4 shows the construction of B_p, a comparator network which sorts a bitonic sequence of length p, from two copies of $B_{p/2}$ according to this description. The correctness proof and complexity analysis is left to Exercise 2.3.

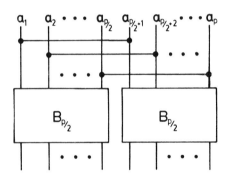

Figure 2.2.4 Batcher's bitonic sorting network.

The bitonic sorting network can be used to construct an $O(\log^2 n)$ depth, $O(n \log^2 n)$ size sorting network built from min-max and max-min comparators (see Exercise 2.4). These can be converted to min-max comparators using Theorem 2.1.1. There is some confusion in the literature over the nomenclature "bitonic sorting network". We use it, as did Batcher, to denote a comparison network which sorts bitonic sequences. It has become popular to use it to describe the sorting network which is constructed from bitonic sorters.

2.3. Waksman's Permutation Network

Consider the problem of permuting n inputs. We will use a network similar to the comparator network defined in the previous section. Instead of comparators the basic building blocks will be *switches*. A switch, like a comparator, can either pass its two inputs directly to the outputs, or swap them. A comparator swaps if the right input is smaller than the left input. In contrast, a switch is subject to outside control. A switch can either be set to *on,* indicating that it is to swap its inputs, or *off* indicating that it is to pass the inputs through directly, unchanged in any way. A network built from switches according to the following constraints is called a *switching network.*

1. The values to be sorted are treated as atomic units. They may neither be divided nor duplicated.
2. The values travel in n *channels,* which we will in our diagrams represent by vertical lines. The inputs will be presented at the top of the network, and will appear in some permuted order at the bottom.
3. The channels are labelled 1 through n, in ascending order from left to right. The network is divided vertically into a finite number of *levels,* which are numbered consecutively, starting at 0. The 0th level consists of the inputs. Each of the subsequent levels contains one or more switches. Each switch is placed on two channels. At most one switch is placed on any channel at any particular level. We will depict a switch using a horizontal line between the two channels, with heavy dots emphasizing the end-points, in the same manner as we depicted comparators in the previous section.

We will say that channel i *carries value v at level j* on input $x_1,...,x_n$ if either

(i) j = 0 and $x_i = v$, or

(ii) j > 0, there is no switch on channel i at level j, and channel i carries value v at level j-1, or

(iii) j > 0 and there is a switch on channel i at level j, that switch is "off" and channel i carries value v at level j-1, or

(iv) j > 0 and there is a switch between channels i and k at level j, that switch is "on" and channel k carries value v at level j-1.

The output of the network consists of the n values carried by the channels at the final level, in left-to-right order. As with comparator networks, the *depth* of a switching network is the number of levels, and the *size* is the number of switches. An n-input switching network is called a *permutation network* if, for every permutation Π on n objects, the switches of the network can be set in such a manner that the output of the network consists of the inputs whose positions have been permuted according to Π. That is, on input $x_1,...,x_n$ the output of the network is $x_{\Pi^{-1}(1)},...,x_{\Pi^{-1}(n)}$.

The following is the recursive description of a permutation network with n inputs, due to Waksman [131]. Suppose n is a power of 2. If n = 1, then the network consists of a single channel with no switches. If n > 1, place a level of switches between channel 2i–i and channel 2i, $1 \leq i \leq n/2$. Separately, take the left-outputs and right-outputs from these switches, and recursively permute them. Finally, place switches between channel 2i–1 and channel 2i, for $2 \leq i \leq n/2$. Figure 2.3.1 shows the construction of P_n, a switching network which permutes n inputs, from two copies of $P_{n/2}$ according to this description.

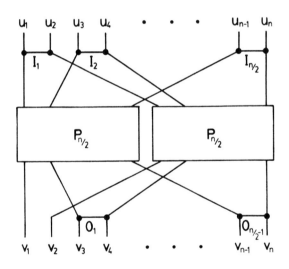

Figure 2.3.1 Waksman's permutation network.

Theorem 2.3.1 The switches of Waksman's permutation network can be set to realize any permutation of n inputs.

Proof. The proof follows by induction on n. Suppose the inputs are $u_1,...,u_n$, and the outputs are $v_1,...,v_n$, and that we number the first layer of switches $I_1,...,I_{n/2}$, and the last layer of switches $O_1,...,O_{\frac{n}{2}-1}$. The induction hypothesis is

16

trivially true when $n = 1$. Now suppose $n > 1$. Take any permutation on n objects. Start with v_1. Set the switches of the left-hand copy of $P_{n/2}$ to route it to the appropriate I-switch. Set that I-switch to route it to the appropriate input. Say that input is u_j. Now consider $u_{j+(-1)^j}$, the "partner" of u_j in switch $I_{\lceil i/2 \rceil}$. It has been routed to the right-hand copy of $P_{n/2}$. Set the switches of that sub-network to route it to the appropriate O-switch (or to v_2, if necessary). Set that O-switch to send it to the appropriate output. Continue this process, at each stage selecting the "partner" of the previously processed channel in the appropriate I-switch or O-switch. If the partner has already been chosen (or we end up at v_2), start again from any other input or output value. Continue in this manner until all of the input-output routings have been made. By the induction hypothesis, the switches of the sub-networks can be set in such a manner that the appropriate sub-permutations are realized. $\square$

Let $D(n)$ denote the depth, and $S(n)$ denote the size of Waksman's permutation network on n inputs. Then $D(1) = 0$, and for $n > 1$, $D(n) = D(n/2)+2$. Therefore, by induction, $D(n) = 2 \log n$. Also, $S(1) = 0$, and for $n > 1$, $S(n) = 2 S(n/2) + n{-}1$. Therefore, by induction, $S(n) = n \log n - n{+}1$. Since the lower-bounds of Exercise 2.2 hold equally well for permutation networks, these results are asymptotically optimal.

2.4. Parallel Prefix Computation

Suppose we have an "addition gate", which computes the sum of two inputs. It is easy to construct a combinational circuit with addition gates, of depth $\lceil \log n \rceil$ and linear size, to sum n inputs (using a binary tree). However, suppose that we want a circuit with n inputs and n outputs, such that on input $<x_1,...,x_n>$ the output is $<y_1,...,y_n>$, where for $1 \leq i \leq n$, $y_i = \sum_{j=1}^{i} x_j$. This is called the *parallel prefix problem*. The obvious solution uses n trees, has logarithmic depth and quadratic size. However, it is possible to obtain logarithmic depth and linear size. The following is a recursive description of a parallel prefix circuit on n inputs, due to Fischer and Ladner [70].

Suppose n is a power of 2. On input $<x_1,...,x_n>$, first compute x_i+x_{i+1} for each odd i, $1 \leq i \leq n{-}1$. Compute the prefix-sum of these values, using a sub-network with $n/2$ inputs. The ith output of the sub-network becomes the $(2i)^{th}$

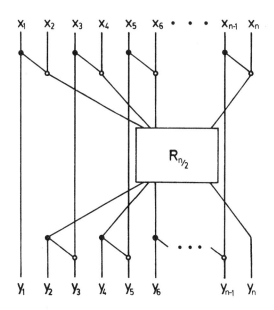

Figure 2.4.1 The parallel prefix circuit of Fischer and Ladner.

output of the network, for $1 \leq i \leq n/2$. The first output of the network is just x_1. The $(2j - 1)^{\text{th}}$ output of the network, $2 \leq j \leq n/2$ consists of the jth output of the sub-network added to $x_{2j - 1}$. Figure 2.4.1 gives the recursive construction of an n-input parallel prefix circuit R_n from $R_{n/2}$, according to this description. In that diagram, solid dots denote fan-out, and circles denote addition gates.

The correctness of the construction can be readily verified by induction on n. Let $D(n)$ denote the depth, and $S(n)$ the size of an n-input parallel prefix circuit. Then $D(1) = 0$, and for $n > 1$, $D(n) = D(n/2) + 2$. Therefore, by induction, $D(n) = 2 \log n$. Also, $S(1) = 0$, and for $n > 1$, $S(n) = S(n/2) + n-1$. Therefore, by induction, $S(n) = 2n-2-\log n$. These bounds are easily seen to be asymptotically optimal.

2.5. Exercises

2.1 Prove that the Zero-One Principle (Theorem 2.1.2) holds equally well for merging networks. That is, a comparator network merges two sorted sequences of integers iff it merges two sorted sequences of zeros and ones.

2.2 Show that an n-input sorting or permutation network must have size at least $n \log n - o(n)$. Show that an n-input sorting or permutation network must have depth at least $2 \log n - o(1)$. (Hint: use Stirling's approximation).

2.3 Use the Zero-One Principle to prove the correctness of Batcher's bitonic sorting network. Analyze its size and depth.

2.4 Use Batcher's bitonic sorting network to construct a sorting network which will sort all input sequences, not just bitonic ones. Prove its correctness, and analyze its size and depth.

2.5 (Van Voorhis [130]). Let $S(n)$ denote the minimum size of an n-input sorting network. Prove that $S(n) \geq S(n-1) + \left\lceil \log_2 n \right\rceil$.

We saw in Section 2.2 how to construct a sorting network using comparators. These are gates which input two integers, and output them in sorted order. Suppose that we also have 3-comparators. These are gates which input three integers, and output them in sorted order. In our diagrams, we will draw 3-comparators as horizontal lines, with *three* heavy dots denoting connections to the appropriate channels.

2.6 Prove that the Zero-One Principle (Theorem 2.1.2) still holds. That is, prove that a network built from comparators and 3-comparators sorts iff it can sort all sequences of zeros and ones.

2.7 Prove, using the Zero-One Principle (see Exercise 2.6), that the following network M_p (adapted from Tseng and Lee [123]) will merge three sorted sequences of p integers, where p is a power of 3. M_1 is just a single 3-comparator. M_p is constructed recursively from three copies of $M_{p/3}$ as in Figure 2.5.1. We call this network the *modulo-3 merging network*. Show that its depth is $2 \log_3 p + 1$, and that it uses $p \log_3 p + 1$ 3-comparators and $p \log_3 p + \dfrac{p-1}{2}$ 2-comparators.

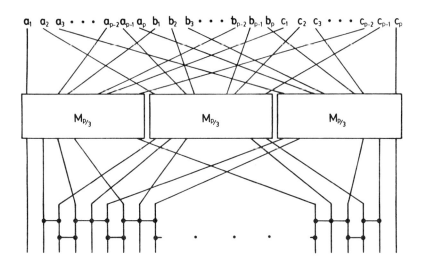

Figure 2.5.1 The modulo-3 merging network.

2.8 Use the merging network of Exercise 2.7 to construct a network for sorting n integers (where n is a power of 3) with depth $\log_3^2 n$. How many 3-comparators and 2-comparators does your sorting network use?

2.9 Suppose we can build a gate which adds k numbers. Construct a circuit for finding the prefix-sum of n numbers with depth $(2 \lceil \log_k n \rceil)$ and linear size.

3   Designing a Parallel Machine Model

In Chapter 2 we saw three primitive parallel machine models which were particularly suited to a limited type of computation. In this chapter we present a general parallel machine model and attempt to justify some of the decisions which contributed to its design. Informally, the model consists of a synchronous network of sequential processors, each of which have random-access to each other's memory. In the first section we give a more formal description, providing illustration by way of an example instruction-set. We define the major resources of interest: *processors* (the number of sequential processors used), *time* (number of instructions executed), *degree* (degree of the interconnection graph), *space* (number of registers required) and *word-size* (the size of those registers). In order to simplify the presentation of algorithms, we describe a high-level pseudo-programming language which we will use in subsequent chapters.

The second section is devoted to a discussion of our choice of a unit-cost measure of time. We choose to charge a single unit of time for each instruction executed, rather than charge according to some notion of "difficulty". This raises an interesting question: for which instruction-sets is this valid? It does not *a priori* seem reasonable to charge a single unit of time for complex instruction sets, but it is not obvious as to exactly where the line should be drawn. We shall see in subsequent chapters that the answer can be provided in several different ways.

Our basic networks have a single program for all processors. In the third section we justify this approach, comparing and contrasting it with the SIMD and MIMD machines of Flynn [32]. In a SIMD machine the processors have program-counters which at any point in time, all contain the same value, with each individual processor either executing the common current instruction or remaining dormant for a step. In contrast, we allow each processor to be at a different point in the program. A MIMD machine has a different program for each processor. Our model is seen to be equivalent to a SIMD one, and to a reasonable subset of the MIMD model.

Finally, in the fourth section we justify our decision to start the computation with all processors active, rather than have them become active at run-time.

This latter approach places a not altogether unreasonable upper-bound on the number of processors used in a computation, in relation to time. If we place a similar restriction on our model, then the two activation conventions are equivalent. However, we will see in Sections 6.1 and 6.2 that it is sometimes profitable to lift the restriction.

3.1. The Basic Model

Our parallel machine model can be viewed as an infinite collection of interconnected, synchronous random-access machines, only finitely many of which are active in any particular finite computation. By "random-access machine" we refer to a variant of the RAM, which is already well-known as a sequential machine model (see, for example, [3,23,113]); and by "synchronous" we mean that the instruction-cycles of the RAMs are synchronized. Every RAM has an infinite number of general-purpose registers $r_0, r_1,...$, each of which is capable of storing a single integer, and a read-only processor identity register PID. The PID of the ith RAM is preset to i, for i $= 0,1,...$.

More formally, a *network* M consists of a program to be executed and a processor-bound which indicates how many processors are to be used. The *program* of M is a finite list of instructions; each instruction has the form either:
(i)   Read a value from a register of a neighbouring processor.
(ii) Write a value to a register of a neighbouring processor.
(iii) Perform an internal computation.
(iv) Transfer of control.
For example, let "$\circ$" denote a binary operation defined on integers. For convenience we divide our example instruction-set into two categories. Local instructions have the form:

$r_i \leftarrow$ constant	(load register with constant)
$r_i \leftarrow r_j \circ r_k$	(binary operation)
$r_i \leftarrow r_{r_j}$	(indirect load)
$r_{r_i} \leftarrow r_j$	(indirect store)
$r_i \leftarrow$ PID	(store PID)
halt	(end execution)
goto m **if** $r_i > 0$	(conditional transfer of control)

Communication instructions have the form:

$$r_i \leftarrow (r_{r_j} \text{ of } r_k) \quad (\text{read})$$
$$(r_{r_i} \text{ of } r_j) \leftarrow r_k \quad (\text{write})$$

The program is to be executed synchronously in parallel by the (finitely many) active processors. As far as local instructions are concerned, their behaviour is that of independent RAMs, that is, references to registers in local instructions are treated as references to their respective local registers. Execution of a read instruction:

$$r_i \leftarrow (r_{r_j} \text{ of } r_k)$$

by processor p has the following effect. Suppose registers r_j, r_k of processor p contain the values q and s respectively. Then the contents of register r_q of processor s are read and placed into register r_i of processor p. Similarly, execution of a write instruction:

$$(r_{r_i} \text{ of } r_j) \leftarrow r_k$$

by processor p has the following effect. Suppose registers r_i, r_j of processor p contain the values q and s respectively. Then the contents of register r_k of processor p are written into register r_q of processor s.

Simultaneous reads (often called *multiple reads* or *concurrent reads*) of the same register are allowed. In the case of simultaneous writes to a single register we adopt some reasonable convention whereby a single processor succeeds and is allowed to write its value, whilst all others fail. For example (after [45]) the lowest-numbered processor attempting to write succeeds, or (as in Chapter 9), the processor which is attempting to write the smallest value succeeds, with ties being broken in favour of the lowest-numbered processor. A write-attempt always takes precedence over a local instruction, should any conflict occur. This is popularly called a CRCW (concurrent-read, concurrent-write) protocol. We will mostly be interested in CRCW networks, although occasionally (for example, in Section 6.3) we will consider CREW (concurrent-read, exclusive-write) networks, in which simultaneous writes are forbidden. EREW (exclusive-read, exclusive-write) models are also often studied in the literature (see, for example, Lev, Pippenger and Valiant [74] and Snir [118]). In the case of read-attempts conflicting with write-attempts, the reads are serviced first. Any attempt to write to a non-existent or halted processor is ignored. Any attempt to read from a non-existent or halted processor returns zero.

Suppose $f:\mathbf{Z}^* \to \mathbf{Z}^*$ and $x = <x_0, x_1, \ldots, x_{n-1}>$, where $x_i \in \mathbf{Z}$ for $0 \leq i < n$. We will say that x has *size* or *length* n, and write $|x| = n$. Let $m = \max_{|x| = n} |f(x)|$ and $f_n:\mathbf{Z}^n \to \mathbf{Z}^m$ denote the restriction of f to n arguments (we adopt the convention that unused output places are filled by zeros). We will variously refer to x as an *input* or *input string*, and each x_i as an *argument* or *input symbol*.

Suppose M is a network with processor-bound $P:\mathbf{N} \to \mathbf{N}$. We assume that P is computable. Let $p = P(n)$. A *computation* of M on input x is defined as follows. The input symbols are placed consecutively into register r_0 of processors $0, 1, \ldots$. If $p < n$ we wrap around into register r_1 of processors $0, 1, \ldots$ etc., utilizing in this fashion as many registers as necessary. That is, we place x_i into register $r_{\lfloor i/p \rfloor}$ of processor $(i \bmod p)$. All other general-purpose registers are set to zero. We then simultaneously activate processors $0, 1, \ldots, p\text{-}1$. These synchronously execute the program of M. For $0 \leq i < m$ let y_i denote the contents of register $r_{\lfloor i/p \rfloor}$ of processor $(i \bmod p)$ when all processors have finally halted. We say that M *computes* f if for all $n \geq 0$ and inputs x with $|x| = n$, $f_n(x) = <y_0, y_1, \ldots, y_{m-1}>$. Recognition of a language over a finite alphabet is defined in the customary manner; we will encode each input symbol as a positive integer, and say that *acceptance* of an input occurs if register r_0 of processor 0 contains the value 1 on termination of the computation.

Note that if $P(n) \geq n$, then the network can determine n, the input-size, in constant time, as follows. We simply adopt the convention that zero is never used as an input value, replacing every non-negative integer i in the input by $i+1$. Each processor j examines its register r_0. If it is non-zero, it then examines register r_0 of processor $j+1$. If that is zero (and exactly one processor will find that this is the case), then the number of inputs is $j+1$, which value it writes to register r_1 of processor 0. Each processor in possession of a positive input value then subtracts one from it, and finally all processors simultaneously read the number of inputs from register r_1 of processor 0. For general $P(n)$, this algorithm can be modified to run in time $O(\frac{n}{P(n)} + 1)$, which can be ignored for computations which depend on all n input symbols, since such a computation requires time $\Omega(\frac{n}{P(n)} + 1)$.

The *interconnection pattern* of M is an infinite family of finite graphs $G = (G_0, G_1, \ldots)$, one for each input-size. For $n \geq 0$, G_n has vertex-set $\{0, 1, \ldots, P(n)\text{-}1\}$, and an edge between vertices i and j if at any time during the computation of M on an input of length n, processor i attempts to read from or write to a register of processor j. Let $D:N \to N$. M is said to have *degree* $D(n)$ if for all $n \geq 0$, G_n has degree $D(n)$.

Let $T,S,W:N \to N$. M is said to compute within *time* $T(n)$ if for all inputs of size n, all active processors have halted within $T(n)$ steps. For $0 \leq t \leq T(n)$, let $S_t(n)$ be the maximum (over all inputs of size n) number of registers of M with non-zero contents after t instructions have been executed. Then M uses *space* $S(n)$ if $S(n) = \max_{0 \leq t \leq T(n)} S_t(n)$. It has *word-size* $W(n)$ if every value which appears in a register during such a computation has absolute value less than $2^{W(n)}$ (note that this includes the inputs, outputs and processor identity registers).

The space bound is a measure of the number of registers used in a computation. It is slightly non-standard; it is more usual to define space to be the number of registers which are assigned non-zero contents at any point during the computation (see, for example, [3] for the case of a single RAM). Our reasons will become more apparent in Chapter 9. The word-size is a measure of the width of (inter- and intra-processor) data paths, and a measure of register size. This can be combined with our unit-cost measure of space to provide an upper-bound on log-cost space.

Consider the example instruction-set given earlier in this section. So far, we have not specified exactly which binary operations can be used for "$\circ$". In particular we will be interested in five types of instruction-sets.

1. The *minimal* instruction-set allows addition, subtraction and shifts of positive values by a single bit.

    $$r_i \leftarrow r_j \pm r_k$$
    $$r_i \leftarrow \left\lfloor r_j / 2 \right\rfloor$$

    Note that the second instruction corresponds to a right-shift by a single bit, and that a left-shift can be achieved by using integer addition.

2. The *restricted arithmetic* instruction-set also allows arbitrary-length shifts.

    $$r_i \leftarrow \left\lfloor r_j * 2^{r_k} \right\rfloor$$

    Note that r_k may be either positive (corresponding to a left-shift) or negative (corresponding to a right-shift). The "floor" operators are not necessary in the former case.

3. The *full arithmetic* instruction-set is the restricted arithmetic instruction-set augmented with multiplication and integer division.

$$r_i \leftarrow r_j * r_k$$

$$r_i \leftarrow \left\lfloor r_j / r_k \right\rfloor$$

4.   The *extended arithmetic* instruction-set is the full arithmetic instruction-set plus exponentiation.

$$r_i \leftarrow r_j^{r_k}$$

5.   The *general* instruction-set includes any instruction which can be simulated by a multi-tape deterministic Turing machine in polynomial time. (That is, a multi-tape deterministic Turing machine can, when given as input the m-bit binary representations of the operands, compute the binary representation of the result in time $m^{O(1)}$.)

A number of questions spring to mind. Given that we have chosen a unit-cost measure of time (that is, we charge one unit of time for each instruction executed, regardless of the type of instruction or the size of its arguments), are these instruction-sets reasonable? Are they powerful enough? Too powerful? Natural? Clearly an unrestricted instruction-set which allows any computable function as a local instruction is too powerful, but what kind of instruction-set *is* reasonable? We will return to these questions in the next section.

Instead of writing algorithms in the low-level RAM language, we will follow the common practice of using a high-level language which can easily be translated into instructions of this form. We use the usual high-level constructs for flow-of-control, based on sequencing, selection and iteration. Variables of the form (x **of processor** i) will be taken as a reference to variable x of processor i. An unmodified variable x will be taken to mean (x **of processor** PID), that is, a local variable. For example, execution of the statement

> **if** y < (y **of processor** $\lfloor \mathrm{PID}/2 \rfloor$)
>   **then** statement$_1$
>   **else** statement$_2$

by a network of P(n) processors causes the ith processor, $0 \le i < P(n)$, to compare its variable y with variable y of processor $\lfloor i/2 \rfloor$. If it finds that the former is less than the latter, then it executes statement$_1$, otherwise it executes statement$_2$. All processors execute this code in parallel. To aid synchronization, we assume that statement$_1$ and statement$_2$ are translated into blocks of code containing the same number of instructions, by filling with NO-OPs (such as $r_0 \leftarrow r_0$)

as necessary. All of the algorithms in this Monograph will maintain synchronization by virtue of this simple arrangement. As a notational convenience we may occasionally use concurrent and conditional assignments. Block-structuring will be indicated by indentation, in the customary fashion.

3.2. The Unit-Cost Measure of Time

In Section 3.1 we defined the running-time of our parallel machines to be the number of instructions executed (synchronously) before all active processors have halted. That is, we charge a single unit of time for each instruction. This is termed a *unit-cost* measure of time. The use of unit-cost charging is potentially a contentious issue. The alternative is *log-cost* charging, whereby the cost of an instruction is expressed as a function of the size of its arguments, thus tying the time required for a particular computation to its word-size.

We follow Cook [22] in the belief that the major parallel resources of interest are *time* and *hardware*. We also believe that the important issues in the design of parallel algorithms are more clear-cut if these two resources are kept completely independent. A hardware measure should take into account the amount of memory used, which will depend upon the word-size. This makes the unit-cost measure of time more attractive, since it alone is independent of word-size, and thus hardware.

Even for purely sequential machines, the selection of unit-cost measures versus log-cost is of fundamental importance. Inter-simulations between various log-cost models (for example [3], Turing machines and log-cost RAMs) can be achieved with only a polynomial increase in time, whereas no such simulation can be obtained between unit-cost and log-cost models. For example, in time t a unit-cost RAM with multiplication can compute (without input) a value as large as $2^{2^{t+\Theta(1)}}$, whereas the same machine with log-cost charging can only compute a value as large as $2^{t+\Theta(1)}$.

From a purely practical standpoint, the choice of charging mechanism depends on the type of computation in question. If the word-size of an algorithm is sufficiently small compared to the word-size of the computer on which it is to be implemented, then the unit-cost measure is more applicable. Alternatively, if the values being manipulated grow very quickly with input-size, requiring the use of multi-word instructions for quite modest input lengths, then the log-cost measure is preferable.

This issue is neatly encapsulated in what Goldschlager and Lister [47] call the "sequential computation thesis". This states that time on all "reasonable" sequential models is polynomially related. This is motivated principally by the polynomial-time simulations of one log-cost model by another, but in fact breaks the models into two disjoint classes, those with unit-cost and those with log-cost measure of time. Members of the same class are polynomially related, but two models from different classes are not. Given this observation, the important question which must be addressed by any theoretical treatment is not "which model is better", but "which model is more accurate for the intended application". We believe that a unit-cost model is more suitable for the individual processors of a parallel machine.

The parallel analogue of the sequential computation thesis is the so-called "parallel computation thesis" [18,45]. This states that time on all "reasonable" parallel models is polynomially related. Furthermore, it attempts to characterize parallel computers by relating parallel time to a sequential resource. More precisely, it states that time on a "reasonable" parallel computer is polynomially equivalent to log-cost sequential (for example, Turing machine) space. This has two implications. Firstly, a machine which is too weak to simulate an $S(n)$ space-bounded Turing machine in time $S(n)^{O(1)}$ is *not powerful enough* to be called a parallel machine. Secondly, a machine which is so strong that a $T(n)$ time-bounded computation cannot be simulated in space $T(n)^{O(1)}$ by a Turing machine is *too powerful* to be called parallel. We will be concentrating mainly on the latter aspect of the parallel computation thesis, since networks with an unrestricted instruction-set are obviously extremely powerful. Henceforth, by "reasonable" we will mean "not too powerful", in the sense that it is "reasonable" to expect a parallel computer to have only a moderate amount of resources at its disposal.

As we shall see in Section 5.3, one way of making our model satisfy the parallel computation thesis is to restrict the processors to the minimal instruction-set of Section 3.1 (this approach was taken by Goldschlager for his SIMDAG [45]). This ensures that the word-size grows by at most one in every time-step, and so the log-cost of the individual instructions executed in any given computation is at most a polynomial in the unit-cost running-time, provided the input integers are sufficiently small. In this case, unit-cost and log-cost are polynomially related. It makes sense to restrict the word-size of parallel processors since (as we saw in the second paragraph of this section) the extra power of unit-cost RAMs over log-cost RAMs seems to stem from their ability to generate large integers quickly. Indeed, a single unit-cost RAM with either the restricted [103] or full arithmetic [50] instruction-sets satisfies the parallel computation thesis, so is itself as powerful as a parallel machine.

We claim that the unit-cost measure of time is valid for parallel processors. We shall call this the *unit-cost hypothesis*. It is framed as a hypothesis (rather than a theorem or proposition) because it cannot be proved or disproved in the formal sense. In particular, it depends upon the way in which the word "valid" is interpreted. We will meet several interpretations in the remainder of this Monograph. Whilst it is intuitively obvious that the unit-cost measure of time is unrealistic for very powerful instruction-sets which allow the computation of infeasible functions in a single step, we may reasonably expect it to be realistic for fairly weak instruction-sets, such as the minimal instruction-set of Section 3.1.

This raises a number of interesting side-issues. We are in effect asking when a unit-cost model is "reasonable". We have seen that restricting the processors to the minimal instruction-set makes our model "reasonable" in the sense that it satisfies the parallel computation thesis. But what do we actually mean by "reasonable"? Do models which satisfy the parallel computation thesis successfully formalize the idea of "parallel computers"? What do we really expect from a parallel machine model? These are amongst the issues that we will address in Chapter 4.

3.3. The Assignment of Programs to Processors

Although every processor of our parallel machine executes the same program, our model does not fall precisely into the SIMD category of Flynn [32]. SIMD is an acronym for "Single Instruction-stream, Multiple Data-stream" computer. In the latter, each processor has the same program, and shares the same program-counter. At each time-step, each processor either executes the common current instruction, or remains dormant for a step. This model is attractive since program-control can thus be left to a single central processor (as in Goldschlager [45]). This central processor broadcasts the current instruction to all processors, which individually decide whether to participate. In our model, the conditional *goto* instruction takes action depending on the value of a local register, the contents of which may vary from processor to processor. Thus different processors may be at different points in the program at any given time. However, it is fairly easy to show that our model is equal in power to a SIMD one, and to a reasonable subset of MIMD models. MIMD is an acronym for "Multiple Instruction-stream, Multiple Data-stream" computer, and refers to a model in which each processor may have a different program.

For the sake of discussion, we will call our assignment of programs to processors a *uniform* one. We use the term "uniform" in the sense of Karp and Lipton [61], meaning that every machine has a finite description. In our case, the finite description consists of the program (a finite list of instructions) and the processor-bound (which can be represented as the Gödel number of a Turing machine which computes the binary representation of $P(n)$, on input n in binary). A MIMD model is non-uniform in the sense that it allows a different program for each processor; thus an infinite family of finite descriptions (one for each input-size) is needed. Some authors (for example [15,22,108]) use the term "uniform" to denote the fact that an external "constructibility" condition has been enforced on a non-uniform model in order to restrict interest to machines with finite descriptions.

A SIMD machine is a uniform one in which, at any given point in time, all active processors are either executing the same instruction, or are dormant. Our high-level pseudo-programming language allows the user to write non-SIMD programs; we believe that this keeps the language simple, elegant and flexible (it may be argued that it gives the user the flexibility to get into trouble, but the same is often said of the *goto* statement in modern programming languages). Furthermore, it is not really necessary to force the programmer to write SIMD programs, since a uniform network can be simulated by a SIMD one without asymptotic time-loss, using the same number of processors and degree, with space and word-size increasing by only a constant.

Suppose M is a $P(n)$-processor uniform network. We will construct a SIMD network to simulate M as follows. Processor i of the SIMD network, $0 \leq i < P(n)$, simulates processor i of M, using variables PC, VPC, NPC, PR, A and V, and an infinite array R. PC keeps track of the program-counter of the simulated processor, whilst for $j \geq 0$, R[j] contains the current contents of its register r_j. VPC (the virtual program-counter) will cycle from 1 to the program length (which is a constant, independent of n); when PC = VPC the PCth instruction of the program of M is simulated. NPC receives the new program-counter value, and if the instruction involves a data-transfer, A and PR receive the address and PID respectively of the register to be updated, and V its new value. At the end of the cycle, the arrays R are updated to reflect the new register contents, using the information in PR, A and V, whilst PC is updated using the contents of NPC. The process is completed at the end of a cycle in which a halt instruction is simulated.

We present the algorithm in the high-level language of Section 3.1. A different interpretation is placed on the control constructs however, in order to make them strictly SIMD. The branches of a selection statement (such as **if** or **case**) are tried one at a time, with a processor executing a particular branch if its register contents satisfy the entry condition; all other processors remain dormant during that period. This is opposed to the general (non-SIMD) uniform case, in which all processors are free to start their respective branches at the same time, or to enter and leave the construct at different times.

Suppose M has the example instruction-set of Section 3.1. Then the program of the simulating network is as follows:

$$A:=V:=0$$
$$PC:=VPC:=1$$
while $PC > 0$ **do**
    for $VPC:=1$ **to** program length **do**
      if $VPC = PC$ **then**
        $PR,A,V:=$**case** PC^{th} instruction of M **of**
              "$r_i \leftarrow constant$":PID,i,constant
              "$r_i \leftarrow r_j \circ r_k$":PID,i,R[j]$\circ$R[k]
              "$r_i \leftarrow r_{r_j}$":PID,i,R[R[j]]
              "$r_{r_i} \leftarrow r_j$":PID,R[i],R[j]
              "$r_i \leftarrow PID$":PID,i,PID
              "$r_i \leftarrow r_{r_j}$ **of** r_k": PID,i,(R[R[j]] **of processor** R[k])
              "$(r_{r_i}$ **of** $r_j) \leftarrow r_k$":R[j],R[i],R[k]
      $NPC:=$**case** PC^{th} instruction of M **of**
           "halt":0
           "**goto** m **if** $r_i > 0$":**if** $R[i] > 0$ **then** m **else** $PC+1$
           "*others* ":$PC+1$
    (R[A] **of processor** PR):=V
    $PC:=NPC$

Thus we see that our uniform model is equivalent to a SIMD one (noting that the SIMD model is a special case of the uniform one). Now, a MIMD model allows a different program for each processor. Let $\Delta\colon N\to N$ be such that $\Delta(i)$ is a reasonable encoding of a RAM program (say, using the example instruction-set of Section 3.1), for $i \geq 0$. By "reasonable encoding" we mean that a universal RAM should be able to decode this program, using negligible resources, into a format which allows efficient simulation. A MIMD variant of our model is identical to that of Section 3.1, except that processor i of a $P(n)$-processor network has program $\Delta(i)$, $0 \leq i < P(n)$. Δ is called the *processor assignment* function.

Let M be a $P(n)$-processor MIMD network which uses resources $R_1(n)$, whose processor assignment Δ is such that $\Delta^* = <\Delta(0),\Delta(1),\ldots,\Delta(P(n)-1)>$ can be computed by a $P(n)$-processor uniform network using resources $R_2(n)$. Then clearly there is a uniform $P(n)$-processor network which can simulate M in resources $R_1(n)+R_2(n)$, simply by computing Δ^*, and then having processor i, $0 \leq i < P(n)$ simulate program $\Delta(i)$. Each processor of the uniform network has an identical program made up of two parts, a part to compute Δ^*, and a universal RAM.

Thus we see that (provided the resources needed to compute Δ are kept to a feasible level, as in, for example, Galil and Paul [38]) a uniform network can efficiently simulate a MIMD one. This can be summarized as follows: if a MIMD network is easy to specify, then it can be specified as a uniform network. Thus a uniform model is equivalent to a practical MIMD model.

3.4. Processor Activation

In our model as presented so far, all $P(n)$ processors are activated simultaneously at the start of the computation, and synchronously execute the first instruction of the program at time $t=1$. We call this the *initial activation* model. An alternative formulation (*lazy activation*) is to start off with some small number of active processors (for example, just processor 0, or just those which receive input), postponing the activation of the remainder until run-time. This convention was adopted by Galil and Paul [38] and Savitch [110].

There are two essentially different ways of approaching lazy activation. The first requires that an active processor explicitly activate an inactive one by executing a special "call" instruction (as in Savitch [110]). This implies that the number of active processors can at most double in each time-step. Alternatively,

Galil and Paul [38] allow the inactive processors to execute a polling-loop, interrogating each of its neighbours in turn in order to decide when to become active. This is really only feasible for networks with constant degree, in which case it is asymptotically equivalent to the first approach.

Note that this implies that a $T(n)$ time-bounded network can have at most $n\, 2^{O(T(n))}$ (in the case when only input-bearing processors are initially active), or $2^{O(T(n))}$ (in the case when only processor 0 is initially active) processors. We will, in later sections, find it useful to consider networks with far more processors.

We will consider a canonical lazy-activation scheme in which:

1. Initially, only processor 0 is activated.
2. In a computation on an input of size n, processor 0 is initially given the value of $P(n)$ as part of its input.
3. If an inactive processor has a value written into it for the first time in a computation during time-step t, it becomes active and executes the first instruction of the program during time-step $t+1$. Thereafter, it is indistinguishable from any other active processor. A processor which has halted cannot be reactivated.

We will see that lazy activation is essentially the same as initial activation, provided $P(n) \leq 2^{O(T(n))}$. If this condition does not hold, it is clear that initially-activated networks are more powerful than lazily-activated ones, by the simple virtue of their being able to produce longer unary strings. Clearly an initial-activation network can simulate a lazy-activation one without asymptotic loss in resources, by simply maintaining an activation flag in each processor. Simulation in the other direction is only slightly more difficult. The problem is to activate $P(n)$ processors and synchronize them so that they begin the execution of the program of M at the same time. If M has $P(n)$ processors and runs in time $T(n)$, we will show that the simulating (lazy) network runs in time $O(T(n)+\log P(n))$, whilst increasing space, word-size and degree by only a constant term.

To simplify the presentation, assume that $P(n)$ is of the form 2^k-1 for some $k > 0$. We will activate $P(n)$ processors using an interconnection pattern in the shape of a complete binary tree (see Figure 3.4.1). A complete binary tree has 2^k-1 processors for some $k \geq 1$; processor i is connected to processors $2i+1$ and $2i+2$ (its *children*) for $0 \leq i < 2^{k-1}-1$, and to processor $\lfloor (i-1)/2 \rfloor$ (its *parent*) for $0 < i \leq 2^k-1$.

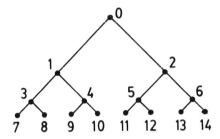

Figure 3.4.1. The binary tree interconnection pattern with 15 vertices.

Each processor has variables C and P. P holds the value of P(n) (we assume that P of processor 0 is set to P(n) at the start of the computation), and C the number of processors activated so far (we assume that C of processor 0 is initialized to zero). The algorithm consists of a single loop. At each iteration, a new level of the tree is activated; C is used to detect termination. Upon exiting the loop, all processors are synchronized, and execution of the program of M can begin.

Processor i activates its children at the next level (processors 2i+1 and 2i+2) using the high-level statements:

$$(C,P) \text{ of processor } 2i+1 := C,P$$

$$(C,P) \text{ of processor } 2i+2 := C,P$$

(Note that we use concurrent assignments as a notational convenience only; four transfers of data take place in sequence). This also initializes their variables C and P so that they can join in the loop at the appropriate stage. Note that the left (odd-numbered) child is activated before the right (even-numbered) child, and so potentially enters the loop earlier. We can avoid this by making odd-numbered processors wait for α steps (where α is a suitably chosen constant) before entering the loop. In order to synchronize the newly-activated processors entering the loop with those already inside it, it is necessary to add another delay, this time of β steps (where β is another suitably chosen constant). Note that the values α, β depend only on the exact form of the RAM instruction-set, and the ability of the compiler to generate succinct code from high-level statements. In a high-level form, the algorithm is:

> Odd-numbered processors wait for α steps
> Wait for β steps
> C:=2C+1
> **while** C < P **do**
>   (C,P) **of processor** 2*PID+1 := C,P
>   (C,P) **of processor** 2*PID+2 := C,P
>   C:=2C+1

To make the synchronization method completely transparent, this program would generate the following code (using an instruction-set similar to that of Section 3.1, with certain minor liberties taken with arithmetic and Boolean expressions to ensure brevity). In this case, $\alpha = 2$ and $\beta = 1$.

1. **goto** 4 **if** PID mod 2 = 0
2. NOOP
3. NOOP
4. NOOP
5. C←2*C+1
6. **goto** 13 **if** C ≥ P
7. (C **of** 2*PID+1)←C
8. (P **of** 2*PID+1)←P
9. (C **of** 2*PID+2)←C
10. (P **of** 2*PID+2)←P
11. C←2*C+1
12. **goto** 6
13. *etc.*

Table 3.4.1 gives a trace of this algorithm for $P(n) = 7$ processors.

Many papers in the current literature use a lazy-activation model, either explicitly, or implicitly by insisting that $P(n) \leq 2^{T(n)}$. However, there are many problems which can be solved in sub-logarithmic time on polynomial-processor machines, once the processors have been activated (see Lemmas 6.1.1 and 6.1.6, Corollary 6.1.7 and Theorem 6.1.10). This class of problems, which is becoming increasingly well-studied in the literature, deserves some consideration.

	PC,P,C of Processor						
Time	0	1	2	3	4	5	6
0	1,7,0						
1	4,7,0						
2	5,7,0						
3	6,7,1						
4	7,7,1						
5	8,7,1	1,-,1					
6	9,7,1	2,7,1					
7	10,7,1	3,7,1	1,-,1				
8	11,7,1	4,7,1	4,7,1				
9	12,7,3	5,7,1	5,7,1				
10	6,7,3	6,7,3	6,7,3				
11	7,7,3	7,7,3	7,7,3				
12	8,7,3	8,7,3	8,7,3	1,-,3		1,-,3	
13	9,7,3	9,7,3	9,7,3	2,7,3		2,7,3	
14	10,7,3	10,7,3	10,7,3	3,7,3	1,-,3	3,7,3	1,-,3
15	11,7,3	11,7,3	11,7,3	4,7,3	4,7,3	4,7,3	4,7,3
16	12,7,7	12,7,7	12,7,7	5,7,3	5,7,3	5,7,3	5,7,3
17	6,7,7	6,7,7	6,7,7	6,7,7	6,7,7	6,7,7	6,7,7
18	13,7,7	13,7,7	13,7,7	13,7,7	13,7,7	13,7,7	13,7,7

Table 3.4.1 Activation and synchronization of 7 processors in a lazy-activation model. Each entry shows the value of the program-counter (PC), and variables P and C for a particular processor, initially (at time 0), and after each of 18 steps. A blank entry indicates an inactive processor. An entry of "-" for a variable indicates that it has not yet been initialized.

Run-time on the initial-activation model more accurately measures the cost of running algorithms as sub-routines; in particular, initial-activation run-time remains accurate under iteration. The cost of activating processors can, if this is desired, be added at the end of the entire computation. For example, consider a

36

sequence of O(log n) sub-computations, each of duration O(log log n), on a polynomial-processor machine. In an initial-activation model, the run-time would be O((log n)(log log n)); simulating this on a lazy-activation machine will not asymptotically affect the run-time. Insisting that each sub-computation cost O(log n) for activating the processors is unnecessary, since each sub-computation can re-use the same set of processors. The O(log^{2}n) run-time obtained using the lazy-activation model for the sub-computations is clearly inaccurate.

We will also be studying networks with an exponential number of processors. It is not surprising that many problems become solvable in sub-logarithmic time with exponential hardware. Our primary motivation for studying algorithms which need exponential hardware is to use them as sub-routines on very small input-sizes. For example, Theorem 6.1.9, which uses exponentially many processors to sum finite objects in constant time, is used as a sub-routine in Theorem 6.1.10 to perform the summation in sub-logarithmic time using a linear number of processors. Lemma 6.2.1, which simulates Turing machines on networks with exponential hardware, can be "slowed down" to derive speedups of of sequential machines on networks which satisfy the parallel computation thesis (see Sections 5.5 and 6.2) and the extended parallel computation thesis (see Sections 9.4 and 9.5). This study would have been more difficult to carry out within the artificial constraints of a lazy-activation model.

3.5. Exercises.

3.1 Show how to compute the following on a single processor with the given instruction-set in constant time.

(i) Compute any two-input Boolean function with the minimal instruction-set.

(ii) Implement the following high-level program using the minimal instruction-set.

if x is odd **then** x:=x+1

(iii) Let x, y and z be positive integers, with y $\geq$ z. Show how to compute the integer whose binary representation consists of the yth through zth bits of the binary representation of x, where the bits are numbered consecutively starting at zero for the least-significant bit, using the restricted arithmetic instruction-set.

3.2 Design a SIMD instruction-set which is powerful enough to implement the high-level SIMD language used in Section 3.3.

3.3 Suppose we add to our high-level programming language a **synch** statement. Any processor encountering a **synch** statement becomes dormant until all other processors reach a **synch** statement. When and if this occurs, all processors then simultaneously execute their next instruction. Can a **synch** statement be implemented in our model? If so, then describe an efficient method for doing so. If not, then explain your reasoning, and describe a set of modifications which make it possible.

3.4 Suppose we add an explicit activation instruction to our model:

activate r_i

which, when executed by processor p, activates the processor whose PID is in register r_i of processor p, and modify our lazy-activation scheme accordingly. Show that this model can simulate an initial-activation machine efficiently.

3.5 Modify the lazy-activation program in Section 3.4 to work when $P(n)$ is not necessarily one less than a power of two.

4 Variants of the Model

The aim of this chapter is to examine a few important variants of our basic network model. In the first section we propose a fixed-structure variant, that is, one in which the interconnection patterns of the networks can be predicted. The more general model computes its own interconnections, which implies that it must, in the worst case, be fabricated as a completely-connected network. In contrast, the degree of a fixed-structure model is an accurate measure of the number of communication lines needed by each processor. It is observed that more efficient fixed-structure networks can be constructed by expending more resources, for example a network with a non-recursive interconnection function can compute arbitrary (non-recursive) single-valued Boolean functions in constant time, given exponentially many processors.

The second section compares our model to the popular shared-memory machine. In a shared-memory machine the processors communicate indirectly via a common shared memory, rather than by direct register access. The two models are easily seen to be almost identical in computing power. In the third section we define a practical variant of the network, which we will call a *feasible network*. We suggest the possibility of constructing a feasible network which is universal for the general model as described in Section 3.1. This suggestion will be followed up in Section 9.2. Various types of universal network are considered, differing in how closely they mimic the communications of the simulated network.

4.1. A Fixed-Structure Model

The basic model described in Section 3.1 falls into Cook's [22] category of machines with *modifiable structure*, since processor interconnections are computed at run-time. A resource-bound for such a machine is made up of two parts, corresponding to the resources required to compute the interconnections and those required to perform the actual computation. In a *fixed-structure* network these two components are separated. The former reflects the cost of building the network, and the latter the cost of using it.

This separation can become significant when the two components differ by a large amount. For example, consider a network with the example instruction-set of Section 3.1, whose only allowable binary operations are (single-bit) two-input Boolean functions, integer division by 2 and multiplication by 2. Let $f:\{0,1\}^* \to \{0,1\}^*$ be defined by $f(x_0, \ldots, x_{n-1}) = \langle y_0, \ldots, y_{n-1} \rangle$ where for $0 \leq i < n$, $y_i = x_i \oplus x_{(i+1) \bmod n}$. An n-processor, constant-degree network can compute f in a constant number of steps, provided processor i knows the value of $(i+1) \bmod n$, $0 \leq i < n$. However, the same network requires $\Omega(\log n)$ steps to actually compute those values, since it can only perform bit-operations. Thus in a model with modifiable structure, the run-time of this network is $\Omega(\log n)$, whilst under a fixed-structure model the run-time is constant. Any reasonable fabrication device which includes addition as part of its instruction-set can compute the interconnections in parallel in a constant amount of time.

A fixed-structure analogue of our basic model can be defined as follows. Galil and Paul [38] call this a model with *predictable communication* since the inter-processor connections need to be known in advance of actually running the machine. Note that all networks have "predictable communication" in the sense that they can be fabricated as a completely-connected machine (with each processor connected to every other), but this may involve an unacceptable increase in degree. Our fixed-structure model has the same format as the basic model of Section 3.1, with a number of minor modifications. Each processor is given a number of additional read-only registers which are preset at the beginning of a computation. These correspond to values which are "hard-wired" into the network during the fabrication process. They consist of the DEGREE register, and an infinite number of port registers $p_0, p_1, \ldots$, each of which is capable of holding a single integer.

More formally, a *fixed-structure network* consists of a program and an interconnection scheme. The *program* is a finite list of instructions, each of which may have the following form, where p is a port register. Either:

1. Read a value from a register of processor p.
2. Write a value to a register of processor p.
3. Perform an internal computation.
4. Transfer of control.

Using the notation of Section 3.1, the read instruction:

$$r_i \leftarrow (r_{r_j} \textbf{ of } r_k)$$

would be interpreted as meaning "read the $(r_j)^{\text{th}}$ register of processor p_{r_k} and place the result into register r_i", and the write instruction:

$$(r_{r_l} \text{ of } r_j) \leftarrow r_k$$

would be interpreted as meaning "write the value from register r_k into the $(r_i)^{th}$ register of processor p_{r_j}".

An *interconnection scheme* consists of three functions, a processor-bound $P: N \rightarrow N$, a degree function $D: N \rightarrow N$ and an interconnection function $G: \Pi(n) \times \Delta(n) \times N \rightarrow \Pi(n)$, where $\Pi(n) = \{ i \mid 0 \leq i < P(n) \}$ denotes the set of processors and $\Delta(n) = \{ d \mid 0 \leq d < D(n) \}$ denotes the set of communication lines attached to each processor. In a $P(n)$-processor computation, processor i is connected to processors $G(i,d,n)$, $0 \leq d < D(n)$. We adopt the convention that if $i \in \{ G(j,d,n) \mid 0 \leq d < D(n) \}$ then $j \in \{ G(i,d,n) \mid 0 \leq d < D(n) \}$. A *computation* of M, where M has interconnection scheme (P,D,G), is defined similarly to Section 3.1, with the following addition. Before the processors are activated, the DEGREE register is set to $D(n)$, and for $0 \leq d < D(n)$, $0 \leq i < P(n)$, register p_d of processor i is set to $G(i,d,n)$. The values of the remaining port registers are undefined. The resources of space and word-size are modified to include the new registers (the word-size of the port registers may be measured according to their absolute contents, or some concise relative encoding, if such is applicable).

Note that a resource bound for computing any given function must include reference to the complexity of the interconnection scheme. This is because, as might be expected, more efficient networks can be built by investing more resources in their construction. Information can be stored in the interconnection pattern, to be used later as a kind of "look-up table". Take for example the problem of computing an arbitrary computable single-valued Boolean function $f: \{0,1\}^* \rightarrow \{0,1\}$. We will show how to compute f on n inputs in a constant number of steps, using $n \, 2^n$ processors.

If $x = <x_0, \ldots, x_{n-1}>$ is an input of size n, let $int(x) = \sum_{i=0}^{n-1} x_i 2^i$ be a binary encoding of x as an integer. The $n \, 2^n$ processors are broken up into 2^n *teams* T_i, $0 \leq i < 2^n$. For $0 \leq i < 2^n$, team T_i consists of the n processors $i \, n + j$, for $0 \leq j < n$. The smallest-numbered processor of each team is a distinguished processor called the *manager* of that team. For each input x, the manager of $T_{int(x)}$ will have the value f(x) encoded as part of its interconnection pattern. Our problem then, given an input x, is to notify the manager of the appropriate team.

This is achieved as follows. Each team manager sets a specified register a to zero. For $0 \leq i < 2^n$, $0 \leq j < n$ the jth member of team T_i compares the jth symbol of the input to the jth bit of i. If these two values are different, it writes a one to register a of its team manager. The manager of $T_{int(x)}$ will be the only manager which is not written to; its register a still contains zero. It then consults its interconnection pattern for the value of f(x), and writes this value to processor 0 for subsequent output.

The following is a high-level implementation of this algorithm. Assume that initially variable x of processor p contains the pth bit (x_p) of the input, $0 \leq p < n$. Each processor has two variables i and j which (as in the previous paragraph) record that processor's team number and position within that team. Variable a of the team managers will be used for communication with its team members. The result f(x) will be found in variable r of processor 0 on termination.

The interconnection pattern is as follows. For $0 \leq i < 2^n$, $0 \leq j < n$, processor i n + j (the jth member of T_i) is connected to processor j (the processor in charge of the jth bit of the input), and processor i.n (its team manager). For each input x, processor n.int(x) is connected to processor f(x) via a special link. It can determine the value of f(x) by reading the PID of that processor.

> a:=r:=0
> i,j:= $\lfloor$PID/n $\rfloor$,PID mod n
> **if** (x **of processor** j) $\neq$ (j^{th} bit of i)
>> **then** (a **of processor** i*n):=1
> **if** (j = 0) and (a = 0)
>> **then** (r **of processor** 0) := PID **of processor** *special link*

Note that even non-recursive functions can be computed in constant time if the fixed-structure network is allowed to be non-uniform. We will normally restrict ourselves to uniform fixed-structure networks, that is, fixed-structure networks whose processor, degree and interconnection functions are computable. The algorithm as presented uses the full arithmetic instruction-set. The restricted arithmetic instruction-set can be substituted by increasing the number of processors in each team to 2^n (see Exercise 4.1). If the minimal instruction-set is used, the run-time is O(log n). Note that the values i.n, $0 \leq i < 2^n$, are not computed at run-time, but are stored as part of the interconnection pattern. The degree can be reduced to a constant by the use of binary trees for routing. The run-time is thus increased to $O(\log n)$ on either the full arithmetic, restricted arithmetic or minimal instruction-sets. The number of processors can be reduced to 2^{n+2} [38]. This increases the run-time to $O(n)$, although it does reduce the degree to a constant, and uses only finite-state machines as processors.

4.2. Shared Memory Machines

A popular alternative model is obtained by constraining processors to communicate via a common memory, rather than communicating by direct processor-to-processor links. Let $P,S,T,W:N \rightarrow N$. A *shared memory machine* consists of an infinite number of processors attached to a globally accessible shared memory. The shared memory consists of an infinite number of memory locations $s_0, s_1, ...,$ each of which can hold a single integer. Each processor possesses an infinite number of general purpose registers, and a unique read-only processor identity register PID which is preset to i in the ith processor, $i \in N$. A *program* for this machine consists of a finite list of instructions; each instruction is of the form either:

1. Read a value from a specified place in the shared memory.
2. Write a value to a specified place in the shared memory.
3. Perform an internal computation.
4. Transfer of control.

The allowable internal computations usually consist of direct and indirect register transfers, logical and arithmetic operations. The communication instructions are of the following form:

$$r_i \leftarrow s_{r_j} \quad (\text{read})$$
$$s_{r_i} \leftarrow r_j \quad (\text{write})$$

More formally, a *shared-memory machine* consists of a program P and a processor bound $P(n)$. A computation proceeds roughly as follows. An input of size n (where the "size" measure depends on the problem in question) is broken up into n unit-size pieces, and the ith piece is stored in shared memory location i, $0 \leq i < n$. All other memory locations and general purpose registers are set to zero. Processors $0,1,...,P(n)-1$ are activated simultaneously; they synchronously execute the program P. When all processors have halted, the output is to be found in some specified place in the shared memory.

The *processor* bound P(n) is a measure of the number of processors used as a function of input-size. The *space* S(n) is the maximum number of non-zero entries in the shared memory and registers at any time during the computation. (Note that this includes the input and the processor identity registers). The machine is said to have *word-size* W(n) if the maximum value in any register or shared memory location during any computation on an input of size n has absolute value less than $2^{W(n)}$. The *time* bound T(n) is the number of instructions executed before all processors have halted, again as a function of input-size.

Similar parallel machine models have appeared in a large number of papers, the earliest of which include Fortune and Wyllie [33], Goldschlager [41], Schwartz [112] and Shiloach and Vishkin [114]. We assume some reasonable protocol for dealing with memory access conflicts, as in those references. Although for our purposes the exact details of the write-conflict resolution scheme are not important, there are situations in which it is important (see Fich et al [29,28] and Li and Yesha [75]). The general consensus of opinion is that whilst the shared-memory model is a powerful theoretical tool, it will not be feasible to construct one using any foreseeable technology.

A shared-memory machine M can be simulated by a network with identical internal instruction-set, without asymptotic loss of resources. Suppose M has P(n) processors. Then the network has P(n)+1 processors. Processor 0 remains idle throughout the computation, whilst processor i, $1 \leq i \leq P(n)$ simulates the action of processor i-1 of M. The processors possessing input values first store them into the registers of processor 0 according to the input-convention of the shared-memory machine, in time $O(\frac{n}{P(n)} + 1)$. If $P(n) = \Omega(n)$, then this is a constant. Otherwise each processor has $\Omega(n/P(n))$ inputs, and thus the machine must run in time $\Omega(n/P(n))$ if it is to access all of the input symbols. In either case, the running-time of the machine is increased by at most a constant multiple. Any reference to shared memory location m is replaced by a reference to register r_m of processor 0. The extra processor can be eliminated by having processor 0 reserve the odd-numbered registers for its own use, and the even-numbered registers for the contents of the shared memory. A reference to shared memory location m is then replaced by a reference to register r_{2m} of processor 0.

Alternatively, the shared memory contents can be divided up amongst the processors of the network, provided the instruction-set is sufficiently powerful. Suppose M has P(n) processors and space S(n). Processor i of the network, $0 \leq i < P(n)$, simulates processor i of M, and in addition holds the values of shared memory locations i+jP(n), j $\geq$ 0. A reference to shared memory location m is replaced by a reference to register $r_{2 \lfloor m/P(n) \rfloor}$ of processor m mod P(n); each processor reserves its even-numbered registers for memory locations, and the odd-numbered registers for its own use. This assumes that the instruction-set is at least as powerful as the full arithmetic instruction-set of Section 3.1. If the restricted arithmetic instruction-set is used, P(n) should be replaced by $2^{\lceil \log P(n) \rceil}$. For a minimal instruction-set, the time-loss is $O(\log P(n))$ per instruction, using P(n) processors. If sufficiently many processors are used (so that each processor holds at most one memory location) this time-loss can be reduced to a constant multiple.

Similarly, a network M can be simulated by a shared-memory machine without asymptotic loss in resources, provided the instruction-set is sufficiently powerful. The registers of the network are stored in the common memory; each processor of the shared-memory machine need only have a constant number of local registers. Note that the same trick serves to reduce the local memory requirements of all shared-memory machines, subject to similar conditions. The processors which require input values according to the input-convention of the network can read them from the shared memory. Any reference to register r_i of processor j is replaced by a reference to shared-memory location i P(n) + j.

This replacement costs only a constant number of steps per access for machines with the full arithmetic instruction-set. As before, if P(n) is replaced by $2^{\lceil \log P(n) \rceil}$ it also costs a constant number of steps with the restricted arithmetic instruction-set. For machines with the minimal instruction-set, a similar result can be obtained by storing, along with each register r_i, the contents of r_i multiplied by P(n). This requires time proportional to $\lceil n/P(n) \rceil \log P(n)$ to set up for the initial input string. Thereafter, these values can be maintained and used for register access with a constant loss in time for each step of M. Alternatively, the multiplication by P(n) can be computed at access-time, at a cost of $O(\log P(n))$ per access.

In view of the close relationship between networks and shared-memory machines, particularly since the shared-memory machine can be viewed as a sub-model of the network machine, we will henceforth use the shared-memory model whenever possible.

4.3. A Practical Model

In the last section we saw a theoretically elegant but impractical variant of the network model. Here we will discuss a restricted, more practical variant of the network model. Many restrictions have been made in the literature, motivated, it is often claimed, by practical considerations. These include the following:

(1) Restrictions on degree. It is widely accepted that a completely-connected network is impractical. Some authors (for example, Galil and Paul [38]) think that degree should be constant (i.e. independent of input-size).

(2) Restrictions on the interconnection pattern. In the case of fixed-structure networks (see Section 4.1) it is desirable to restrict oneself to networks with interconnection patterns which are in a sense easy to compute (see, for example, [38]). This is also the case for uniform circuits [108] and conglomerates [45]. One advantage of this approach is that it avoids the kind of network described in Section 4.1, which can compute a large class of functions (including even non-recursive ones) in an unnaturally small amount of time.

(3) Restrictions on register access. Even if higher-degree networks are acceptable, should every processor necessarily have the freedom of being able to read *any* register of its neighbours? An alternative is to provide each processor with a special communication register COM, which is the *only* register accessible to other processors. The only allowable communication instructions are:

$$r_i \leftarrow (\text{COM of } r_j) \quad (\text{read})$$
$$(\text{COM of } r_i) \leftarrow r_j \quad (\text{write})$$

This approach was taken, for example, by Galil and Paul [38], Karp and Lipton [61] and Upfal [124]. We will call networks of this kind *restricted-access* networks.

(4) Restrictions on multiple register access. Some authors (for example, Fortune and Wyllie [33]) insist that simultaneous writes to a single register be disallowed, others (for example, Lev, Pippenger and Valiant [74]) insist that simultaneous reads of a single register also be banned.

We are now ready to define our practical model. A *feasible network* M is a fixed-structure network (see Section 4.1) with interconnection scheme (P,D,G), such that:

(i)   Each processor has a constant number of general-purpose registers.

(ii) The degree, D(n), is a constant.

(iii) The interconnection function G can be computed in polynomial time (that is, time polynomial in log P(n)) by a deterministic Turing machine.

These three conditions ensure that the networks are, in a sense, easy to construct. Each processor has a small amount of memory, and a small number of easy-to-compute interconnections. Machines with similar characteristics have appeared in many papers, including [37,86,104,112,122].

Even if we accept the feasible network as being feasibly constructible, it is unlikely that the fabrication costs would be so low that the average user would be willing to build a new network for each application. More likely, the user would prefer to present each new machine (in the form of a program) to a universal parallel computer which can simulate it at a small cost in resources. The user would thus be able to trade the fabrication cost of a feasible network for a small increase in resources at run-time.

A further advantage is to be gained if we can find an efficient feasible network which is universal for the general model of Section 3.1. From a practical point of view, it would provide the user of a feasible network with a flexible high-level programming language. Programs which are written in a high-level programming language similar to that of Section 3.1 could, although they may correspond to networks which are not feasibly constructible, be run on a feasible universal machine with only a small extra cost in resources. By building a single feasible network the user gains the use of a flexible and elegant virtual architecture corresponding to a completely-connected network. From a theoretical point of view, we obtain a practical motivation for studying the more esoteric parallel machine models of Chapter 3.

Note that the universal network is far more attractive than the machines that it can simulate. It it is a fixed-structure network with a small number of easy-to-compute interconnections per processor. The number of registers per processor is constant, and therefore the problem of providing access to arbitrary registers of neighbouring processors vanishes; we can insist that the universal network be restricted-access without asymptotic time-loss. Because the degree is constant, the problem of whether to allow simultaneous access to those communication registers also vanishes. Accesses in the universal network can be restricted to exclusive reads without asymptotic time-loss (see Exercise 4.3). Also, the requirement that the universal network is synchronized is no longer essential (see [38]).

Exactly what do we mean by a "universal machine"? Suppose U is a $P(n)$ processor (feasible) network, M is an arbitrary network, and $x = <x_0,...,x_{n-1}>$ is an input of size n. A *simulation* of M on input x by U is to proceed as follows. Let $p=P(n)$. Place x_i into register $r_{\lfloor i/p \rfloor}$ of processor (i mod p). Place into the remaining registers of processor 0 a concise finite encoding of the program of M. Set all other general-purpose registers to zero, and simultaneously activate processors 0,1,...p–1 on the program of U. Suppose M computes a function f, and $f_n(x) = <y_0, \ldots, y_{m-1}>$ (for definitions see Section 3.1). U is said to be *universal* if for all networks M and inputs x, when all processors of U have halted, register $r_{\lfloor i/p \rfloor}$ of processor (i mod p) contains y_i, for $0 \leq i < m$.

We are interested in a particular kind of simulation, which we shall call "step-wise". A simulation of a $T(n)$ time bounded network M on an input of size n is said to be *step-wise* if:

(1) For $0 \leq i < S(n)$, $0 \leq \tau \leq T(n)$ each register i of M has a corresponding *dedicated processor* $d(i,\tau)$ in U. Note that we may allow $d(i,\tau) = d(j,\tau)$ when $i \neq j$.

(2) Suppose $t:\mathbf{N}\rightarrow\mathbf{N}$. The simulation consists of three phases:

  (a) Initialization. This includes the assignment of, and routing of the input values to the dedicated processors as well as any pre-computations required for phase (b).

  (b) Computation. The computation phase is to take $t(n)T(n)$ steps. For $0 \leq \tau \leq T(n)$ we require that after $t(n)\tau$ steps of this phase, processor $d(i,\tau)$ has a distinguished register which contains the contents of register i of M after τ steps of M, $0 \leq i < S(n)$.

  (c) Termination. This includes routing of the output from the dedicated processors to the output processors.

Such a universal network is said to have *delay* t(n). The *set-up time* is the time required for phases (a) and (c) combined. A step-wise simulation is also said to be *literal* if a data-transfer from registers i to register j of M, $0 \leq i,j < S(n)$, during time-step τ, $1 \leq \tau \leq T(n)$, gives rise to a communication between processors $d(i,\tau-1)$ and $d(j,\tau)$ of U between time-steps $(\tau-1)t(n)+1$ and $\tau t(n)$ of phase (b). More formally, define a directed multi-graph G_n as follows (G_n is to reflect the information flow between processors of U during the simulation of time-step τ of M). G_n has vertex-set $\{0,1,...,P_U(n)-1\}$ (where U has $P_U(n)$ processors), and an edge from vertex u to vertex v, labelled δ, if during time-step $(\tau-1)t(n)+\delta$ of phase (b), processor v of U reads a value from processor u, $1 \leq \delta \leq t(n)$. (Recall that processors of U use only exclusive-reads for inter-processor communication). We require that there be a path from $d(i,\tau-1)$ to $d(j,\tau)$ in G_n with monotonic increasing labels on the edges. Thus in a literal simulation, a data transfer between registers of the simulated network can give rise to a data transfer between the corresponding dedicated processors within the simulation of that time-step. In a *non-literal* simulation, the required data may (for example) have started out during the simulation of the previous step of M, and been kept up-to-date by auxiliary processors along the way (see Sections 10.2, 10.3).

Later, we will consider a more restrictive form of literal simulation in which the dedicated processor assignment does not change with time. We will call this type of simulation *strongly-literal*. In Section 10.1 we give an upper-bound of $O(\log P(n))$ on the delay for a strongly-literal simulation of a $P(n)$ processor, constant-degree, restricted-access network, and match this with a lower-bound in Section 10.2.

Our characterization of simulations into *strongly-literal, literal* and *non-literal* categories is motivated by (although different from) the *type 1, type 2* and *type 3* characterization used by Meyer auf der Heide [52].

4.4. Exercises

4.1 Show that a non-uniform fixed-structure network with the restricted arithmetic instruction-set can compute any n-input Boolean function in constant time with $2^{O(n)}$ processors (see Section 4.1).

4.2 Show that a shared-memory machine can be restricted to have only a constant number of registers per processor without increasing any resource by more than a constant multiple, provided its instruction-set is powerful enough. What increase in running-time is obtained for the minimal instruction-set? What increase in running-time is obtained for the restricted arithmetic instruction-set? How many registers per processor are sufficient?

4.3 Show that register accesses in a feasible network can be restricted to exclusive reads only, without asymptotic time-loss.

5   Space and Parallel Time

Suppose we consider a parallel machine as an acceptor for a language over a finite alphabet (see Section 3.1). *The parallel computation thesis is an attempt to characterize the language recognition capabilities of time-bounded parallel computers. Informally, it states that "sequential space is polynomially related to parallel time". This enables us to take advantage of the large body of knowledge relating to sequential space complexity, in particular, P-completeness. P-complete problems are problems in P which have the property that if any of them can be recognized in poly-log space (equivalently, poly-log parallel time), then so can every problem in P. (We use the term "poly-log" to describe $\log^{O(1)} n$, a polynomial in the logarithm of n.) Thus P-complete problems probably do not have an exponential speed-up in parallel.

In Section 5.1 we introduce small-space sequential computations, and in Section 5.2 meet the concept of log-space reduction and P-completeness. Section 5.3 examines a P-complete problem, the *circuit-value problem,* and some of its variants. Finally, in Section 5.4 we relate space to parallel time.

5.1. Small-Space Sequential Computations

The *space* required by a deterministic Turing machine is usually defined to be the maximum (over all inputs x of size n) of the number of tape cells scanned by any tape head. It would be just as realistic to define space using the number of bits of memory used in a RAM program, or any other "reasonable" model of sequential computation. Indeed, most "reasonable" models of sequential computation seem to have polynomially-related time and space bounds. This extension of the classical Church-Turing thesis is called the *sequential computation thesis* by Goldschlager in [47]. Our decision to use the Turing machine as our model of sequential computation is therefore not critical, to within a polynomial. Note that for a standard Turing machine the space requirement is bounded above by the running-time, and is at least n (since at least n cells are required to store the input). However, for some problems, the amount of work-space required is exponentially smaller than the space required for the input and output. We will study these problems in more detail.

In order to distinguish between work-space and space used solely for the storage of inputs, we will use a Turing machine model with a read-only input tape, a one-way infinite work-tape and a write-only output tape. We measure *space* as the maximum, over all inputs x of size n, of the number of work-tape cells used in processing x. Nondeterminism is defined in the usual way, with space defined to be the maximum, over all inputs x of size n, of the minimum, over all accepting computations on input x, of the number of work-tape cells used in that accepting computation (with space taken to be zero if no such accepting computation exists). Note that (by the tape reduction theorem [57]), we can increase the number of work-tapes to any constant k without affecting the space-bound by more than a constant multiple. And, as we shall see, constant multiples in space-bounds can be ignored.

Definition. DSPACE(S(n)) is the class of languages which can be recognized in space S(n) by a deterministic Turing machine. Similarly, NSPACE(S(n)) is the class of languages which can be recognized in space S(n) by a nondeterministic Turing machine.

Theorem 5.1.1 For all $c \in N$, $c \geq 2$, DSPACE(S(n))$\subseteq$DSPACE(S(n)/c).
Proof. See Hopcroft and Ullman [57]. □

A *configuration* of a Turing machine is a snapshot of its internal settings at a particular point in time. That is, it consists of the positions of the input, output and work-tape heads, the contents of the work-tape and the internal state of the finite-state control. Note that a configuration of an S(n) space-bounded Turing machine can be described in O(S(n)+log n) bits if it is used as a language acceptor. It is clear that DSPACE(log n)$\subseteq$P, since a deterministic Turing machine that uses work-space O(log n) has at most polynomially many configurations, each of which can occur at most once in any computation (otherwise an infinite loop would occur). Furthermore, it is easy to see that NSPACE(log n)$\subseteq$P. Suppose M is a nondeterministic Turing machine which uses space O(log n). Given an input x, define the *computation graph* of M on input x to have a vertex for every configuration of M on input x, and an edge from vertex u to vertex v precisely when configuration v follows from configuration u on input x according to the rules of M. A depth-first search can be carried out on this graph to ascertain whether a vertex corresponding to an accepting configuration can be reached

breadth

from the initial configuration using the edges of the computation graph. Since M runs in logarithmic space, it can have at most polynomially many configurations, and hence the depth-first search can be carried out in polynomial time (those unfamiliar with depth-first search can consult Aho, Hopcroft and Ullman [3]). The following are popular conjectures, all of which remain open problems:

NSPACE(log n) $\neq$ DSPACE(log n).

P $\neq$ DSPACE(log n).

P $\neq$ NSPACE(log n).

Consider the following problem:

THE GRAPH ACCESSIBILITY PROBLEM (GAP).

INSTANCE: A directed graph G = (V,E), and two distinguished vertices, u,v$\in$V.
QUESTION: Does there exist a path from u to v in G?

We use the number of vertices in V as a measure of input-size. We will require that a reasonable encoding scheme is used, such as an edge-list or adjacency matrix, so that $|V|$ is to within a polynomial an accurate measure of the number of bits needed to describe an instance of GAP. The chief requirement is that edge-queries can be answered using space logarithmic in the size of the graph. For convenience, suppose that the vertices are numbered 1 through n, and that the edges are represented by an adjacency matrix. Clearly GAP$\in$P (simply use depth-first search). Also, it is clear that GAP$\in$NSPACE(log n). Consider the following pseudo-code algorithm.

```
x:=u
while x ≠ v do
    guess a value for y
    if (x,y)∉E then REJECT
    x:=y
ACCEPT
```

It uses logarithmic space, and will nondeterministically guess a path from u to v if one exists. But how much space is needed to solve GAP deterministically? Consider the following recursive algorithm:

procedure path(i,j,k)

    comment returns true if there is a path from vertex i to j of length at most k

    if k = 0 **then** return(i = j) **else**

    if k = 1 **then** return((i,j)∈E) **else**

       return (∃ l path(i,l, $\lceil k/2 \rceil$) and path(l,j, $\lfloor k/2 \rfloor$))

The existential quantifier is evaluated by sequentially trying each possible vertex l in turn. The depth of recursion is $O(\log k)$, and at each level of recursion we use a constant number of variables, each requiring $O(\log n)$ bits. GAP can be solved by computing path(u,v,n), which therefore uses space $\log^2 n$.

In the remainder of this chapter, we will express our algorithms using a so-called *expression language,* that is, we will omit the *returns*, deeming a procedure to return the expression that it contains.

Definition. A function $S:N \rightarrow N$ is called *space-constructible* if a deterministic Turing machine can, on input n in unary, output $S(n)$ in unary using space $S(n)$. Most useful functions, for example, polynomials and poly-logs, are space-constructible.

Theorem 5.1.2 (Savitch's Theorem [109]). If $S(n)$ is space-constructible, $S(n) = \Omega(\log n)$, then $NSPACE(S(n)) \subseteq DSPACE(S(n)^2)$.

Proof. (Sketch). Let M be an $S(n)$ space-bounded nondeterministic Turing machine. Modify it so that its accepting configuration is unique, by ensuring that before it enters the accept state, it erases all work-tapes, and returns all heads to their initial positions. The computation graph of this new machine on input x of length n has $2^{O(S(n))}$ vertices, and a path from the initial configuration to the final one iff M accepts x. By using the algorithm for GAP, we can determine if such a path exists in space $(\log 2^{O(S(n))})^2$. The computation graph need not be computed explicitly since edge-queries can be answered in a small amount of space (see Exercise 5.1). □

The following conjectures are still open.

    $P \not\subseteq DSPACE(\log^2 n)$.

    $DSPACE(\log^2 n) \not\subseteq P$.

    $DSPACE(\log^2 n) \neq DSPACE(\log n)$.

    $DSPACE(\log^2 n) \not\subseteq NP$.

Definition. POLYLOGSPACE $= \bigcup_{k \geq 1} DSPACE(\log^k n)$.

Note that Theorem 5.1.2 implies that POLYLOGSPACE is invariant under non-determinism. It is conjectured that P $\not\subseteq$ POLYLOGSPACE and POLYLOGSPACE $\not\subseteq$ P, but all that is known is that P $\neq$ POLYLOGSPACE [14].

5.2. Log-Space Completeness

The question of whether P $\subseteq$ POLYLOGSPACE is still open, and as we shall see later, is of fundamental importance to parallel computation. The current status is similar to that of the NP $\subseteq$ P question. It is widely conjectured that NP $\not\subseteq$ P, evidence being provided by the existence of *NP-complete* problems, which are the hardest problems in NP in the sense that if they are members of P, then so is every problem in NP. It is also widely conjectured that P $\not\subseteq$ POLYLOGSPACE, evidence being provided by the existence of so-called *P-complete* problems, which are the hardest problems in P in the sense that if they are members of POLYLOGSPACE, then so is every problem in P. A stronger concept of reduction is needed to show P-completeness; the concept of a polynomial-time reduction is replaced by a log-space reduction. To emphasize this, a P-complete problem is often called *log-space complete for P*. Using this nomenclature, an NP-complete problem would be called "polynomial-time complete for NP".

Definition. Let Σ be a finite alphabet. A language A $\subseteq \Sigma^*$ is *log space reducible* to B $\subseteq \Sigma^*$ if there exists a function f computable in logarithmic space such that for all x $\in \Sigma^*$, x $\in$ A iff f(x) $\in$ B. We write A $\leq_{\log}$ B.

Definition. Let C be a class of languages. We say that B is *log-space hard for* C if for all A $\in$ C, A $\leq_{\log}$ B. If, in addition, B $\in$ C, we say that B is *log-space complete for* C. We will use the terms "P-complete" and "log-space complete for P" interchangeably.

Before proceeding further, we should verify that the above notion of log-space completeness matches our intuitive description, namely, that if a P-complete problem is a member of POLYLOGSPACE then P $\subseteq$ POLYLOGSPACE. That is, we must prove that if A $\leq_{\log}$ B and B $\in$ POLYLOGSPACE then A $\in$ POLYLOGSPACE. An intuitively appealing, but erroneous approach is the following. Construct a Turing machine which on input x computes f(x) in log space, and then simulates the poly-log space recognizer for B on its output. This approach works perfectly well for polynomial-time reductions (see, for example, Lemma 2.1 of Garey and Johnson [39]), but fails here since it necessitates writing

54

f(x) (which may be extremely large; since f(x) is computable by a log-space Turing machine, it may have size as large as a polynomial in n) on the work-tape. However, we can avoid writing down f(x) by noting that we only need one symbol of f(x) at a time; the one under the input head. This can be recomputed by simulating the Turing machine for f, discarding the output bits that are not currently required. Let $S:\mathbf{N}{\rightarrow}\mathbf{N}$. We say that S is *closed under polynomials* if $S(n^{O(1)}) = O(S(n))$. Note that $S(n) = \log^{O(1)}n$ is closed under polynomials.

Theorem 5.2.1 (Stockmeyer and Meyer [121], Jones [59]) Suppose $S(n) = \Omega(\log n)$, and S is closed under polynomials. If $A \leq_{\log} B$ and $B{\in}DSPACE(S(n))$ then $A{\in}DSPACE(S(n))$.

Proof. Since $A \leq_{\log} B$, there exists a function f computable in logarithmic space such that for all $x{\in}\Sigma^*$, $x{\in}A$ iff $f(x){\in}B$. If $y{\in}\{0,1\}^*$, $y = y_k y_{k-1}...y_0$, let the integer whose binary representation is y, denoted int(y), be $\sum_{i=0}^{k} y_i 2^i$. Suppose we have a deterministic Turing machine which computes f in log space. It can easily be converted into an acceptor M_f for the language:

$$L_f = \{<x,i,s> \mid x{\in}\Sigma^*, s{\in}\Sigma, i{\in}\{0,1\}^* \text{ and the int}(i)^{th} \text{ symbol of f(x) is s}\}$$

which also runs in logarithmic space.

Suppose $B{\in}DSPACE(S(n))$. Then there is a deterministic Turing machine M_B which recognizes B in space $S(n)$. Create a new Turing machine M_A. M_A has the following action on input x. It keeps the binary representation i of some integer on its work-tape (henceforth we will not distinguish between the integer i and its binary representation). This is the number of the input tape cell that the input head would be pointing to if it had input f(x) instead of x. It is initially set to zero. It also keeps the ith symbol of f(x) on the work-tape. It computes this initially by simulating M_f to determine whether $<x,0,s>{\in}L_f$, for each symbol $s{\in}\Sigma$ in turn.

M_A simulates M_B step-by-step, with the following modifications:

1. Where the transitions of M_B depend upon the current input symbol, the corresponding transitions of M_A depend upon the current symbol of f(x), which can be found on the work-tape.
2. Where the transitions of M_B demand that its input head be moved one cell to the left or right, M_A subtracts one from or adds one to the value of i, respectively, and recomputes the ith symbol of f(x).

55

Then M_A recognizes A, is deterministic and uses space $O(\log n)$ to store i, $O(\log n)$ as work-space for the simulation of M_f, and $O(S(\,|\,f(x)\,|\,))$ for the simulation of M_A. Since a deterministic logarithmic-space Turing machine must run in polynomial time, $|\,f(x)\,| = n^{O(1)}$. Since S is closed under polynomials, and $S(n) = \Omega(\log n)$, M_A uses space $S(n)$. $\square$

Theorem 5.2.2 $\leq_{\log}$ is transitive.

Proof. Similar to the proof of Theorem 5.2.1 (see Exercise 5.3). $\square$

Corollary 5.2.3 If A is log-space complete for P, and $B \in P$, $A \leq_{\log} B$, then B is log-space complete for P.

5.3. The Circuit-Value Problem

Informally, the circuit-value problem is the following. Given a combinational circuit (that is, a circuit without feedback loops) built from two-input Boolean gates, and an assignment to its inputs, compute its output. Let B_2 denote the set of two-input Boolean functions. More formally, a *circuit* over base $B \subseteq B_2$ is a sequence $C = \langle g_1,...,g_n \rangle$ where each g_i is either a variable $x_1, x_2,...$ (in which case it is called an *input*) or $f(j,k)$ for some function $f \in B$ (in which case it is called a *gate*), $i > j,k$. Note that we have numbered the gates of a combinational circuit in such a manner that every gate is numbered higher than the gates from which it receives its inputs. This enforces the restriction that there are no feedback loops. An *input assignment* is an assignment of values $v(x_i) \in \{0,1\}$ to the variables x_i of C. The *value* of a circuit C at gate g_i, $v(C,g_i)$ is given by

$$v(C,x_j) = v(x_j)$$

$$v(C,f(j,k)) = f(v(C,g_j),v(C,g_k))$$

The *value* of a circuit C is defined to be $v(C) = v(C,g_n)$. The *circuit-value problem* over base B is defined as $CVP_B = \{\,C\,\mid\,v(C) = 1\,\}$. We will use CVP or "the circuit-value problem" to denote the circuit-value problem over a complete base (in classical switching theory, a base B is *complete* if every two-input Boolean function can be realized using a combinational circuit built from gates which realize functions from B). McColl [81] gives an easy method due to Emile Post for determining whether a given basis is complete. If B consists of two-input AND and OR functions, then CVP_B is called the *monotone circuit-value problem,* denoted MCVP. We can easily generalize the above description to include unbounded fan-in gates (that is, gates which realize Boolean functions with an arbitrary number of inputs). In particular, if the base B consists of unbounded fan-in AND and OR then CVP$_B$ is called the *unbounded fan-in circuit-value problem,* or UCVP. We can encode every instance of the circuit-value problem as a list of gate descriptions, where each gate description consists of the identification number of a gate, the function that it computes and the identification numbers of the gates from which it receives its inputs. The number of gates is thus, to within a polynomial, a reasonable measure of the number of bits needed to describe a problem instance.

Theorem 5.3.1 UCVP is log-space complete for P.

Proof. Clearly UCVP$\in$P. It remains to show that, for all L$\in$P, L $\leq_{\log}$ UCVP. Suppose L$\in$P. Then there is a single-tape Turing machine M which accepts L in polynomial time. We will use the formalism of Hopcroft and Ullman [57], with the minor exception that we will number the tape-cells of our Turing machine starting from zero and place the inputs, one per cell, consecutively starting in cell 0, with all other cells blank. We insist that M remains in the accept state after it enters it for the first time. Suppose that M has state-set Q $= \{q_0, q_1, ..., q_\alpha\}$, with q_0 the initial state and q_α the accept state, tape-alphabet $\Gamma = \{s_0, s_1, ..., s_\beta\}$, with s_0 the distinguished blank symbol, and transition function $\delta: Q \times \Gamma \to Q \times \Gamma \times \{L, R\}$. Given an input x for M, we will construct, in logarithmic space, a circuit C and an input y such that C outputs 1 on input y iff M accepts x, that is, iff x$\in$L.

We will use the construction of Ladner [69] to produce a circuit which simulates M. Suppose that M runs in time T(n), a polynomial, and that x $= x_1 x_2 ... x_n$ is an input to M, with $x_i \in \Gamma$ for $1 \leq i \leq n$. Our circuit C will have fourteen different types of gates. In what follows, "at time t" will mean "immediately after the tth transition of M".

1. Gate D(i,j,t), $0 \leq i \leq \alpha$, $0 \leq j \leq \beta$, $0 \leq t \leq T(n)$, will be true iff M is in state q_i scanning symbol s_j at time t. D(i,j,0) is an input, which is set to 1 if $i = 0$ and $x_1 = s_j$ and is set to 0 otherwise. D(i,j,t) for $1 \leq t \leq T(n)$ is a two-input AND gate, with inputs from Q(i,t) and S(j,t).

2. Gate Q(i,t), $0 \leq i \leq \alpha$, $0 \leq t \leq T(n)$, will be true iff M is in state q_i at time t. Q(i,0) is an input, with Q(0,0) set to 1 and Q(i,0) set to 0 for $1 \leq i \leq \alpha$. Q(i,t), $1 \leq t \leq T(n)$, is an OR gate with at most $\alpha\beta$ inputs. The inputs are from those D(j,k,t–1) with $0 \leq j \leq \alpha$, $0 \leq k \leq \beta$ such that there exists

57

$0 \leq 1 \leq \beta$, $d \in \{L,R\}$ such that $\delta(q_j,s_k) = (q_i,s_l,d)$.

3. Gate S(j,t), $0 \leq j \leq \beta$, $0 \leq t \leq T(n)$, will be true iff M is scanning symbol s_j at time t. S(j,0) is an input, which is set to 1 if $x_1 = s_j$ and set to 0 for all other j. S(j,t) is an OR gate with T(n)+1 inputs, from P(m,j,t) where $0 \leq m \leq T(n)$.

4. Gate P(m,j,t), $0 \leq m,t \leq T(n)$, $0 \leq j \leq \beta$, is true if M is in cell m scanning symbol s_j at time t. P(m,j,0) is an input, which is set to one if $m = 0$ and $x_1 = s_j$, and to zero otherwise. P(m,j,t), $1 \leq t \leq T(n)$ is a two-input AND gate with inputs from C(m,j,t) and H(m,t).

5. Gate C(m,j,t), $0 \leq m,t \leq T(n)$, $0 \leq j \leq \beta$, is true iff cell m contains symbol s_j at time t. C(m,j,0) is an input, which is set to one if either $0 \leq m \leq n$ and $x_m = s_j$, or $n < m \leq T(n)$ and $j = 0$. C(m,j,t) is a two-input OR gate with inputs from W(m,j,t) and E(m,j,t).

6. Gate W(m,j,t), $0 \leq m \leq T(n)$, $1 \leq t \leq T(n)$, $0 \leq j \leq \beta$, is true iff symbol s_j was written into cell m during the tth step. W(m,j,t) is a two-input AND gate with inputs from O(j,t) and H(m,t–1).

7. Gate O(j,t), $1 \leq t \leq T(n)$, $0 \leq j \leq \beta$, is true iff symbol s_j was written during the tth step. O(j,t) is an OR gate with at most $\alpha\beta$ inputs. The inputs are from those gates D(i,k,t–1) such that there exist $0 \leq 1 \leq \alpha$ and $d \in \{L,R\}$ such that $\delta(q_i,s_k) = (q_l,s_j,d)$.

8. Gate E(m,j,t), $0 \leq m \leq T(n)$, $1 \leq t \leq T(n)$, $0 \leq j \leq \beta$, is true iff cell m retained the symbol s_j during the tth step. E(m,j,t) is a two-input AND gate with inputs from U(m,t–1) and C(m,j,t–1).

9. Gate U(m,t), $0 \leq m,t \leq T(n)$, will be true if M is not scanning cell m at time t. U(m,0) is an input, which is set to zero if $m = 0$, and is set to one otherwise. U(m,t) for $1 \leq t \leq T(n)$ is an OR gate with at most T(n) inputs. The inputs are from H(i,t) where $0 \leq i \leq T(n)$ and $i \neq m$.

10. Gate H(m,t), $0 \leq m,t \leq T(n)$, will be true iff M is scanning cell number m at time t. H(m,0) is an input, with H(0,0) set to 1, and H(m,0) set to 0 for $1 \leq m \leq T(n)$. H(m,t), $1 \leq t \leq T(n)$ is a two-input OR gate with inputs from F(m,t) and G(m,t).

11. Gate F(m,t), $1 \leq m,t \leq T(n)$, will be true if the head enters cell m from the left on the tth transition. F(m,t) is a two-input AND gate with inputs from H(m–1,t–1) and R(t).

12. Gate G(m,t), $0 \leq m < T(n)$, $1 \leq t \leq T(n)$, will be true if the head enters cell m from the right on the tth transition. G(m,t) is a two-input AND gate

with inputs from $H(m+1,t-1)$ and $L(t)$.

13. Gate $L(t)$, $1 \le t \le T(n)$, will be true if the head moves left on the tth transition. $L(t)$ is an OR gate with at most $\alpha\beta$ inputs. The inputs are from those $D(i,j,t-1)$ with $0 \le i \le \alpha$, $0 \le j \le \beta$ such that there exists $0 \le k \le \alpha$, $0 \le l \le \beta$ such that $\delta(q_i,s_j) = (q_k,s_l,L)$.

14. Gate $R(t)$, $1 \le t \le T(n)$, will be true if the head moves right on the tth transition. $R(t)$ is an OR gate with at most $\alpha\beta$ inputs. The inputs are from those $D(i,j,t-1)$ with $0 \le i \le \alpha$, $0 \le j \le \beta$ such that there exists $0 \le k \le \alpha$, $0 \le l \le \beta$ such that $\delta(q_i,s_j) = (q_k,s_l,R)$.

The output of the circuit is gate $Q(\alpha,T(n))$. It is easy to prove by induction that the gates play the roles ascribed to them in the above description, in particular that gate $Q(\alpha,T(n))$ has output 1 iff M is in state q_α at time $T(n)$, that is, M accepts input x. The construction of the circuit takes space which is logarithmic in $T(n)$ given $x = x_1x_2...x_n$. Since $T(n)$ is a polynomial in n, this implies that our reduction can be performed in space logarithmic in n. Note that, as expected, our circuit has size a polynomial in n (it has $O(T(n)^2)$ gates and $O(T(n))$ inputs, to be precise). We have used only AND and OR gates in our construction. Hence for all L$\in$P, L $\le_{log}$ UCVP, thus UCVP is P-complete. $\square$

Corollary 5.3.2 (Goldschlager [42]) MCVP is log-space complete for P.
Proof. Clearly MCVP$\in$P. It is easy to prove that UCVP $\le_{log}$ MCVP (see Exercise 5.4). Therefore, by Corollary 5.2.3, MCVP is P-complete. $\square$

Corollary 5.3.3 (Ladner [69]) CVP is log-space complete for P.
Ladner initially proved that CVP was P-complete from first principles, and Goldschlager [42] demonstrated that CVP $\le_{log}$ MCVP (using "double-rail logic", see Section 11.1), thus implying by Corollary 5.2.3 that MCVP is log-space complete for P. It is known precisely which of the two-input bases B$\subseteq$B$_2$ make the circuit-value problem P-complete (Goldschlager and Parberry [48]). Ignoring the trivial two-input Boolean functions, CVP$_B$ is P-complete except when either:

1. B consists of Boolean OR,
2. B consists of Boolean AND, or
3. B consists of parity-functions; that is, any or all of exclusive-or, equivalence and negation.

In each of these three cases, CVP$_B\in$DSPACE($\log^2 n$).

Corollary 5.3.3 holds even when the circuit is required to be planar, that is, constructed without crossing wires. More formally, a *planar circuit* over base

59

$B \subseteq B_2$ is a sequence of levels $C = <l_0,l_1,...,l_d>$. Level l_0 is a sequence $x_1,x_2,...,x_n$ of *inputs*. Level l_i, $1 \leq i \leq d$ consists of a sequence $<g_1^i,...,g_s^i>$ of *gates*, where each $g_j^i = f(k_{2i-1},k_{2i})$, for some function $f \in B$, and $k_i = k_{i-1}$ or $k_i = k_{i-1}+1$. An *input assignment* is an assignment of values $v(x_i) \in \{0,1\}$ to the variables x_i of C. The *value* of a circuit C at gate g_j^i, $v(C,g_j^i)$ is given by:

$$v(C,g_j^0) = v(x_j)$$

and for $i \geq 1$, if $g_j^i = f(a,b)$ then:

$$v(C,g_j^i) = f(v(C,g_a^{i-1}),v(C,g_b^{i-1})).$$

The *value* of a circuit C is defined to be $v(C) = v(C,g_1^d)$. The *planar circuit-value problem* over base B is defined as $PCVP_B = \{ C \mid v(C) = 1 \}$. We will use PCVP or "the planar circuit-value problem" to denote the planar circuit-value problem over a complete base.

Theorem 5.3.4 (Goldschlager [42]) The planar circuit-value problem is log-space complete for P.

Proof. (Sketch) Clearly PCVP∈P. We will show that CVP $\leq_{log}$ PCVP. We will make use of a *planar crossover circuit*. This is a planar combinational circuit with two inputs and two outputs, whose outputs consist of the two inputs interchanged. Figure 5.3.1 shows a planar crossover circuit built from three exclusive-or gates.

On input $x,y \in \{0,1\}$, the left output computes $x \oplus (x \oplus y) = y$, and the right output computes $(x \oplus y) \oplus y = x$. McColl [81] has determined exactly which of the two-input Boolean bases admit planar crossover circuits.

The reduction proceeds as follows. Suppose we are given a combinational circuit and its inputs. The input assignment for the planar circuit will be identical to the input to the original. The planar circuit will be divided into a series of "phases", each phase being a planar combinational circuit of size polynomial in the size of the original circuit. The number of phases will be bounded above by the size of the original circuit. Phase 0 just consists of the inputs. Phase i, $i \geq 1$ has a copy of the inputs to the circuit, plus the value of gates j, $1 \leq j \leq i-1$, and will output the value of gates j, $1 \leq j \leq i$. Thus the contribution of each phase is to compute the output of one gate in the original circuit. This is achieved by using planar crossovers to route the two values needed by that gate together (remembering that we have numbered the gates of the combinational circuit in such a manner that every gate is numbered higher than the gates from which it receives its inputs) and placing the appropriate gate there.

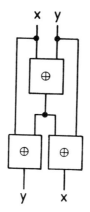

Figure 5.3.1 Planar crossover circuit.

This reduction can be carried out using logarithmic space. Hence CVP $\leq_{\log}$ PCVP, and so by Corollary 5.3.3 and Corollary 5.2.3, PCVP is P-complete. □

Curiously, whilst the monotone and planar circuit-value problems are log-space complete for P, and hence are unlikely to be in POLYLOGSPACE, the circuit-value problem for circuits which have both of these properties (the *monotone-planar circuit-value problem,* MPCVP) can be solved in $O(\log^2 n)$ space [43]. Finally, let us consider the tree circuit-value problem (TCVP), the circuit-value problem restricted to circuits which have no fan-out.

Lemma 5.3.5 In any tree of N vertices, and k < N, there is a vertex with at least k vertices beneath it, each of whose children have at most k vertices beneath it.
Proof. Work up level-by-level from the leaves. Eventually such a vertex must be found. □

Theorem 5.3.6 TCVP∈DSPACE($\log^2 n$).
Proof. Suppose we have a tree-circuit whose gates (including inputs) are numbered $g_1,...,g_n$. Let S denote the set of true inputs and T denote he set of false inputs. We claim that the circuit has output 1 iff eval(n,S,T,n) returns true, where procedure eval is defined as follows.

procedure eval(i,S,T,m)

    comment returns true if g_i has output 1 in a tree-circuit of size m

                    assuming that all gates in S have output 1 and all gates

                    in T have output 0

if $g_i \in S$ **then** true

    else if $(g_i \in T) \bigvee (m = 1)$ **then** false

        else $\exists j$ with $1 \leq j \leq n$ such that the following holds:

            Suppose $g_j = f(g_k, g_l)$ and let

            $V = f(\text{eval}(k,S,T, \lfloor m/2 \rfloor), \text{eval}(l,S,T, \lfloor m/2 \rfloor))$.

            Then $(V \bigwedge \text{eval}(i,S \cup \{j\},T, \lceil m/2 \rceil)) \bigvee$

                $(\neg V \bigwedge \text{eval}(i,S,T \cup \{j\}, \lceil m/2 \rceil))$

We claim that eval(i,S,T,m) returns true if g_i has output 1 in a tree-circuit of size m, assuming that all gates in S have output 1, and all gates in T have output 0. The proof is by induction on m, using Lemma 5.3.5 with $N = \lfloor m/2 \rfloor$. Since the parameter m is halved on each recursive call, the depth of recursion is O(log n). The existential quantifier can be computed by repeatedly trying each candidate gate in turn. We solve the tree circuit-value problem by calling eval with i denoting the output gate, S the set of true inputs, T the set of false inputs and m = n. Thus the procedure uses O(log n) space at each level of recursion, which implies that the total space requirement is O(log²n). The bulk of S and T (the true and false inputs respectively) is kept on the input tape, with the remainder threaded into the run-time stack. □

Lynch [79] has shown that the tree circuit-value problem can actually be solved in logarithmic space. However, the above technique is widely applicable to more difficult problems (see Exercise 5.6).

5.4. The Parallel Computation Thesis

In Section 3.2 we raised the following important question: what constitutes a "reasonable" model of parallel computation? In particular, what is a reasonable instruction-set for our processors, given that we have chosen a unit-cost measure of time? Goldschlager, in [45] placed certain restrictions on his SIMDAG's (a variant of the shared-memory model considered in Section 4.2) to ensure that they satisfy the *parallel computation thesis,* which can be stated as follows: time on any "reasonable" parallel model is polynomially equivalent to sequential (log-cost) space. Evidence for this thesis is provided by a multiplicity of "reasonable" models, including alternating Turing machines [18] uniform circuits [15] and vector machines [103] in addition to Goldschlager's SIMDAG and conglomerate.

As we shall see later in this section, in order to make networks and shared-memory machines satisfy the parallel computation thesis, it is necessary to place upper-bounds on the word-size and type of instructions allowed. These restrictions can be accepted as "reasonable" purely on practical grounds; one can argue that the word-size of problems tackled in practice should not grow too rapidly with input-size, and that the instruction-set should not be too powerful.

The parallel computation thesis also provides us with a powerful theoretical tool. Suppose that we are interested in those problems from P which have an exponential speed-up in parallel, that is, those members of P which can be solved in time $\log^{O(1)} n$ by a "reasonable" parallel machine. If a "reasonable" machine is one which satisfies the parallel computation thesis, then these are precisely the members of P which can be solved in poly-log space by a Turing machine. Thus log-space complete problems probably do not have an exponential speed-up on any "reasonable" parallel machine, where the parallel computation thesis is used as a criterion for "reasonableness". Thus, for example, the circuit-value problem probably does not have an exponential speed-up in parallel on a "reasonable" machine, whereas the monotone-planar circuit-value problem does.

The Graph Accessibility Problem also has an exponential speedup in parallel. We present a poly-log time parallel program for GAP on a shared-memory machine. An instance of GAP is described as follows. The vertices of $G = (V,E)$ are numbered from 0 to n–1 consecutively. The shared-memory machine is given n, the numbers of the two vertices $0 \leq u,v < n$, and an adjacency matrix for G, that is, an array A where A[i,j] is true iff $(i,j) \in E$. A is kept in the shared memory; all other values can be maintained locally by all processors. The following algorithm is to be run on n^3 processors.

$$i,j,k := \left\lfloor PID/n^2 \right\rfloor, \left\lfloor (PID \bmod n^2)/n \right\rfloor, PID \bmod n$$

A[i,i]:=true

L:=1

while $L < n$ **do**

    if A[i,k] $\wedge$ A[k,j] **then** A[i,j]:=true

    L:=2*L

Note the use of simultaneous writes. After the tth iteration of the while-loop, $L = 2^t$ and for all $0 \leq x,y < n$, A[x,y] is true iff there is a path of length at most L from x to y (proof by induction on t). Thus after $\lceil \log n \rceil$ iterations, A[u,v] is true iff there is any path from u to v. This result can be moved to the correct place in the shared-memory machine according to the output convention. The running-time is thus $O(\log n)$ using the full arithmetic instruction-set. The word-size is $O(\log n)$ and the space-bound is $O(n^3)$. The full arithmetic instruction-set can be replaced by the minimal instruction-set without asymptotically affecting the resource bounds, since the integer divisions and multiplications in the first line can be computed in time $O(\log n)$ by each processor using standard sequential algorithms (see, for example, Wirth [133]), and multiplications implicit in the array accesses can be pre-computed by each processor before entering the while-loop.

Earlier in this section we referred to some additional conditions which ensure that networks satisfy the parallel computation thesis. What exactly are these conditions?

Theorem 5.4.1 (Goldschlager [45]) Suppose S(n) can be computed by a network with the minimal instruction-set, of word-size $O(S(n))$, in time $O(S(n))$, on input a single integer n. Then an S(n) space-bounded nondeterministic Turing machine can be simulated in time $O(S(n))$ by a network with the minimal instruction-set and word-size $O(S(n))$.

Proof. (Sketch) Similar to the proof of Savitch's Theorem (Theorem 5.1.2), noting from the above that the Graph Accessibility Problem (see Section 5.1) can be solved in logarithmic time and word-size. □

Corollary 5.4.2 An S(n) space-bounded deterministic Turing machine can be simulated by a network with the minimal instruction-set, of word-size $O(S(n))$, in time $O(S(n) \log S(n))$.

Proof. Use the technique of Theorem 5.4.1 successively with $S(n) = 1,2,4,8,...$
□

Conversely, we have:

Theorem 5.4.3 (Goldschlager [45]) A $T(n)$ time-bounded network M with word-size $W(n)$ can be simulated by a deterministic Turing machine using space $T(n)(W(n)+\log T(n)) + S(n)$, where $S(n)$ is the space required for the Turing machine to simulate a single instruction of a processor of M.

Proof. We will prove the result for a model in which the lowest-numbered processor wins in the case of a write-conflict (as in Goldschlager [45]). The proof will require only minor modifications for other conflict-resolution schemes. When we say "at time t", we will mean "after t instructions have been executed". Assume that the instructions of M's program have been numbered consecutively, 1, 2,..., x, where $x \in \mathbf{N}$. Suppose we modify M so that register r_0 of processor 0 remains at zero during the course of the computation, and is reset to 1 if the input is accepted, -1 if it is rejected, from which time it remains unchanged until all processors have terminated (see Exercise 5.5). Consider the following mutually recursive procedures.

procedure instruction(i,t)
    comment returns program-counter of processor i at time t
    if $t = 0$ **then** 1 **else**
        h:=instruction(i,t–1)
        case h^{th} instruction **of**
            "**goto** m **if** $r_j > 0$": **if** register(i,j,t–1) > 0 **then** m **else** h+1
            "halt":h
            others :h+1

procedure input(i)
    Move input head to the ith tape cell and return
    the character scanned there (0 for a blank)

procedure register(i,j,t)

    comment returns contents of register r_j of processor i at time t

    if t $= 0$ **then**

        if j $= 0$ **then** input(i) **else** 0

    else comment check for attempts to write there

    winner:=P(n)

    for w:=P(n)–1 **downto** 0 **do**

        h:=instruction(w,t–1)

        if $\left(\text{h}^{\text{th}} \text{ instruction is } (r_{r_x} \text{ of } r_y) \leftarrow r_z \right) \wedge$

            $\left(\text{register(w,y,t–1)} = \text{i} \right) \wedge \left(\text{register(w,x,t–1)} = \text{j} \right)$

        then

            winner:=w

            value:=register(w,z,t–1)

    if winner $<$ P(n) **then** value **else comment** evaluate local instruction

    h:=instruction(i,t–1)

    case h^{th} instruction **of**

        "$r_j \leftarrow$ constant":constant

        "$r_j \leftarrow r_k \circ r_l$": register(i,k,t–1)$\circ$register(i,l,t–1)

        "$r_j \leftarrow r_{r_k}$": register(i,register(i,k,t–1),t–1)

        "$r_{r_k} \leftarrow r_l$": **if** register(i,k,t–1) $=$ j **then** register(i,l,t–1) **else** register(i,j,t–1

        " $r_j \leftarrow (r_{r_k} \text{ of } r_l)$": register(register(i,l,t–1),register(i,k,t–1),t–1)

        others : register(i,j,t–1)

The correctness of the above procedures can be proved by induction. To discover whether the network accepts a particular input, call procedure register(0,0,T(n)), where T(n) is the running-time of the network. Since T(n) may not necessarily be easy to compute, we can try T(n) $= 1,2,...$ in turn, without asymptotically affecting the space-bound (as soon as a non-zero value is returned, it can be used to determine acceptance or rejection). At each recursive procedure-call, the value of t is reduced by 1, and so the depth of recursion is at most T(n)+1. We use a constant number of variables in each procedure, each of either O(W(n)) or O(log T(n)) bits. We need a further O(log n) cells for a pointer into the input. The total amount of work-space needed is thus proportional to T(n)(W(n)+log T(n))+S(n)+log n, where S(n) is the space required for the Turing machine to simulate a single instruction of a processor of M. The log n can be ignored. since W(n) $= \Omega$(log n) (at least log n bits are needed to address the n inputs to a network). □

These Theorems enables us to throw some light on the unit-cost hypothesis. As far as the parallel computation thesis is concerned, it is reasonable to charge a single unit of time for instructions which can be computed by a Turing machine in space $T(n)^{O(1)}$, where $T(n)$ is the number of steps in the intended computation. Given this condition, networks satisfy the parallel computation thesis provided $W(n) = T(n)^{O(1)}$. Note that this allows networks with as many as $2^{T(n)^{O(1)}}$ processors; although those who support lazy activation (see Section 3.4) insist that $P(n) = 2^{O(T(n))}$, and some authors insist that $P(n) = n^{O(1)}$ (for example, [24,25,74,102]).

A number of similar restrictions on networks and shared-memory machines have been used in the literature to define so-called "reasonable" machines, including:

(1) *Restrictions on the instruction-set.*

Restrictions on instruction-set are often motivated by a desire to see that the unit-cost hypothesis holds.

(a) The first premise is that individual processors should behave like log-cost sequential machines. In particular, the resource of time should be polynomially related to time on an accepted log-cost sequential machine model, such as the deterministic Turing machine (c.f. the sequential computation thesis, Section 3.2). Thus instructions which are valid for a $T(n)$ unit-cost time-bounded computation should individually take no more than $T(n)^{O(1)}$ steps on a deterministic Turing machine.

(b) Instructions should be computable in space $T(n)^{O(1)}$ by a Turing machine. This helps to ensure that the parallel computation thesis holds. Note that this condition is weaker than condition (a) above.

(2) *Bounds upon processors and time.*

Upper-bounds on the number of processors are usually motivated by the observation that, given enough processors, every computable function can be computed in constant time (see Section 6.2), which makes time a singularly uninteresting resource.

(a) $P(n) \leq 2^{O(T(n))}$. This is a consequence of the lazy activation approach (see Section 3.4).

(b) $P(n) = n^{O(1)}$, $T(n) = \log^{O(1)} n$. Parallel machines with these two properties are sometimes called *small* and *fast* respectively. See, for example, [24,25,102,108].

(3) *Bounds upon word-size.*

Upper-bounds on word-size are usually motivated by the observation that (as previously noted in Section 3.2) single-processor machines with the full [50] or restricted [103] arithmetic instruction-sets satisfy the parallel computation thesis, and so can be considered "reasonable" parallel machines in themselves. This makes the processor-bound an uninteresting resource.

(a) $W(n) = O(T(n))$. This can be achieved indirectly (as in Goldschlager [45]) by restricting the instruction-set and the size of the input symbols.

(b) $W(n) = T(n)^{O(1)}$. This condition guarantees that the parallel computation thesis holds, subject to the additional conditions on the instruction-set mentioned in 1(b) above.

(c) $W(n) = n^{O(1)}$. This ensures that the input encoding is "concise" in the sense of [39]. If the input symbols are allowed to be integers with more than a polynomial number of bits, then n is no longer a reliable (to within a polynomial) measure of input-size.

5.5. Exercises

5.1 Complete the proof of Savitch's Theorem (Theorem 5.1.2) by giving an explicit procedure which can be used to simulate a nondeterministic Turing machine.

5.2 Complete the proof of Theorem 5.4.1.

5.3 Prove that $\leq_{log}$ is transitive (Theorem 5.2.2).

5.4 Prove that UCVP $\leq_{log}$ MCVP (Corollary 5.3.2).

5.5 Show that a network which is used as a language acceptor (see Section 3.1) can be modified so that register r_0 of processor 0 remains at zero during the course of the computation, and is reset to 1 if the input is accepted, -1 if it is rejected, from which time it remains unchanged until all processors have terminated, without affecting its language recognition capabilities, or asymptotically changing the processors, word-size, space or running-time (c.f. Theorem 5.4.3).

A *context-free grammar* (in Chomsky Normal Form) is a 4-tuple $G = (N,T,P,S)$, where N and T are disjoint finite sets, called *nonterminal* and *terminal* symbols respectively, $S \in N$ is the distinguished *start symbol* and P is a finite set of *productions* of the form $A \rightarrow BC$ or $A \rightarrow a$, where $A,B,C \in N$, $a \in T$. The *language* $L(G)$ generated by G is defined in the usual manner (see, for example, Hopcroft and

Ullman [57]). A *context-free grammar with ε-productions* is defined similarly, with the addition of productions of the form A→ε, where ε denotes the empty string. The context-free membership problem (CFMEMBER) is defined to be {G,s | s∈L(G)}. The space complexity of the context-free membership problem depends very much on whether ε-productions are permitted.

5.6 Show that if no ε-productions are allowed, then CFMEMBER can be solved in $\log^2 n$ space. (Hint: apply Lemma 5.3.5 to the parse-tree).

5.7 (Goldschlager [44]) Show by reduction from the monotone circuit-value problem (see Section 5.3) that if ε-productions are allowed, then CFMEMBER is log-space complete for P.

6 Parallel Computation with Shared-Memory Machines

In this chapter we investigate some upper and lower-bounds on the time required by shared-memory machines to compute some interesting functions. The first two sections are concerned with upper-bounds, and the last two with lower-bounds. The first section contains some elementary upper-bounds for such functions as the summation of n integers (which we will find useful in the second section, and in Chapter 11). The second section contains simulations of time-bounded deterministic Turing machines on parallel machines with large word-size, and on machines which satisfy the parallel computation thesis. The third and fourth sections contain lower-bounds, the former on the time required to perform the Boolean OR of n inputs on a machine without simultaneous writes, and the latter on the time required to sum n integers on a machine with simultaneous writes.

6.1. Some Upper-Bounds

In this section we will derive upper-bounds for computing some interesting functions in parallel using shared-memory machines. We will find many of these useful in the next section. The following results are from [91,94,96,99]. Unless explicitly stated otherwise, the shared-memory machines use the restricted arithmetic instruction-set.

Lemma 6.1.1 A CREW shared-memory machine with $\lceil \log n \rceil$ processors can compute $\lceil \log n \rceil$ or $\lfloor \log n \rfloor$ in constant time with word-size $O(\log n)$, when given as input a single positive integer n.

Proof. Suppose $n \geq 1$; $\lfloor \log n \rfloor$ is computed as follows. Processor i, $i \geq 0$, computes the value $v = \lfloor n/2^i \rfloor$ using a single shift instruction. If it finds that $v > 0$ and $\lfloor v/2 \rfloor = 0$, then $i = \lfloor \log n \rfloor$. Computation of $\lceil \log n \rceil$ from $\lfloor \log n \rfloor$ is simple; if $n = 2^i$ then $\lceil \log n \rceil = i$, otherwise $\lceil \log n \rceil = i+1$. The required value can then be written into shared-memory cell s_0 by processor i. $\square$

Lemma 6.1.2 A shared-memory machine with word-size $O(n(b+\log n))$ can add n b-bit numbers in constant time.

Proof. We use the techniques of [91,93,94]. Suppose that we are given n b-bit integers $x_0,...,x_{n-1}$. Let us assume, for the purposes of this proof, that they are all positive. The modifications necessary for the inclusion of negative integers are simple but tedious. We can assume without loss of generality that n is a power of two.

Firstly, it is easy to determine n, the number of inputs. We can adopt the convention that zero is never used for an input value (if necessary we can encode non-negative integers by adding one to them). Processor i reads shared memory cells i and i+1. If the latter contains zero whilst the former contains a non-zero value, then $i = n$. Processor i can then write its PID into shared-memory location 0, where it can be read simultaneously by all processors. Note that if n is not a power of two, then we can compute $\lceil \log n \rceil$ using Lemma 6.1.1, and then with a single processor compute $2^{\lceil \log n \rceil}$, the power of two immediately above n, using a shift operation. This will have a negligible effect on our resource bounds.

The sum of n b-bit numbers can have no more than $b+\log n$ bits. Each processor requires this value. The value log n can be computed using Lemma 6.1.1; it remains to determine the value of b. We do this by finding the largest input integer. We use the first n^2 processors, divided into n equal-sized teams. Each processor can determine whether it participates in this sub-computation by comparing its PID to n^2. Since n is a power of two and both n and log n are known to all processors, n^2 can be computed with a single shift operation. Next, each processor determines which team it is in, and its identity number within its team, as follows. Each processor extracts the last log n bits of its PID using two shifts and a subtraction. It treats this value as its identity number within its team. It treats the remaining leading bits of its PID as its team identity number. That is, it has divided its PID in constant time into two values (i,j) where $0 \leq i,j < n$, and acts as the jth member of the ith team.

The ith team uses shared memory location n+i for communication (remembering that the cells 0 through n–1 contain the input). The 0th processor in team i (which we will call the *manager* of that team) sets shared-memory n+i to zero. The ith team $0 \leq i < n$ determines whether the ith input integer x_i is the largest overall. The jth processor in the ith team compares x_j with x_i, for $0 \leq i,j < n$. If the former is greater than the latter, then it writes a one into shared-memory location· n+i. Finally, the team-manager reads shared-memory location n+i. If that location still contains zero, it knows that x_i is the largest input. It can then write this value into shared-memory location 0, where it can be read by all processors. This has taken constant time, and can be performed provided the word-size is at least $2\log n$. The value of b can finally be obtained by finding the logarithm of this largest input value using Lemma 6.1.1.

Now the value $b+\log n$ is known to all processors. Let us assume for the purposes of this proof that it is a power of two. If not, then it can easily be rounded up to a power of two by using Lemma 6.1.1 and a shift operation. The number of bits in this value is also easily obtained using Lemma 6.1.1. The processors now divide themselves into $2^{n(b+\log n)}$ teams of n processors. Each team interprets its team identification number (which has $n(b+\log n)$ bits) as a sequence of n $(b+\log n)$-bit integers, $y_0, y_1, \ldots, y_{n-1}$. The ith member of each team, $1 \leq i < n$ extracts y_i and y_{i-1}, while the 0th processor extracts y_0. The ith processor will have to perform a shift of $i(b+\log n)$ bits. In order to do this, it will have to first compute this shift amount. Since the latter factor is a power of two, and its logarithm is known, the multiplication can be implemented using a shift operation. The ith processor of each team, $1 \leq i < n$ verifies that $y_i = y_{i-1}+x_i$, while the 0th processor verifies that $y_0 = x_0$. Those processors which find a discrepancy report to their team-managers via the shared-memory as described in the previous paragraph. Exactly one team will find no discrepancy. Its team-manager knows that its team identity number represents a valid prefix-sum string for the given inputs. It then extracts the total sum (the last integer in the sequence) which it finally writes into shared-memory location 0 for output.

All of the operations described take place in constant time. The PIDs of the processors have $O(n(b+\log n))$ bits, and are the largest words used in the computation. $\square$

Lemma 6.1.3 A shared-memory machine with word-size $O(b^2)$ can multiply two b-bit positive integers in constant time.

Proof. We will use the standard shift-and-add algorithm. For simplicity, let us assume that the two input integers x_1 and x_2 are both positive. The machine first finds the value of b by taking the logarithm of the largest input (using Lemma 6.1.1). Processor i, $0 \leq i < b$, does the following.

(a) Extract the ith bit of x_2 (where the bits are numbered consecutively from left-to-right starting with zero) using shifts and a subtraction.

(b) If the value obtained in (a) is non-zero, then left-shift x_1 by i places (that is, multiply it by 2^i), and write the result into shared-memory location i+1.

The sum of these values is computed in constant time using Lemma 6.1.2. $\square$

Lemma 6.1.4 A shared-memory machine, when given as input a single integer n, can compute $\left\lceil n^{1/c} \right\rceil$ in constant time and word-size $O(\log^2 n)$, for any natural number c > 1.

Proof. We use n teams of processors. Team i, $0 \leq i < n$, checks to see whether $i = \left\lceil n^{1/c} \right\rceil$. It does this by computing i^c (using c–1 multiplications). For this purpose, each team has $2^{O(\log^2 n)}$ processors (by Lemma 6.1.3). If $i^c \geq n$, yet $i^{c-1} < n$, then $i = \left\lceil n^{1/c} \right\rceil$. $\square$

For our purposes, it will be sufficient to show that a shared-memory machine with linear word-size can add n constant-bit integers in constant time. However, a much stronger result is possible without much extra effort.

Lemma 6.1.5 For every $0 < \lambda \leq \dfrac{1}{2}$ there exists $\mu > 0$ such that a shared-memory machine with word-size $n^{1-\mu}$ can add n $n^{1-\lambda}$-bit integers in constant time.

Proof. Suppose we have as input n positive integers, each of $n^{1-1/c}$ bits, for some positive integer $c \geq 2$. Since the technique used is elementary, for a cleaner presentation of this proof we will omit the floor and ceiling operators necessary to ensure that all values are integers. The sum of these integers (and every partial sum) has at most $O(n^{1-1/c})$ bits.

The shared-memory machine first determines n, and computes $m = n^{\frac{1}{c+1}}$. After this pre-computation, the summation is performed in two phases.
Phase 1.
Divide the input into n/m groups of m numbers, and sum each group. After c iterations of this process, we are left with n/m^c partial sums.
Phase 2.
Add the n/m^c partial sums.

By Lemma 6.1.4, the pre-computation takes constant time, and negligible word-size (for large enough n). By Lemma 6.1.2, phases 1 and 2 can be performed in constant time. The word-size required for the former is proportional to

$$mn^{1-1/c} = n^{1 - \frac{1}{c^2+c}},$$

and for the latter is proportional to

$$\frac{n}{m^c}n^{1-1/c} = n^{1 - \frac{1}{c^2+c}}.$$

Thus n $n^{1-1/c}$-bit integers can be summed in constant time with word-size $O(n^{1 - \frac{1}{c^2+c}})$. $\square$

Suppose $x_i \in \mathbf{N}$, $1 \leq x_i \leq n$ for $1 \leq i \leq n$. Define prev:$\mathbf{Z}^n \to \mathbf{Z}^n$ by $prev(x_1,...,x_n) = <y_1,...,y_n>$ where $y_i = j$ if $x_j = x_i$, $j < i$, and $x_k \neq x_i$ for $j < k < i$, (and 0 if no such j exists). Define last:$\mathbf{Z}^n \to \mathbf{Z}^n$ by $last(x_1,...,x_n) = <y_1,...,y_n>$ where $y_i = j$ if $x_j = i$ and $x_k \neq i$ for $j < k \leq n$, (and 0 if no such j exists).

Lemma 6.1.6 A shared-memory machine can compute $prev(x_1,...,x_n)$ and $last(x_1,...,x_n)$ in constant time with word-size $O(\log n)$.

Proof. We will prove the result for prev (the algorithm used for last is similar). The values $y_1,...,y_n$ described above are computed as follows. Divide the processors into n^2 teams, one for each ordered pair $<i,j>$, $1 \leq i,j \leq n$. Each team has n processors, one for each k, $1 \leq k \leq n$. The kth processor of each team, $j < k < i$ remains active, the rest do not participate in the following. We reserve a shared-memory location for each team, initialized to zero. The kth processor of each team, $j < k < i$ verifies that $x_k \neq x_i$. If it finds that $x_k = x_i$, it writes a one into the shared memory location reserved for its team. All team members do this simultaneously. The lowest-numbered member of its team then reads that value, verifies that it is still zero, and checks that $x_j = x_i$. If so, then it writes the value j to the ith shared memory cell, for output. $\square$

We close this section by investigating the problem of adding together n numbers from a finite subset of the integers, which we will call the *finite semigroup summation problem*. Let $T(n,P(n))$ be the time required to sum n elements of an arbitrary (finite or infinite) semigroup using $P(n)$ processors. For convenience we will write $T(n)$ for $T(n,n)$. We will say that $f:\mathbf{Z} \to \mathbf{Z}$ is *constant-time constructible* if a shared-memory machine with n processors can compute $f(n)$ from a single integer n in constant time. By Lemmas 6.1.1, 6.1.3 and 6.1.4, any polynomial in n, $\log n$, and roots of n is constant-time constructible.

Lemma 6.1.7. Suppose f:N→N, $f(n) \leq n$ for all $n \geq 0$ is constant-time constructible. Then $T(n) \leq T(\lceil n/f(n) \rceil) + T(f(n),n) + O(1)$.

Proof. Suppose we are to sum n elements with n processors. The shared-memory machine computes $f(n)$. The processors divide themselves into $f(n)$ *teams*. The ith team, $0 \leq i < f(n)$, consists of those processors with PID mod $f(n) = i$. Thus there are $f(n)$–1 teams of $\lceil n/f(n) \rceil$ processors, and one team of at most $\lceil n/f(n) \rceil$ processors. Each team independently computes the sum of its inputs, in time $T(\lceil n/f(n) \rceil)$ (we assume that $T(n)$ is monotone nondecreasing). This leaves $f(n)$ partial sums, which can be added together in time $T(f(n),n)$. □

Corollary 6.1.8 (Shiloach and Vishkin [114]). The maximum of n integers can be found in time $O(\log \log n)$ with n processors, and in constant time with $n^{1+\epsilon}$ processors (for any real number $\epsilon > 0$).

Proof. It is easy to compute the maximum of n elements in constant time using n^2 processors (see Exercise 6.2). Thus, by using Lemma 6.1.7 with $f(n) = \lceil \sqrt{n} \rceil$, the time required to find the maximum of n elements using n processors is given by:

$$T(n) \leq T(\lceil \sqrt{n} \rceil) + T(\lceil \sqrt{n} \rceil, n)$$

$$= T(\lceil \sqrt{n} \rceil) + O(1)$$

$$= O(\log \log n).$$

By limiting the depth of recursion to $\lceil \log_2 k \rceil$, for some constant $k \geq 1$, the time can be reduced to $O(\log k)$ with $n^{1+\frac{1}{k}}$ processors. □

Theorem 6.1.9 (Vishkin and Wigderson [129]) The finite semigroup summation problem can be solved in constant time with $2^{O(n)}$ processors.

Proof. The proof uses the techniques of Lemmas 6.1.2 and 6.1.5 (see Exercise 6.3). □

Theorem 6.1.10 (Reif [106], Parberry [96]). The finite semigroup summation problem can be solved in time $O(\log n/\log \log n)$ using n processors.

Proof. By Lemma 6.1.7 with $f(n) = O(\log n)$, and Theorem 6.1.9. □

Thus, for example, the exclusive-or of n bits can be computed in time $O(\log n/\log \log n)$ using n processors. A matching lower-bound for polynomially many processors with limited instruction-set can be derived from the result of Yao [134].

Theorem 6.1.10 can be generalized to the case of summing n constant-bit elements of an infinite semigroup with the property that any n-element sum can be described in $O(\log n)$ bits (since Theorem 6.1.9 holds with the processor-bound modified to $2^{O(n \log n)}$, the proof follows from Lemma 6.1.7 with $f(n) = O(\log n/\log \log n)$.) Thus, for example, n single-bit integers can be added together in time $O(\log n/\log \log n)$ using n processors.

6.2. Simulation of Sequential Machines

In Chapter 5 we considered the following question: which problems in P have an exponential speed-up in time on a "reasonable" parallel machine, where the latter is defined to be a network which satisfies the parallel computation thesis? The only answer which we were able to obtain was "probably not all of them". Here we tackle an easier question: what speed-ups of sequential machines *are* offered by our parallel machines (reasonable or otherwise). Firstly, we shall demonstrate that shared-memory machines with large word-size are immensely powerful.

We will say that $T:N \to N$ is *word-size constructible* if a shared-memory machine with word-size $O(T(n))$ can compute $T(n)$ in constant time from a single integer n. Note that by Lemmas 6.1.1, 6.1.3 and 6.1.4, many useful functions are word-size constructible.

Lemma 6.2.1 (Parberry and Schnitger [99]). Suppose $T(n)$ is word-size constructible. Then a shared-memory machine with the restricted arithmetic instruction-set can simulate a $T(n)$ time-bounded k-tape deterministic Turing machine in constant time and word-size $O(T(n))$.

Proof. (Sketch) Suppose we list and number the transitions or rules of the Turing machine in some reasonable fashion. We divide the processors into $2^{O(T(n))}$ teams, one for each sequence of $T(n)$ rules $r_0, r_1, ..., r_{T(n)-1}$. Each team has $2^{O(T(n))}$ processors. Firstly, each team determines the head positions for each of the k tapes at each instant of time by applying the algorithm of Lemma 6.1.5 to the sequence of head motions derived from its rule-sequence. It then verifies that:

1. The sequence of states determined by the sequence of rules is a valid one. That is, rule r_0 requires that the Turing machine be in its initial state, and for $1 \leq i < T(n)$ if rule r_{i-1} leaves the Turing machine in state q, then rule r_i requires that the Turing machine be in state q.

2. For each of the k tapes, and for each time t, $0 \leq t < T(n)$:

   (i) If this is the first time that the head visits this cell, then the symbol read by rule r_t is the symbol found in that cell in the initial configuration.

   (ii) If the last time the head visited this cell was at time $s < t$, then the symbol written by rule r_s is the symbol read by rule r_t.

The information necessary for this verification is provided by computing prev using the algorithm of Lemma 6.1.6. Exactly one team will find that its sequence of rules is valid. It can then determine if the final state is accepting, and sets the contents of shared memory location 0 to 0 or 1 accordingly. By Lemmas 6.1.5 and 6.1.6 the simulation requires constant time and word-size $O(T(n))$. $\square$

This result can obviously be extended to the simulation of deterministic Turing machines which compute results, rather than act as acceptors for a language (the final configuration can be constructed from the valid sequence of rule numbers by use of the algorithm for function last in Lemma 6.1.6), and to the simulation of nondeterministic Turing machines. The word-size has been improved to $O(T(n)/\log^* T(n))$ for $T(n) = \Omega(\log^* n)$ (Parberry and Schnitger [99]).

It is clear that this result depends strongly on the large word-size. But what if we limit the word-size by requiring that the parallel computation thesis holds? That is, we require that the shared-memory machine run in time $T(n)$ and have word-size $W(n)$, where $W(n) = T(n)^{O(1)}$. Dymond and Tompa [26] have shown that speed-up by a square-root is possible in the case where word-size is linear in parallel running-time. We will show that an arbitrary polynomial speed-up is possible if word-size is allowed to be polynomial in time. First, we present a general speed-up result.

Theorem 6.2.2 (Parberry [94]) Suppose $B:\mathbf{N}\rightarrow\mathbf{N}$ is word-size constructible, and a shared-memory machine with word-size $W(n)$ can simulate a $B(n)$ time bounded deterministic Turing machine in time $C(n)$. Then a shared memory machine with word-size $O(W(n)+B(n)+\log T(n))$ can simulate a $T(n)$ time bounded deterministic Turing machine in time $O(T(n)/B(n) + C(n))$.

Proof. (Outline). Let M be a $T(n)$ time-bounded k-tape deterministic Turing machine. We will store the current configuration of M in the first $kT(n)+k+1$

words of the shared memory (corresponding to the $T(n)$ tape cells on each tape, k head positions and the control state). The simulation will consist of $\lceil T(n)/B(n) \rceil$ phases, each corresponding to $B(n)$ steps of M. The initial configuration is easy to compute from the input, and the simulation will endeavour to maintain it from phase to phase.

A *zone* consists of that portion of the tape which may be altered during the current phase, that is, the $k(2B(n)-1)$ tape-cells that are within distance $B(n)$ from a head at the start of the phase. During each phase the simulation will be conducted using these zones - at the end of each phase the final zone will be used to update the stored configuration. To be more precise, a zone consists of $k(2B(n)-1)$ tape symbols, k head-pointers (each of $O(\log B(n))$ bits), and the current state of the finite-state control.

Before the first phase, some pre-computation is carried out. The machine first computes $B(n)$. We divide the processors into $2^{O(B(n))}$ teams, one for each possible zone. The ith team, $1 \le i \le 2^{O(B(n))}$ simulates $B(n)$ steps of M from the ith zone, in time $C(n)$ and word-size $W(n)$. From this information a look-up table is constructed in the shared memory. The ith entry of that table is the zone which follows in $B(n)$ steps from the ith zone of M.

Each phase is broken up into three parts.

(1) Determine the initial zone from the initial configuration of the phase. The processors are broken up into $2^{O(B(n))}$ teams (one for each possible zone), each of $2B(n)-1$ processors. The lowest-numbered processor of each team is a distinguished processor called the *manager* of that team. Processors which are not members of a team remain idle.

The ith member of the jth team ($i,j \ge 0$) has $i = \text{PID mod } (2B(n)-1) + 1$ and $j = \lfloor \text{PID}/(2B(n)-1) \rfloor + 1$. Each processor first computes i and j. The value j is interpreted as the encoding of a zone (note that j is the same for all members of any particular team). The ith processor of each team, $1 \le i \le (2B(n)-1)$ decodes the head positions and the ith symbol of each tape from this zone. Every processor of every team then compares its symbols to the corresponding symbols of the stored configuration. If they disagree, the processor is said to *fail*. Failed team members report to their respective managers via the shared memory using the technique from the proof of Lemma 6.1.2.

The team manager whose zone has the correct state, head-pointers equal to $B(n)$, and whose shared memory location remains at zero knows that its value of j is an encoding of the initial zone of the phase. It writes this value to the shared memory for safe-keeping.

(2) Determine the final zone of the current phase. Processor 0 can obtain this information from the ith entry in the look-up table, where i is the initial zone of the current phase computed in (1) above.

(3) Determine the final configuration of the phase from the final zone. Processor i, $1 \leq i \leq k$ updates the stored head positions, whilst processor $k+j+cT(n)$, $1 \leq c \leq k$, $1 \leq j \leq T(n)$ determines whether the jth tape cell of the cth tape is within $B(n)$ cells of the head, and if so, updates its value. Processor 0 updates the current state of the finite-state control.

The machine is then in a position to begin the next phase. $T(n)$ steps of M are simulated by repeating this for $\lceil T(n)/B(n) \rceil$ phases. The pre-computation takes time $O(C(n))$, and each of $\lceil T(n)/B(n) \rceil$ phases takes a constant amount of time, provided the restricted arithmetic instruction-set is used. The maximum word-size during the computation is the larger of $O(W(n)+B(n))$ (for the pre-computation), $O(B(n))$ (for the processor identity registers during each phase) and $O(\log T(n))$ (to access the stored configuration). $\square$

Theorem 6.2.3 Let $B:N \rightarrow N$ be word-size constructible. A $T(n)$ time-bounded deterministic Turing machine can be simulated in time $O(T(n)/B(n))$ by a shared-memory machine with word-size $O(B(n)+ \log T(n))$.

Proof. The proof of Lemma 6.2.1 can be modified to work for (deterministic) Turing machines which actually compute values (instead of just being acceptors). The desired result then follows by application of Theorem 6.2.2. $\square$

Corollary 6.2.4 If $T(n)$ is word-size constructible, then a $T(n)$ time-bounded deterministic Turing machine can be simulated in time $T(n)^{1-\epsilon}$, for any real number $\epsilon > 0$, by a shared-memory machine which satisfies the parallel computation thesis.

Proof. The result follows by Theorem 6.2.3 with $B(n) = T(n)^{\epsilon}$. Note that if $T(n)$ is word-size constructible , then so is $B(n)$ (consider Lemma 6.1.4). $\square$

That is, an arbitrary polynomial speedup of sequential computation is possible on a parallel machine which satisfies the parallel computation thesis. This is a strong result since, as we observed in Chapter 5, there are problems in P (such as the circuit-value problem) which probably do not have an exponential speedup on such a machine.

Corollary 6.2.5 (Dymond and Tompa [26]) If $T(n)$ is word-size constructible, then a $T(n)$ time-bounded deterministic Turing machine can be simulated in time $O(\sqrt{T(n)})$ by a lazy-activation shared-memory machine with the minimal instruction-set (which satisfies the parallel computation thesis).

Proof. The result follows by Theorem 6.2.3 with $B(n) = \sqrt{T(n)}$, noting that for a lazy-activation machine, the running-time must be at least the logarithm of the number of processors. This gives sufficient time for the minimal instruction-set to be substituted for the restricted arithmetic instruction-set. □

Corollary 6.2.6 If $T(n)$ is word-size constructible, then a $T(n)$ time-bounded deterministic Turing machine can be simulated in time $O(T(n)/\log T(n))$ by a lazy-activation shared-memory machine with the minimal instruction-set, using $n^{O(1)}$ processors and word-size $O(\log n)$.

Proof. The result follows by Theorem 6.2.3 with $B(n) = \log n$. □

6.3. A Lower-Bound Without Simultaneous Writes

Consider the problem of computing the Boolean OR of n bits in parallel on a shared-memory machine. It is clear that constant time can be achieved with n processors if simultaneous writes are allowed. (First, some processor sets shared-memory location 0 to 0. Then each processor examines a different bit. Those processors whose bit is 1 attempt to write a 1 into shared-memory location 0.) However, the situation changes radically if simultaneous writes are not allowed.

The material in this section comes from Cook, Dwork and Reischuk [20]. For exactness, we will count a sequence of three instructions "read, compute, write" as a single time-unit for the remainder of this chapter (any or all of the three instructions may be NO-OPs). It is easy to construct an n processor, $\lceil \log n \rceil$ time algorithm using a complete binary tree. This intuitively appears optimal. However, a slightly faster algorithm is possible.

Define the Fibonacci numbers as follows: $F_0 = 0$, $F_1 = 1$, and for $m \geq 0$, $F_{m+2} = F_{m+1} + F_m$. The following algorithm will OR together F_{2t+1} inputs in t steps using $1 + F_{2t+1}$ processors. Since $F_t \sim (\frac{1+\sqrt{5}}{2})^t$ this means that it can OR together more than 2.6^t bits in t steps, which is faster than the naive algorithm in the previous paragraph. We use a local variable y as work-space, and local variables f and g for the current Fibonacci numbers. We also use an n-cell shared

80

array M, with M[0],...,M[n–1] containing the n input bits at the start of the computation.

$$y,f,g:=0,0,1$$
while $f < n$ **do**
$$y:=y \vee M[PID+f]$$
if $(PID > g \wedge y = 1)$ **then** $M[PID-g]:=1$
$$f,g:=f+g,f+2g$$

It is easy to prove by induction that after the tth iteration of the while-loop, $t \geq 0$, local variables f and g of every processor contain F_{2t} and F_{2t+1} respectively. Let y_i^j and M_i^j denote the value of y of processor i and M[i] respectively after the jth iteration. Also let OR(i,j) denote $x_i \vee x_{i+1} \vee ... \vee x_j$. We claim that:

$$y_i^j = OR(i,i+F_{2j}-1)$$

$$M_i^j = OR(i,i+F_{2j+1}-1)$$

The proof is by induction on j. The hypothesis is true for $j = 0$ since $y_i^0 = 0$ and $M_i^0 = x_i$. Now suppose that the hypothesis is true for the $(j–1)^{st}$ iteration. Note that during the jth iteration, f and g contain the values $F_{2(j-1)}$ and $F_{2(j-1)+1}$ respectively. Then:

$$y_i^j = y_i^{j-1} \vee M_{i+F_{2j-2}}^{j-1}$$

$$= OR(i,i+F_{2j-2}-1) \vee OR(i+F_{2j-2},i+F_{2j-2}+F_{2j-1}-1) \qquad \text{(by the ind. hypoth.)}$$

$$= OR(i,i+F_{2j}-1) \qquad \text{(by the definition of Fibonacci number)}$$

And:

$$M_i^j = M_i^{j-1} \vee y_{i+F_{2j-1}}^j$$

$$= OR(i,i+F_{2j-1}-1) \vee OR(i+F_{2j-1},i+F_{2j-1}+F_{2j}-1) \qquad \text{(by the ind. hypoth.)}$$

$$= OR(i,i+F_{2j+1}-1) \qquad \text{(by the definition of Fibonacci number)}$$

The correctness of the algorithm and the complexity analysis follows immediately from the Claim. Each iteration of the while-loop can be implemented as a single read-compute-write step, and after j iterations, M[0] contains the OR of F_{2j+1} bits.

The strength of this algorithm lies in the if-statement. Data is communicated by processors *choosing not to write* at that point. It is clear that processors can communicate a single-bit value by this mechanism without the use of a direct chain of reads and writes between them. For example, suppose that processor A wishes to communicate a value $v \in \{0,1\}$ to processor C. We use an extra processor B and two shared-memory locations s_B and s_C.

(i)   Processor P sets s_P to 0, for $P \in \{B,C\}$.

(ii) If A has a 0, it writes 1 into s_B.

(iii) B then reads s_B. If it is a 0, it writes 1 into s_C.

(iv) C then reads s_C.

A simple case analysis shows that s_C contains 0 iff the value possessed by A was 0. There is no direct chain of reads and writes between A and C, regardless of the value to be communicated.

We have seen that the naive lower-bound of $\lceil \log n \rceil$ is incorrect. However, a lower-bound of $\Omega(\log n)$ does hold. We define the *state* of a processor to be the contents of its registers, and its program-counter. Let $I = (x_0,...,x_{n-1}) \in \{0,1\}^n$ be an input string. Define $I(u) = (x_0,...,x_{u-1},\bar{x}_u,x_{u+1},...,x_{n-1})$, where $\bar{0} = 1$ and $\bar{1} = 0$ to be the input which is identical to I except in the uth bit. If $0 \leq u < n$ we say that u *affects processor p at time t on input I* if the state of p at time t is different on inputs I and I(u). Similarly, we say that u *affects shared-memory cell c at time t on input I* if the contents of c at time t is different on inputs I and I(u). Let:

$$Y(c,t,I) = \{u | \exists \text{ processor } p_u \text{ that writes into c at time t on } I(u)\}$$

$$Z(c,t,I) = \{(u,v) | u,v \in Y(c,t,I) \text{ and } p_u \neq p_v\}$$

Lemma 6.3.1 For all $(u,v) \in Z(c,t,I)$, either u affects p_v at t on I(v) or v affects p_u at t on I(u).

Proof. Consider what happens on input I(u)(v).

Case 1. Neither p_u nor p_v write into cell c at time t.

By hypothesis, p_u writes into cell c at time t on I(u). Changing the vth bit of I(u) causes p_u not to write, so v affects p_u at time t on I(u) (and symmetrically u affects p_v at time t on I(v)).

Case 2. p_v writes into c at time t.

By hypothesis, p_u writes into c at time t on I(u). Changing the vth bit of I(u) must cause p_u not to write (otherwise there would be a write-conflict on p_v), so v affects p_u at time t on input I(u).

Case 3. p_u writes into c at time t.

By hypothesis, p_v writes into c at time t on $I(v)$. Changing the uth bit of $I(v)$ must cause p_v not to write (otherwise there would be a write-conflict with p_u), so u affects p_v at time t on input $I(v)$. $\square$

Define:

$$R(p,t,I) = \{u|u \text{ affects processor p at time t on I}\}$$

$$L(c,t,I) = \{u|u \text{ affects cell c at time t on I}\}.$$

Also let:

$$P_t = \max_{p,I} |R(p,t,I)|$$

$$C_t = \max_{c,I} |L(c,t,I)|$$

Lemma 6.3.2 $P_0 = 0$, $C_0 = 1$ and for $t \geq 0$

$$P_{t+1} \leq P_t + C_t \tag{1}$$

$$C_{t+1} \leq 3P_t + 4C_t \tag{2}$$

Proof. The proof is by induction on t. The hypothesis is true for $t = 0$. Inequality (1) is also clear, since to affect a processor we must either must have affected it earlier or have affected the shared-memory cell that it is currently reading. Inequality (2) is slightly more difficult. Consider each cell c in turn. There are two cases to consider. Either:

Case 1. Some processor p writes into cell c at time t+1.

Then to affect cell c at time t+1 we must affect processor p at time t+1 (noting that we count a read-compute-write sequence as a single time-step). Therefore $C_{t+1} \leq P_{t+1}$. Since we have already shown that $P_{t+1} \leq P_t + C_t$, the required result certainly follows.

Case 2. No processor writes into cell c at time t+1.

We will first analyze $|Z(c,t+1,I)|$. Suppose $(u,v) \in Z(c,t+1,I)$. By Lemma 6.3.1 either u affects p_v at t+1 on $I(v)$ or v affects p_u at t+1 on $I(u)$. Without loss of generality assume that u affects p_v at t+1 on $I(v)$. There are $|Y(c,t+1,I)|$ choices for v, and hence at most $|Y(c,t+1,I)|$ choices for p_v. But each processor p_v can be affected by at most $|R(p_v,t+1,I(v))| \leq P_{t+1}$ different choices for u. Therefore:

$$|Z(c,t+1,I)| \leq 2|Y(c,t+1,I)|P_{t+1} \tag{3}$$

83

(The factor of two is appropriate since each (u,v) also appears in $Z(c,t+1,I)$ as (v,u)). However, for each u there are at least $|Y(c,t+1,I)| - P_{t+1}$ choices for v, since at most P_{t+1} of the candidates for v can be disqualified by having $p_u = p_v$. Therefore:

$$| Z(c,t+1,I) | \ge | Y(c,t+1,I) | (| Y(c,t+1,I) | - P_{t+1}) \tag{4}$$

Hence by (3) and (4):

$$| Y(c,t+1,I) | (| Y(c,t+1,I) | - P_{t+1}) \le 2 | Y(c,t+1,I) | P_{t+1}$$

That is:

$$| Y(c,t+1,I) | \le 3P_{t+1} \tag{5}$$

Now, to affect a cell at time t+1, we must either have affected it earlier, or must be able to cause a processor to write into it by changing a single bit of the input. Therefore:

$$| L(c,t+1,I) | \le | L(c,t,I) | + | Y(c,t+1,I) |$$

Therefore by (5) and the induction hypothesis (2):

$$| L(c,t+1,I) | \le C_t + 3P_{t+1}$$
$$\le 3P_t + 4C_t \qquad \text{(by (1))}$$

From which we can conclude that $C_{t+1} \le 3P_t + 4C_t$ as required. $\square$

Theorem 6.3.3 If simultaneous writes are not allowed, then the time required to compute the Boolean OR of n inputs on a shared-memory machine is at least $\log_b n$, where $b > 4.79$.

Proof. Suppose we have a shared-memory machine which can compute the Boolean OR of n inputs without the use of simultaneous writes in time $T(n)$. Take $I = (0,0,...,0)$, the all-zero input vector. Then $L(0,T(n),I) = n$. But the solution to the recurrence relations in Lemma 6.3.2 tells us that $C_{T(n)} \le b^{T(n)}$, where $b > 4.79$ (see Exercise 6.5). Therefore $n \le b^{T(n)}$, as required. $\square$

Thus we have seen how to compute the Boolean OR of n bits in time $0.73\log n$ without the use of simultaneous writes, while Theorem 6.3.3 tells us that any such algorithm must take time at least $0.44\log n$. Lower-bounds for other functions appear in Simon [116] and Snir [118].

6.4. A Lower-Bound With Simultaneous Writes

We saw in the previous section that lower-bounds for shared-memory machines can be surprisingly subtle even when multiple writes are not allowed. The first lower-bounds on models with simultaneous writes were for severely restricted machines. For example, Vishkin and Wigderson [129] bounded the total amount of successful communication in each time-step, and Meyer auf der Heide and Reischuk [55] gave a lower-bound of $\Omega(\log n)$ for integer summation on a machine with limited local instruction-set. We will give a proof of this result for networks with an unlimited local instruction-set, from [91,96]. Meyer auf der Heide and Wigderson [56] subsequently extended the lower-bound of [129] to parallel machines which compute a larger class of functions using the "lowest-numbered processor wins" convention for handling multiple writes. More recently, a much tighter lower-bound for integer summation has been obtained by Beame [11].

Theorem 6.4.1 A restricted-access network of $P(n)$ processors requires time $\lceil \log_3 n \rceil$ to add together n positive integers of size $O(P(n)(\log P(n))(\log n))$.

Proof. Suppose M is a $P(n)$ processor network which can sum n elements in time $T(n)$, and let $x = <x_0,...,x_{n-1}>$ be an input string consisting of n symbols, each of which is a member of S. We assume that the processors are numbered $0,1, \ldots , P(n)-1$, and that the output will be found in processor 0 at the end of the computation. Let G_x be the directed graph with vertices (p,t), $0 \leq p < P(n)$, $0 \leq t < T(n)$, and an edge from (p_1,t_1) to (p_2,t_2) if $t_2 = t_1+1$ and either $p_1 = p_2$ or during time-step t_1 of the computation of M on input x, either processor p_2 reads a value from p_1, or p_1 successfully writes a value to p_2. G_x is called the *communication graph* of the network on input x. The ith symbol of x is said to be *reachable* if there is a path from vertex $(i,0)$ to vertex $(0,T(n))$ in G_x.

Note that it is not necessarily the case that all of the symbols of any particular input are reachable since, as in the previous section, information can be communicated by a processor choosing not to write. Suppose the integers to be added together are drawn from a set S of size N. We claim that (provided N is sufficiently large) there is an input string in which all symbols are reachable. For a contradiction, suppose that every input x has at least one unreachable symbol. Define the *reachable set* of x to be $R_x = \{i \mid x_i$ is reachable$\}$. Let

$Q_x \subseteq \{0,1,...,n-1\}$ be such that $|Q_x| = n-1$ and $R_x \subseteq Q_x$. Then there is a unique i such that $0 \leq i < n$ and $i \notin Q_x$. For definiteness, suppose Q_x is chosen so that i is minimal. Call Q_x the *critical set* of x, $<x_0, \ldots, x_{i-1}, x_{i+1}, ..., x_{n-1}>$ the *critical string* of x, and x_i the *unreachable symbol* of x.

Suppose we fix an input x. How many input strings y are there such that $G_x = G_y$? If $G_x = G_y$ then clearly $R_x = R_y$ and the critical set for x is also criti-cal for y. Suppose there are two inputs y_1 and y_2 with identical critical strings, such that $G_x = G_{y_1} = G_{y_2}$. Then, by a simple cut-and-paste argument, both y_1 and y_2 must sum to the same value since (once the communication graph is fixed) the unreachable symbol cannot affect the output. But by the cancellation law, if we have two inputs y_1 and y_2 with identical critical strings and identical sums, then they must have identical unreachable symbols. Therefore $y_1 = y_2$, from which we deduce that there are at most as many candidates for y as there are different critical strings. Since there are at most N^{n-1} different critical strings, we can conclude that at most N^{n-1} different inputs can give rise to the same com-munication graph.

Let $G(n)$ be the number of possible communication graphs on n inputs. By the pigeonhole principle, at least one graph must be used for at least $N^n/G(n)$ input strings. If N is chosen such that $N > G(n)$ then this value is greater than N^{n-1}, which contradicts the result of the previous paragraph. Thus there must be an input string for which all symbols are reachable. Since for all x, G_x has in-degree 3, this implies that $T(n) \geq \left\lceil \log_3 n \right\rceil$.

Exactly how large can $G(n)$ be? Each communication graph has $T(n)$ layers, each corresponding to a single step of the network. How many different choices for each layer are there? Clearly there are $P(n)^{P(n)}$ choices for the subgraph corresponding to the read operations. The subgraph corresponding to the write operations forms a bipartite matching (if X and Y are finite, disjoint sets of ver-tices, a *bipartite matching* is a graph $G = (V,E)$ where $V = X \cup Y$, $E \subseteq X \times Y$, and each element of $X \cup Y$ appears in at most one edge of E). Let $M(x,y)$ be the number of bipartite matchings from a set of size x to a set of size $y \geq x$. Then $M(1,y) = y+1$ and for all $x > 1$, $M(x,y) = M(x-1,y) + y\,M(x-1,y-1)$ Therefore $M(x,y) \leq (2y-x+3)2^{x-2}y!$ (proof by induction on x). If we further define $M(x) = M(x,x)$, we see (by Stirling's approximation) that $M(x) \leq x^{x+O(1)}$. Thus there are $P(n)^{P(n)+O(1)}$ choices for the subgraph corresponding to the write opera-tions, and so $G(n) \leq \left(P(n)^{2P(n)+O(1)}\right)^{T(n)}$. □

Corollary 6.4.2 Every n^c processor restricted-access network requires time at least $\lceil \log_3 n \rceil$ to add together n positive integers of size $O(n^c \log^2 n)$ The addition of n arbitrary integers requires time at least $\lceil \log_3 n \rceil$ regardless of the processor bound.

Note that the proof of Theorem 6.4.1 (and hence Corollary 6.4.2) will extend to functions on n inputs with the property that fixing n–1 of the inputs and the output fixes the remaining input. The technique of Theorem 6.4.1 also applies equally well to shared-memory machines.

Theorem 6.4.3 A shared-memory machine with P(n) processors requires time $\lceil \log_2 n \rceil$ to add together n positive integers of size $O(P(n).\log P(n).\log^2 n)$.

Proof. Similar to the proof of Theorem 6.4.1, noting that a shared-memory machine with P(n) processors which runs for time T(n) can access at most P(n)T(n) different shared-memory cells. See Exercise 6.4. □

Corollary 6.4.4 Every n^c processor shared-memory machine requires time at least $\lceil \log_2 n \rceil$ to add together n positive integers of size $O(n^c \log^3 n)$ The addition of n arbitrary integers requires time at least $\lceil \log_2 n \rceil$ regardless of the processor bound.

6.5. Exercises

6.1 Show that function *last* from Section 6.1 can be computed in constant time with polynomially many processors and word-size $O(\log n)$.

6.2 Show that the maximum of n integers can be found in constant time by a shared-memory machine with n^2 processors and word-size $O(\log n)$.

6.3 Prove Theorem 6.1.9. That is, show that the finite semigroup summation problem can be solved in constant time with $2^{O(n)}$ processors.

6.4 Complete the proof of Theorem 6.4.3. That is, show that a shared-memory machine with P(n) processors requires time $\lceil \log_2 n \rceil$ to add together n positive integers of size $O(P(n)(\log P(n))(\log^2 n))$.

6.5 Show that the solution to the recurrences in Lemma 6.3.2: $P_0 = 0$, $C_0 = 1$ and for $t \geq 0$:

$$P_{t+1} = P_t + C_t$$

$$C_{t+1} = 3P_t + 4C_t$$

is the following:

$$P_t = \frac{b^t}{\sqrt{21}} - \frac{\bar{b}^t}{\sqrt{21}}$$

$$C_t = \frac{3+\sqrt{21}}{\sqrt{21}} b^t + \frac{-3+\sqrt{21}}{2\sqrt{21}} \bar{b}^t$$

where $b = (5+\sqrt{21})/2$ and $\bar{b} = (5-\sqrt{21})/2$.

7 Programming Techniques for Feasible Networks

In Chapter 4 we suggested the possibility of finding a feasible network which is universal for the general network model. Before we actually tackle this problem, we will first investigate some of the methods at our disposal. This chapter consists of four sections. The first section deals with possible interconnection patterns, concentrating on the shuffle-exchange of Stone [122] and the cube-connected cycles of Preparata and Vuillemin [104]. The latter paper also provides us with some useful programming tools; a large class of fast algorithms on the multi-dimensional cube (called *composite* algorithms) which can be simulated without loss of resources on either the cube-connected cycles or shuffle-exchange. This will allow us to express the program of our universal network in a moderately high-level form which is to a certain extent independent of interconnection pattern.

The second section deals with recurrent interconnection patterns, that is, interconnection patterns with the property that each finite graph in the infinite family is constructed from disjoint subgraphs isomorphic to a smaller member of the family, plus some extra vertices and edges. We present a recurrent interconnection pattern called the cube-connected lines, which is equal to the cube-connected cycles in its ability to simulate composite algorithms. It is shown that a recurrent interconnection pattern constructed without the use of extra vertices cannot share this property. The material in this section is from Parberry [95].

The third section contains some composite sub-algorithms which we will later find useful in the construction of universal networks. The fourth and final section contains some elementary theorems which allow a reduction in the number of processors in networks with the shuffle-exchange, cube-connected cycles or cube-connected lines interconnection patterns, at a cost in time. A reduction in processors from $P_1(n)$ to $P_2(n)$ results in a delay of $O(P_1(n)/P_2(n))$. Thus constant multiples in processor bounds can be ignored without asymptotic time-loss, a fact that we will use often in later chapters.

7.1. Interconnection Patterns and Programming Tools

As suggested in Section 4.4, our aim is to construct a feasible network which can efficiently simulate any general network. There are a number of interconnection patterns available in the literature which we might use for this universal network. These appear to be roughly equal in computing power. Rather than tie ourselves to one particular interconnection pattern, we will express our algorithms in a high-level language which can be implemented efficiently on several interconnection patterns.

Fortunately, the literature provides us with some tools. Preparata and Vuillemin [104] consider various algorithms which use a multi-dimensional cube as the interconnection pattern. Although this has non-constant degree, they find that a large class of useful algorithms have strong properties which allow them to be simulated without asymptotic time-loss on a feasibly-buildable network which they call the *cube-connected cycles*.

To simplify our notation, we will use the concept of an "interconnection template". An *interconnection template* is an infinite sequence of finite graphs $F = (F_1, F_2, ...)$ such that for $i \geq 1$, $F_i = (V_i, E_i)$ with $|V_i| = c^i$ for some constant $c \in N$, $c > 0$. For every processor-bound $P(n)$, we can use F to construct an $O(P(n))$ processor interconnection pattern $G = (G_0, G_1, ...)$ by taking $G_n = F_m$ where $m = \left\lceil \log_c P(n) \right\rceil$, for all $n \in N$. We will see that the constant-multiple increase in processors inherent in this construction can be removed for each of the interconnection patterns considered in this chapter. We will occasionally fail to differentiate between an interconnection template, the interconnection pattern constructed from it, and a network based on that interconnection pattern, relying on context to resolve any ambiguity.

First, let us introduce some useful technical notation. Suppose v and i are non-negative integers. If $i \geq 1$, let v_i denote the ith least-significant bit in the binary representation of v, that is, $v_i = \left\lfloor v/2^{(i-1)} \right\rfloor \bmod 2$. Where convenient, we may choose to blur the distinction between the integer v and a binary representation $v_k v_{k-1} \cdots v_1$ (where $k \geq \lfloor \log v \rfloor + 1$) of v. Also let $v^{(i)}$ denote the integer which differs from v precisely in the ith (least-significant) bit, that is, $v^{(i)} = v + 2^{i-1} - v_i 2^i$. If $v \in \{0,1\}$, let $\bar{v}$ denote $v^{(1)}$, the complement of v.

Suppose k is a non-negative integer. The *k-cube* C_k has vertex-set $\{ v \mid 0 \le v < 2^k \}$, and each vertex v is joined to vertices $v^{(i)}$ for $1 \le i \le k$. C_k has 2^k vertices and degree k; it is this high degree which makes it unsuitable for the construction of a realistic interconnection pattern. However, it has played an important part in motivating the degree-3 interconnection templates which we shall meet below. Figure 7.1.1 shows the four-dimensional cube (commonly called the hyper-cube) C_4, which has 16 vertices and degree 4.

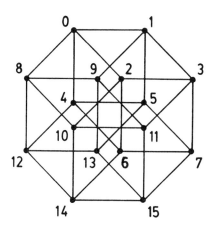

Figure 7.1.1 The hyper-cube, C_4.

Consider a network based on the k-cube, with a constant number of registers per processor. The link between processors v and $v^{(i)}$ is said to be in *dimension* i. Suppose $j \le k$. An algorithm is termed *simple-ascend* (after [104]) if all data transfers occur synchronously along dimension 1, then dimensions 2,3,....,j in monotone increasing order. Similarly it is called *simple-descend* if the data transfers occur in the opposite order, from j down to 1. An algorithm is called *simple* if it is either simple-ascend or simple-descend, or consists of a constant number of ascend or descend passes. It is called *composite* if it is either simple or made up from local instructions and composite modules. We learn from [104] that there are fast composite algorithms for a rich selection of data routing problems (such as permutations, merging and sorting).

The *shuffle-exchange* SE_k of Stone [122] has vertex-set $\{ v \mid 0 \le v < 2^k \}$, and each vertex v is joined to vertices $v^{(1)}$, $(2v) \bmod 2^k + v_k$ and $\lfloor v/2 \rfloor + v_1 2^{k-1}$.

Relative to processor v, these three edges are called *exchange, shuffle* and *unshuffle* edges respectively. SE_k has 2^k vertices and degree 3. Figure 7.1.2 shows the 8 vertex shuffle-exchange SE_3.

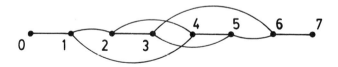

Figure 7.1.2 The 8 vertex shuffle-exchange, SE_4.

In the remainder of this chapter we will call the processors of the simulated network *processes* in order to distinguish them from the *processors* of the simulating machine. This is consistent with the view that the simulated network is presented to the simulator as a program, not as a physical collection of processors and wires.

Theorem 7.1.1 A shuffle-exchange with 2^k processors can simulate a 2^k process composite algorithm with constant delay.

Proof. (Outline) Suppose $j \leq k$. Without loss of generality we will prove the result for algorithms whose data transfers occur synchronously along dimensions $1, 2, \ldots, j-1, j, j-1, \ldots, 2, 1$ in turn. Both simple-ascend and simple-descend class algorithms fit into this category with constant delay, the former by taking the last j data transfers to be null, and the latter the first j. Applying the same technique to each simple module shows that the result also holds for composite algorithms.

Each processor will be assigned the task of simulating one process. Since each process has only a constant number of registers, it is possible to have a simulation in which the processor assignments are flexible. To move a process from one processor to another, we need only transfer the contents of its registers. If this transfer is to take place between neighbouring processors, the entire process can be moved in constant time. We start off with processor i of the shuffle-exchange simulating process i, $0 \leq i < 2^k$. Most importantly where composite algorithms are concerned, we also end up in this configuration. Initially, we can manage the data transfers along dimension 1, since for $0 \leq i < 2^k$, processor i is connected to processor $i^{(1)}$ via an exchange link.

Next we simply move the entire process from processor i to processor $i_1 i_k i_{k-1} \cdots i_2$ via the unshuffle edge out of processor i (which the processor at the other end views as a shuffle edge). After this has been done in parallel for all i, $0 \le i < 2^k$, we see that process $i^{(2)}$ is then resident in processor $(i_1 i_k i_{k-1} \cdots i_2)^{(1)}$, which is adjacent to processor $i_1 i_k i_{k-1} \cdots i_2$ via the exchange link. Thus the necessary transfers between processes i and $i^{(2)}$ can take place over the exchange links. After a second unshuffle of processes, data transfers in dimension 3 can take place over the exchange links. This continues up to dimension j, and then is reversed back down to dimension 1. $\square$

The *cube-connected cycles* CCC_k of Preparata and Vuillemin [104] is defined as follows. Let r be such that $2^{r-1}+r-1 < k \le 2^r+r$. CCC_k has vertex-set $\{ (v,p) \mid 0 \le v < 2^{k-r}, 0 \le p < 2^r \}$, and each vertex (v,p) is joined to vertices:
(i) $(v^{(p+1)},p)$, provided $0 \le p < k-r$,
(ii) $(v,(p+1) \bmod 2^r)$, and
(iii) $(v,(p-1) \bmod 2^r)$.

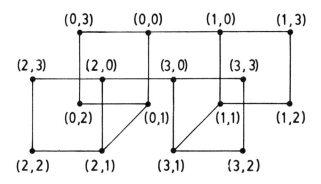

Figure 7.1.3 The 16 vertex cube-connected cycles, CCC_4.

The first link is called a *cube* edge, the remaining two *cycle* edges. Relative to processor (v,p), the first cycle-edge is called *upcycle*, the second *downcycle*. CCC_k has 2^k vertices and degree 3. Figure 7.1.3 shows the 16 vertex cube-connected cycles, CCC_4. Note that every processor (v,p) can be numbered canonically by concatenating the binary representations of v and p. The processors of a fixed-structure network based on the cube-connected cycles do not need to compute v

and p from their PIDs since the connections are "hard-wired" into the machine via the port registers.

Theorem 7.1.2 A cube-connected cycles with 2^k processors can simulate a 2^k process composite algorithm with constant delay.

Proof. Preparata and Vuillemin [104] prove this result when the upper dimension in the simple modules is equal to k. A straightforward modification to the pipelining argument and to LOOPOPER gives us the desired result (Exercise 7.1). □

By application of these theorems we have:

Theorem 7.1.3 A feasible network with at most $2^{\lceil \log n \rceil}$ processors can permute n items according to some fixed permutation in time O(log n) (provided some pre-computation is allowed).

Proof. The algorithm is just a simulation of the permutation network of Waksman [131] (covered in Section 2.3). See Schwartz [112] or Preparata and Vuillemin [104]. (Exercise 7.2). □

Theorem 7.1.4 A feasible network with at most $2^{\lceil \log n \rceil}$ processors can perform the pre-computation mentioned in Theorem 7.1.3 in time $O(\log^4 n)$.

Proof. See, for example, Nassimi and Sahni [87], Schwartz [112], Opferman and Tsao-Wu [89] or Lev, Pippenger and Valiant [74]. □

Theorem 7.1.5 A feasible network with at most $2^{\lceil \log n \rceil}$ processors can sort n items in time $O(\log^2 n)$.

Proof. The algorithm is a composite realization of the odd-even or bitonic sorting algorithms of Batcher [10] (covered in Section 2.2). See, for example, Schwartz [112] or Preparata and Vuillemin [104]. (Exercises 7.3, 7.4). □

7.2. Recurrent Interconnection Patterns

Informally, an interconnection pattern is said to be *recurrent* if every graph in the series is constructed from isomorphic copies of smaller graphs in the series. Recurrent interconnection patterns are desirable since they are in a sense "upward-compatible", that is, more processors can be "plugged in" to the network without altering the existing links. Recurrent networks can also be easily divided (either physically or virtually) into smaller machines for different

94

applications. Neither the cube-connected cycles nor the shuffle-exchange is recurrent (Seigal [115]).

More formally, An interconnection template $F = (F_1, F_2, ...)$ with $P(n)$ processors is said to be *recurrent* if for all n,m with $0 \leq m \leq n$, F_n has $\Omega(P(n)/P(m))$ disjoint subgraphs isomorphic to F_m. The simplest form of recurrence one might choose is to have F_n constructed from *precisely* $P(n)/P(m)$ such subgraphs. Unfortunately, we will see that this type of recurrent interconnection template is much less powerful than the shuffle-exchange or cube-connected cycles interconnection templates.

Suppose c is a fixed positive integer (independent of n). More precisely, a *recursive* interconnection template is one in which F_n $(n > 0)$ is made up of exactly c disjoint copies of F_{n-1} (with some fixed graph for F_1), joined by extra edges from some graph $\hat{F}_n$. We will call a network *recursive* if its interconnection pattern is constructed from a recursive interconnection template.

Theorem 7.2.1 A constant degree recursive network with $P(n)$ processors cannot permute $P(n)$ items in $O(\log P(n))$ steps.

Proof. For a contradiction, suppose $F = (F_1, F_2, ...)$ is a $P(n)$-processor, degree-d recursive interconnection template that can be used to permute $P(n)$ items in time $O(\log P(n))$. The following simple and elegant technique is due to Meertens [82].

Without loss of generality assume $P(1) = c$ (note that this means $P(n) = c^n$). For convenience, write P_n for $P(n)$. Let E_n denote the number of edges in F_n, $\hat{E}_n$ denote the number of edges in $\hat{F}_n$, and $\Gamma_n = E_n/P_n$. Note that $\Gamma_n \leq d/2$. (Let S_n be the sum over all vertices v in F_n of the number of edges incident with v. Clearly $S_n \leq d\,P_n$. But every edge is counted twice, so $S_n = 2\,E_n$).

We claim that for $n \geq 1$, $\hat{E}_n = \Omega(c^n/n)$. Consider one of the subgraphs of F_n isomorphic to F_{n-1}. Pick a permutation that takes a data item from each vertex of the subgraph (there are c^{n-1} of them) to a vertex of F_n outside that subgraph. These data items must pass along the edges of $\hat{G}_n$, since these are the only edges linking the subgraph with the rest of G_n. Thus in one step, at most $\hat{E}_n$ items can be moved. By hypothesis we can move all the items in $O(n)$ steps. There are c^{n-1} items to be moved. Hence $c^n = O(\hat{E}_n n)$. This is sufficient to prove the above claim.

Therefore:

$$E_n = \hat{E}_n + c\, E_{n-1}$$

$$= \sum_{i=1}^{n-1} c^i \hat{E}_{n-i}$$

$$= \Omega\Big(\sum_{i=1}^{n-1} c^i c^{n-i}/(n-i)\Big) \qquad\qquad \text{(by the claim)}$$

$$= \Omega\Big(\sum_{i=1}^{n-1} c^n/i\Big) \qquad\qquad\qquad \text{(by re-indexing)}$$

Thus $\Gamma_n = E_n/P_n = \Omega\Big(\sum_{i=1}^{n-1} 1/i\Big)$, which diverges as $n \to \infty$. But this contradicts the fact that $\Gamma_n \leq d/2$, a constant independent of n. Thus no such parallel machine can exist. $\square$

This is in contrast to the corresponding result for the cube-connected cycles and shuffle-exchange (see Theorem 7.1.3).

Although recursive interconnection patterns are thus in a sense weaker than the shuffle-exchange or cub-connected cycles, the same is not necessarily true of recurrent interconnection patterns. The following is a recurrent interconnection template appearing in Reif and Valiant [107] and Parberry [95] that is as powerful as the cube-connected cycles, at least in its ability to simulate composite algorithms. The *cube-connected lines*, CCL_k is simply a copy of CCC_k with the edges from vertices $(v,0)$ to $(v,2^r-1)$, $0 \leq v < 2^{k-r}$ deleted (we call the remaining cycle edges *line edges*, and the deleted cycle edges *external edges*). That is, the cycles of the cube-connected cycles are broken, and thus become lines. CCL_k has 2^k vertices and degree 3. Figure 7.2.1 shows the 16-vertex cube-connected lines graph, CCL_4.

It is fairly easy to see that CCL_k is recurrent. We need to differentiate the special case of CCL_k when k is of the form 2^r+r, for some r. In this case we call CCL_k a *full* cube-connected lines graph.

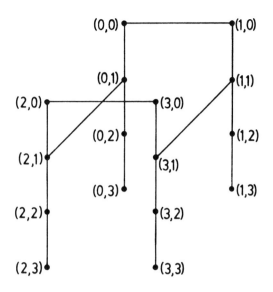

Figure 7.2.1 The 16 vertex cube-connected lines graph, CCL_4. Line-edges are drawn vertically; the remainder are cube-edges.

Lemma 7.2.2 If $k = 2^r + r$ then CCL_{k+1} has exactly one subgraph isomorphic to CCL_k.

Proof. Suppose $k = 2^r + r$. CCL_k has vertices (v,p) with $0 \le v < 2^{k-r}$, $0 \le p < 2^r$. Vertex (v,p) is joined to vertices:

(i) $(v^{(p+1)}, p)$, $0 \le v < 2^{k-r}$, $0 \le p < 2^r$,

(ii) $(v, p+1)$, $0 \le v < 2^{k-r}$, $0 \le p < 2^r - 1$, and

(iii) $(v, p-1)$, $0 \le v < 2^{k-r}$, $0 < p < 2^r$.

CCL_{k+1} has vertices (v,p) with $0 \le v < 2^{k-r}$, $0 \le p < 2^{r+1}$. Vertex (v,p) is joined to vertices:

(i) $(v^{(p+1)}, p)$, $0 \le v < 2^{k-r}$, $0 \le p < 2^r$,

(ii) $(v, p+1)$, $0 \le v < 2^{k-r}$, $0 \le p < 2^{r+1} - 1$, and

(iii) $(v, p-1)$, $0 \le v < 2^{k-r}$, $0 < p < 2^{r+1}$. Thus

CCL_k looks exactly like CCL_{k-1} with lines extended to double the length using vertices without cube edges (see Figure 7.2.2). So CCL_{k+1} has exactly one subgraph isomorphic to CCL_k. $\square$

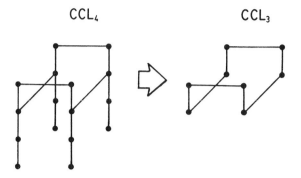

Figure 7.2.2 CCL_4 has one subgraph isomorphic to CCL_3.

Lemma 7.2.3 If k is not of the form 2^r+r then CCL_{k+1} has two disjoint subgraphs isomorphic to CCL_k.

Proof. Without loss of generality, suppose $k < 2^r+r$. CCL_k has vertices (v,p) with $0 \leq v < 2^{k-r}$, $0 \leq p < 2^r$. Vertex (v,p) is joined to vertices

(i) $(v^{(p+1)},p)$, $0 \leq v < 2^{k-r}$, $0 \leq p < k-r$,

(ii) $(v,p+1)$, $0 \leq v < 2^{k-r}$, $0 \leq p < 2^r-1$, and

(iii) $(v,p-1)$, $0 \leq v < 2^{k-r}$, $0 < p < 2^r$.

CCL_{k+1} has vertices (v,p) with $0 \leq v < 2^{k-r+1}$, $0 \leq p < 2^r$. Vertex (v,p) is joined to vertices

(i) $(v^{(p+1)},p)$, $0 \leq v < 2^{k-r+1}$, $0 \leq p < k-r+1$,

(ii) $(v,p+1)$, $0 \leq v < 2^{k-r+1}$, $0 \leq p < 2^r-1$, and

(iii) $(v,p-1)$, $0 \leq v < 2^{k-r+1}$, $0 < p < 2^r$.

Thus deleting the cube-edges from (v,p) to $(v^{(p+1)},p)$ with $p = k-r$ from CCL_{k+1} gives two disjoint graphs isomorphic to CCL_k (see Figure 7.2.3). $\square$

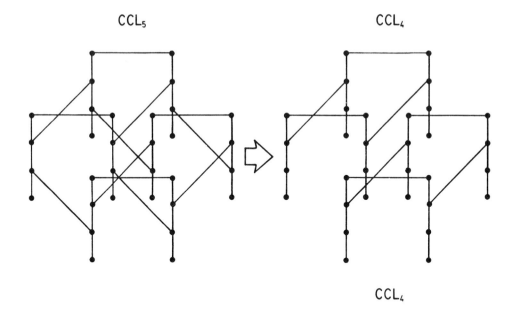

Figure 7.2.3 CCL_5 has two subgraphs isomorphic to CCL_4.

Lemma 7.2.4 If $k = 2^r + r$, and $j = 2^s + s$, where $r \geq s$ then CCL_k has exactly 2^{k-j} disjoint subgraphs isomorphic to CCL_j.

Proof. Suppose $k = 2^r + r$ and $j = 2^s + s$ for some $r \geq s \geq 0$. CCL_j has vertices (v, p), $0 \leq v < 2^{2^s}$, $0 \leq p < 2^s$. Vertex (v, p) is joined to vertex

(i) $(v^{(p+1)}, p)$, $0 \leq v < 2^{2^s}$, $0 \leq p < 2^s$,

(ii) $(v, p+1)$, $0 \leq v < 2^{2^s}$, $0 \leq p < 2^s - 1$, and

(iii) $(v, p-1)$, $0 \leq v < 2^{2^s}$, $0 < p < 2^s$.

CCL_k has vertices (v, p), $0 \leq v < 2^{2^r}$, $0 \leq p < 2^r$. Vertex (v, p) is joined to vertex

(i) $(v^{(p+1)}, p)$, $0 \leq v < 2^{2^r}$, $0 \leq p < 2^r$,

(ii) $(v, p+1)$, $0 \leq v < 2^{2^r}$, $0 \leq p < 2^r - 1$, and

(iii) $(v, p-1)$, $0 \leq v < 2^{2^r}$, $0 < p < 2^r$.

Deleting the line-edges between vertices $(v, i.2^s - 1)$ and $(v, i2^s)$ for $0 \leq v < 2^{2^r}$, $0 \leq i < 2^{r-s}$ breaks CCL_k into 2^{k-j} graphs isomorphic to CCL_j (see Figure 7.2.4). Thus a full CCL_k has 2^{k-j} disjoint subgraphs isomorphic to a full CCL_j. $\square$

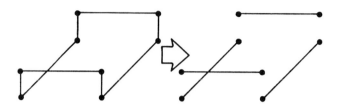

Figure 7.2.4 CCL_3 has four subgraphs isomorphic to CCL_1.

Theorem 7.2.5 For $0 \leq j \leq k$, CCL_k has at least 2^{k-j-1} disjoint subgraphs isomorphic to CCL_j.

Proof. (Sketch) The result follows easily using the above Lemmas. First reduce CCL_k into subgraphs isomorphic to the next smaller full CCL, using Lemmas 7.2.2 and 7.2.3. If CCL_j is encountered along the way, then this is sufficient. Next, using Lemma 7.2.4, reduce the full CCL immediately below CCL_k into subgraphs isomorphic to the full CCL immediately above CCL_j. The latter can be reduced to CCL_j by application of Lemma 7.2.3.

In this entire process we only once have to reduce a non-full CCL to subgraphs isomorphic to full ones. Thus CCL_k consists of 2^{k-j-1} subgraphs isomorphic to CCL_j. $\square$

Note that any attempt to increase the number of subgraphs from 2^{k-j-1} to 2^{k-j} is doomed to failure. For if CCL_k had 2^{k-j} subgraphs isomorphic to CCL_j, it would then be recursive. Thus by Theorem 7.2.1 it would be much weaker than the cube-connected cycles for computing permutations. However we have:

Theorem 7.2.6 A cube-connected lines with 2^k processors can simulate a 2^k processor composite algorithm without asymptotic time loss.

Proof. The proof is almost identical to that for the cube-connected cycles [104]. In that proof:

1. The pipelining phase utilizes a synchronous cyclic shift around the cycles. This can be replaced with a linear shift along the corresponding lines of the cube-connected lines graph, with wrap-around at the ends (at most doubling the time requirement).

2. Communication within the cycles is performed using a procedure called LOOPOPER. A close examination of this procedure reveals that it never

uses external edges, and thus can be executed on the cube-connected lines graph.

A complete proof will be deferred to Exercise 7.5. □

Thus, in particular, a network based on the cube-connected lines interconnection pattern can permute n items in time O(log n). A degree-4 graph with similar properties was earlier devised by Meyer auf der Heide [52,53].

7.3. Some Useful Algorithms

Having developed the idea of a composite algorithm in Section 7.1, we are now ready to describe some simple sub-algorithms which we will find useful in the next three chapters. The algorithms are given for the k-cube, but can be simulated without asymptotic loss of resources on either the shuffle-exchange, cube-connected cycles or cube-connected lines interconnection patterns, as described in Sections 7.1 and 7.2. It is important to note that the algorithms are SIMD in nature; synchronization is maintained by the fact that (as we earlier insisted in Section 3.1) the code generated for each branch of a selection statement (such as if-then-else, even if the "else" branch is null) has the same number of instructions.

Algorithm 1. Broadcast.

Suppose processor 0 has a value v which it wishes to broadcast to all 2^k processors of a k-cube. This can be achieved in time $O(k)$ by the following simple-ascend algorithm, which terminates with variable V of every processor equal to v.

$$V := \textbf{if } PID = 0 \textbf{ then } v \textbf{ else } 0$$
$$\textbf{for } b := 1 \textbf{ to } k \textbf{ do}$$
$$\textbf{if } PID_b = 1 \textbf{ then } V := (V \textbf{ of processor } PID^{(b)})$$

If $0 \le i < 2^k$, define the b-block (after [86,88]) of processor i to be the set of 2^b processors { $\lfloor i/2^b \rfloor 2^b + j \mid 0 \le j < 2^b$}. It is easy to prove by induction that after the bth iteration of the for-loop, variable V of all processors in the b-block of processor 0 is equal to v, for $b = 0,1,...,k$. (By the 0th iteration, we mean the point immediately before the loop is entered for the first time). Table 7.3.1 shows a trace of the algorithm for k=4. The concept of a b-block will play an important part in the next two algorithms.

	V of processor															
b	0	1	2	3	4	5	6	7	8	9	10	11	12	13	14	15
0	V															
1	V	V														
2	V	V	V	V												
3	V	V	V	V	V	V	V	V								
4	V	V	V	V	V	V	V	V	V	V	V	V	V	V	V	V

Table 7.3.1 A trace of Algorithm 1 on 16 processors. Each line of the table shows the contents of variable V of each processor after b iterations of the for-loop. A blank entry indicates that V is uninitialized.

Algorithm 2. Local Rank.

Suppose every processor of a k-cube holds an integer value in some variable V. For simplicity, suppose that these values are in non-decreasing order, that is, if $i < j$ then (V **of processor** i) $\leq$ (V **of processor** j) (this restriction can be removed, see Exercise 7.6). The *local rank* of processor i, $0 \leq i < 2^k$ is defined to be the number of processors j, $0 \leq j < i$, such that for all processors p with $j \leq p \leq i$, V of processor p equals V of processor i. The following is a simple-ascend class algorithm which sets variable R of each processor to its local rank, and runs in time $O(k)$.

> VT:=V
> R:=RT:=0
> **for** b:=1 **to** k **do**
>   **if** $(PID_b = 1)$ and (VT **of processor** $PID^{(b)}$) $= V$
>   **then** R := R+(RT **of processor** $PID^{(b)}$)+1
>   **if** (VT **of processor** $PID^{(b)}$) $= VT$
>   **then** RT := RT+(RT **of processor** $PID^{(b)}$)+1
>   **else if** $PID_b = 0$ **then** (VT,RT) := (VT,RT) **of processor** $PID^{(}$

At the end of the bth iteration of the for-loop, $0 \leq b \leq k$, variable R of processor i, $0 \leq i < 2^k$ holds that processor's local rank within its b-block. At the same time, variables VT and RT contain the values V and R (respectively) of the top-most processor in its b-block (that is, processor $\lfloor i/2^b \rfloor 2^b + 2^b - 1$). The correctness of the algorithm follows by induction. Table 7.3.2 shows a trace for k=3, with V of processor i initially equal to 0,0,0,6,6,6,6,1 for i = 0,1,...,7 respectively.

b	Variable	Processor							
		0	1	2	3	4	5	6	7
	R	0	0	0	0	0	0	0	0
0	VT	0	0	0	6	6	6	6	1
	RT	0	0	0	0	0	0	0	0
	R	0	1	0	0	0	1	0	0
1	VT	0	0	6	6	6	6	1	1
	RT	1	1	0	0	1	1	0	0
	R	0	1	2	0	0	1	2	0
2	VT	6	6	6	6	1	1	1	1
	RT	0	0	0	0	0	0	0	0
	R	0	1	2	0	1	2	3	0
3	VT	1	1	1	1	1	1	1	1
	RT	0	0	0	0	0	0	0	0

Table 7.3.2 A trace of Algorithm 2 on 8 processors. Each table entry shows the contents of variables R, VT and RT of each processor after b iterations of the for-loop.

Algorithm 3. Fan-out.

Suppose every processor of a k-cube holds two integer values x and y (which may be different for each processor). Our aim is to produce a value fanout(i) for each processor i, where for $0 \leq i < 2^k$, fanout(i) is defined to be the y-value of the smallest numbered processor j such that for all p with $j \leq p \leq i$, x of processor p is equal to x of processor i. For simplicity, suppose that the x-values are in non-decreasing order, that is, if i < j then (x **of processor** i) $\leq$ (x **of processor** j) (this restriction can be removed, see Exercise 7.7). The following is a simple-ascend class algorithm which sets variable Y of processor i to fanout(i), $0 \leq i < 2^k$, in time O(k).

Y:=y
XT,YT := x,y
for b:=1 **to** k **do**
    if $(PID_b = 1) \wedge (XT$ **of processor** $PID^{(b)} = x)$
        then Y := YT **of processor** $PID^{(b)}$
    if $(XT = XT$ **of processor** $PID^{(b)}) <> (PID_b = 1)$
        then (XT,YT) := (XT,YT) **of processor** $PID^{(b)}$

At the end of the bth iteration of the for-loop, $0 \le b \le k$, variable Y of processor i contains the value of fanout(i) restricted to its b-block. At the same time, variables XT and YT contain the values of X and Y (respectively) of the highest-numbered processor in its b-block (that is processor $\lfloor i/2^b \rfloor 2^b + 2^b - 1$). The correctness of the algorithm follows by induction. Table 7.3.3 shows a trace for k = 3 with (x,y) of processor i equal to (0,99), (0,89), (0,69), (6,95), (6,19), (6,28), (6,56), (1,44) for i = 0,1,...,7 respectively.

b	Variable	Processor							
		0	1	2	3	4	5	6	7
	Y	99	89	69	95	19	28	56	44
0	XT	0	0	0	6	6	6	6	1
	YT	99	89	69	95	19	28	56	44
	Y	99	99	69	95	19	19	56	44
1	XT	0	0	6	6	6	6	1	1
	YT	99	99	95	95	19	19	44	44
	Y	99	99	99	95	19	19	19	44
2	XT	6	6	6	6	1	1	1	1
	YT	95	95	95	95	44	44	44	44
	Y	99	99	99	95	95	95	95	44
3	XT	1	1	1	1	1	1	1	1
	YT	44	44	44	44	44	44	44	44

Table 7.3.3 A trace of Algorithm 3 on 8 processors. Each table entry shows the contents of variables X, XT and YT of each processor after b iterations of the for-loop.

Algorithm 4. Scatter.

For the moment we briefly step away from the main theme of this chapter, and allow the processors of our networks to have more than a constant number of registers each. In particular, we want each of the 2^k processors of a k-cube to have an array of 2^k elements. Suppose processor 0 has 2^k items of data in its array, and wishes to scatter these amongst processors $0,1,...,2^k-1$ in such a manner that each processor receives precisely one value. The algorithm consists of k stages. At the end of the ith stage, the 2^i processors p, $0 \le p < 2^i$, are each in possession of 2^k data items. Stage i consists of processor p, $0 \le p < 2^i$ sending 2^{k-i} of its data items to processor $p^{(i)}$. In the following implementation, processor 0 starts off with 2^k items of data in an array $d[1..2^k]$. Each processor receives its value into variable $d[1]$.

> **for** i:=1 **to** k **do**
>   **for** j:=1 **to** 2^{k-i} **do**
>   **if** $PID_i = 1$
>   **then** $d[j] := \left(d[j+2^{k-i}] \text{ of processor } PID^{(i)} \right)$
>   **else** $d[j+2^{k-i}]:=0$

Table 7.3.4 shows a trace for k = 3, with $d[i]$ of processor 0 initially containing i, $1 \le i \le 8$.

The algorithm runs in time $O(\sum_{i=1}^{k} 2^{k-i}) = O(2^k)$ on a k-cube, but is not strictly simple-ascend (because dimension i is used 2^{k-i} times in succession, not merely once). This makes very little difference as far as the shuffle-exchange is concerned (see the proof of Theorem 7.1.1). A minor modification to the proofs of Theorems 7.1.2 and 7.2.3 serves to give the same result for the cube-connected cycles and cube-connected lines interconnection patterns, the key point being the fact that after the ith iteration, $0 \le i \le k$, only 2^i processors are in possession of data items (see Exercise 7.8).

7.4. Reducing the Number of Processors

In this section we examine a particular kind of time-processor trade-off, namely, the question of whether a reduction in the number of processors of a network based on the shuffle-exchange, cube-connected cycles or cube-connected lines

i	j	d[j] of Processor							
		0	1	2	3	4	5	6	7
	1	1							
	2	2							
	3	3							
0	4	4							
	5	5							
	6	6							
	7	7							
	8	8							
	1	1	5						
1	2	2	6						
	3	3	7						
	4	4	8						
2	1	1	5	3	7				
	2	2	6	4	8				
3	1	1	5	3	7	2	6	4	8

Table 7.3.4 A trace of Algorithm 4 on 8 processors. Each table entry shows the contents of d[j] of each processor for various values of j after i iterations of the outer for-loop. A blank entry indicates that d[j] has not yet been initialized.

interconnection patterns can be made at a reasonable cost in time. We find that, due to the highly regular form of the interconnection patterns, a small network based on these interconnection patterns can simulate a larger one by having each processor of the former simulate many of the latter. These processor-reduction theorems have many applications. Firstly, as pointed out in [38], in many situations the input to a parallel computer cannot be read in parallel (this assumption has been made, for example, in [84,90,132]). In this case our results can be applied to slow down various fast parallel algorithms to the speed at which the input becomes available, and thus decrease the number of processors without any observable increase in time. Secondly, we can remove the need for constant factors in processor bounds. For example, Galil and Paul [38] are able to reduce the number of processors in their universal network from O(p) to p while increasing time by only a constant multiple. We are able to extend this result by showing that the number of processors in any network based on many popular interconnection patterns can be reduced by a constant factor without asymptotic time-loss.

Constant multiples in processor-bounds pervade the current literature, due to the fact that the commonly used interconnection templates come only in certain sizes, typically 2^k or $k2^k$ for some non-negative integer k. Thus we are restricted to processor bounds which are powers of two (which may almost double the processor requirements) if we use any of the shuffle-exchange, cube-connected cycles or cube-connected lines interconnection patterns. For example, we have seen in Theorem 7.1.3 that it is possible to permute n items on a $2^{\lceil \log n \rceil}$ processor cube-connected cycles, cube-connected lines or shuffle-exchange in time O(log n) by simulating Waksman's [131] permutation network. In this case it may be necessary to use as many as $2n-2$ processors. Our results enable us to remove these "hidden" constants without asymptotic time loss. The results of this section are from [30,67,68,91]. Our technique is motivated by the following result.

Theorem 7.4.1 For all $d \geq 0$, C_k can simulate C_{k+d} with delay $O(2^d)$.

Proof. In order to simulate a single step of C_{k+d}, every processor i, $0 \leq i < 2^k$ will synchronously execute a single step of processes $2^d i + j$, for $0 \leq j < 2^d$. This takes place in two stages.

(1) For $0 \leq j < 2^d$ simulate the communication between process $2^d i + j$ and its neighbouring processes. Suppose, for example, process $2^d i + j$ wishes to communicate with process $(2^d i + j)^{(m)}$ for some m with $1 \leq m \leq k + d$. If $m \leq d$ then no inter-processor communication is necessary. Otherwise $d < m \leq k + d$ and so process $(2^d.i + j)^{(m)} = 2^d.i^{(m-d)} + j$ is being simulated by processor $i^{(m-d)}$. Since processor $i^{(m-d)}$ is a neighbour of processor i in C_k, the desired communication can be carried out in O(1) steps, the exact constant being dependent on the type of instruction-set in use. Note that communications with process $2^d i + j$ may be initiated by processes $2^d i^{(m-d)} + j$, $1 \leq m \leq k$, resident in every neighbour $i^{(m)}$ of processor i. We assume that the communication protocol of C_k deals with these possible clashes in the same manner as that of C_{k+d}. Clashes involving a communication between two processes resident in the same processor are to be dealt with in a manner which is compatible with this protocol.

(2) Finally, simulate the current step of processes $2^d i + j$, $0 \leq j < 2^d$, making possible use of the information obtained in (1). This is assumed to take $O(1)$ steps per process (the constant again being dependent on the instruction-set).

At this point, C_k is ready to simulate the next step of C_{k+d}. Thus we have simulated a single step of a 2^{k+d} processor network C_{k+d} on a 2^k processor C_k with a time-loss of only $O(2^d)$. $\square$

Note that the simulation of Theorem 7.4.1 can be carried out in such a manner that it maintains the simple-ascend or simple-descend property of Section 7.1. Thus it is strong enough to achieve the desired savings in processors for composite algorithms.

As observed earlier in this section, in some instances the input to a parallel machine may not be available in parallel. The example taken by Galil and Paul in [38] is that of matrix multiplication. It is well-known (see Exercise 7.9) that two n $\times$ n matrices can be multiplied in time $O(\log n)$ using $O(n^3)$ processors on any of the graphs listed in Sections 7.1 and 7.2 provided the input can be read in parallel. Suppose, to the contrary, that the input can only be read sequentially, so that there is an *a priori* lower-bound of $\Omega(n^2)$. By applying Theorem 7.4.1 with $k = \lfloor \log (n \log n) \rfloor$ and $d = \lceil 3 \log n \rceil - k$, we have a linear-time (that is, $O(n^2)$) algorithm on n log n processors. If a row (or column) of the input can be read in parallel, Theorem 7.4.1 with $k = \left\lfloor \log(n^2 \log n) \right\rfloor$ and $d = \lceil 3 \log n \rceil - k$ gives us an $O(n)$ time algorithm on $O(n^2 \log n)$ processors. This improvement over the corresponding results in [38] stems from the fact that they have used a universal parallel network, which leads to a significant degradation in performance.

Whilst Theorem 7.4.1 gives the claimed savings in processors for an important class of algorithms on the shuffle-exchange, cube-connected cycles and cube-connected lines, it is possible to produce a stronger result which holds for *all* algorithms on these graphs. Fortunately the interconnection templates are sufficiently like the k-cube for similar techniques to work. The shuffle-exchange, for instance, is particularly amenable.

Theorem 7.4.2 For all $d \geq 0$, SE_k can simulate SE_{k+d} with delay $O(2^d)$.

Proof. In order to simulate one step of SE_{k+d}, every processor i, $0 \leq i < 2^k$ will synchronously simulate one step of processes $2^d i + j$, for $0 \leq j < 2^d$. As in the proof of Theorem 7.4.1, this takes place in two phases - each processor first carries out any communications required by its processes from their respective neighbours, then updates their configurations once all the information has been gathered.

Suppose $0 \leq j < 2^d$ and process $2^d i + j$ wishes to communicate with one of its neighbours in SE_{k+d}. There are three cases to be considered, according to whether process $2^d i + j$ wishes to communicate with its neighbour along the exchange, shuffle or unshuffle edge. Either:

(1) *Exchange edge.* It wishes to communicate with process $(2^d i + j)^{(1)}$. In this case, no inter-processor communication is necessary, since process $(2^d i + j)^{(1)} = 2^d i + j^{(1)}$ is also being simulated by processor i.

(2) *Shuffle edge.* It wishes to communicate with process $i_{k-1} i_{k-2} \cdots i_1 j_d j_{d-1} \cdots j_1 i_k$. This process is being simulated by processor $i_{k-1} i_{k-2} \cdots i_1 j_d$. There are two cases to consider:

   (a) $i_k = j_d$. Processor $i = j_d i_{k-1} i_{k-2} \cdots i_1$ can communicate with processor $i_{k-1} i_{k-2} \cdots i_1 j_d$ directly through its shuffle edge.

   (b) $i_k \neq j_d$. Processor $i = \overline{j_d} i_{k-1} i_{k-2} \cdots i_1$ can communicate indirectly with processor $i_{k-1} i_{k-2} \cdots i_1 j_d$ by utilizing the shuffle edge to processor $i_{k-1} i_{k-2} \cdots i_1 \overline{j_d}$, and the exchange link from there to processor $i_{k-1} i_{k-2} \cdots i_1 j_d$.

(3) *Unshuffle edge.* It wishes to communicate with process $j_1 i_k i_{k-1} \cdots i_1 j_d j_{d-1} \cdots j_2$. This process is being simulated by processor $j_1 i_k i_{k-1} \cdots i_2$. Again, there are two cases to be considered:

   (a) $i_1 = j_1$. Processor $i = i_k i_{k-1} \cdots i_2 j_1$ can communicate directly with processor $j_1 i_k i_{k-1} \cdots i_2$ through its unshuffle edge.

   (b) $i_1 \neq j_1$. Processor $i = i_k i_{k-1} \cdots i_2 \overline{j_1}$ can communicate indirectly with processor $j_1 i_k i_{k-1} \cdots i_2$ by utilizing the exchange link to processor $i_k i_{k-1} \cdots i_2 j_1$ and the unshuffle edge from there to processor $j_1 i_k i_{k-1} \cdots i_2$.

Thus we have shown how to simulate one step of the 2^{k+d} processor SE_{k+d} on the 2^k processor SE_k with a time-loss of only $O(2^d)$, the constant multiple being dependent on the instruction-set used. $\square$

The results for the variants of the cube-connected cycles are proved in a similar manner.

Theorem 7.4.3 For all d $\geq$ 0,

(i) CCC_k can simulate CCC_{k+d}, and

(ii) CCL_k can simulate CCL_{k+d},

with delay $O(2^d)$.

Proof. We will demonstrate the technique for d $=$ 1. This can be looked upon as a recursive algorithm for the processor assignment, along with a proof that the assignment is valid. We consider CCC_k first.

First, suppose that k is of the form $2^r + r$ for some integer r $\geq$ 0. Then the processors of the simulating network are of the form (v,p) where $0 \leq v < 2^{2^r}$, $0 \leq p < 2^r$. In contrast, the processes of the simulated network have the form (v,p) with $0 \leq v < 2^{2^r}$, $0 \leq p < 2^{r+1}$. Processor (v,p), $0 \leq v < 2^{2^r}$, $0 \leq p < 2^r$ will simulate processes (v,p) and (v,2^{r+1}–p–1). As before, each processor synchronously carries out the communications requested by all its processes, and then updates their configurations internally.

Suppose process (v,p) wishes to communicate with one of its neighbours. There are three cases to consider.

(1) *Cube edge.* It wishes to communicate with process ($v^{(p+1)}$,p). This process is being simulated by processor ($v^{(p+1)}$,p) which is directly connected to processor (v,p) via a cube edge.

(2) *Upcycle edge.* It wishes to communicate with process (v,p + 1). If $0 \leq p < 2^r$–1 then process (v,p + 1) is being simulated by processor (v,p + 1), which is directly connected to processor (v,p) by an upcycle edge. Otherwise p $= 2^r$–1 and process (v,2^r) is also being simulated by processor (v,p), so no inter-processor communication is necessary.

(3) *Downcycle edge.* It wishes to communicate with process (v,(p–1) mod 2^{r+1}). If $0 < p < 2^r$ then process (v,p–1) is being simulated by processor (v,p–1), which is directly connected to processor (v,p) by a downcycle edge. Otherwise p $= 0$ and process (v,2^{r+1}–1) is also being simulated by processor (v,p), so no inter-processor communication is necessary.

Now suppose that process (v,2^{r+1}–p–1) wishes to communicate with one of its neighbours. This is handled similarly to (2) and (3) above (remembering that processes of this form have only cycle links).

This completes the case where k is of the form $2^r + r$. Now suppose k is not of that form. Let r be such that $2^{r-1} + r$–1 $< k < 2^r + r$. The processors of the simulating network are of the form (v,p) where $0 \leq v < 2^{k-r}$, $0 \leq p < 2^r$. The processes of the simulated network are of the form (v,p) where $0 \leq v < 2^{k-r+1}$,

110

$0 \leq p < 2^r$. Processor (v,p) will simulate processes (v,p) and $(v + 2^{k-r}, p)$. As always, in order to simulate a single step, each processor first carries out the communications required by its processes, and then updates their configurations internally. Suppose process (v,p) wishes to communicate with one of its neighbours. There are two cases to consider.

(1) *Cube edge.* It wishes to communicate with process $(v^{(p+1)}, p)$. If $p < k-r$ then process $(v^{(p+1)}, p)$ is being simulated by processor $(v^{(p+1)}, p)$. Otherwise $p = k-r$ and process $(v^{(p+1)}, p) = (v + 2^{k-r}, p)$ is also being simulated by processor (v,p), so no inter-processor communication is necessary. Note that p cannot exceed k–r since processes (v,p) with $p > k-r$ have no cube edge.

(2) *Cycle edges.* It wishes to communicate with process $(v, (p \pm 1) \bmod 2^r)$. This process is being simulated by processor $(v, (p \pm 1) \bmod 2^r)$ respectively, which is connected to processor (v,p) by a cycle link.

This completes the simulation of process (v,p). Process $(v + 2^{k-r}, p)$ is handled similarly.

Thus we have shown how to simulate a step of CCC_{k+d} on CCC_k in time $O(2^d)$. Since CCL_k is a subgraph of CCC_k, part (*ii*) of the theorem follows immediately. $\square$

Note that the set-up times for Theorems 7.4.1 and 7.4.2 are far superior to that of Theorem 7.4.3. Not only are the assignments of processes to processors easier to compute, but also the input symbols are placed into the correct processors at the start of a computation according to the convention established in Section 4.1.

7.5. Exercises

7.1 Show that a cube-connected cycles with 2^k processors can simulate a 2^k process composite algorithm with constant delay. (Theorem 7.1.2).

7.2 Show that a feasible network with at most $2^{\lceil \log n \rceil}$ processors can permute n items according to some fixed permutation in time $O(\log n)$ (Theorem 7.1.3), by implementing Waksman's permutation algorithm (Section 2.3).

7.3 Show that a feasible network with at most $2^{\lceil \log n \rceil}$ processors can sort n items in time $O(\log^2 n)$ (Theorem 7.1.5) by implementing Batcher's odd-even sorting algorithm (Section 2.2).

7.4 Show that a feasible network with at most $2^{\lceil \log n \rceil}$ processors can sort n items in time $O(\log^2 n)$ (Theorem 7.1.5) by implementing Batcher's bitonic sorting algorithm (Section 2.2).

7.5 Show that a cube-connected lines with 2^k processors can simulate a 2^k processor composite algorithm without asymptotic time loss. (Theorem 7.2.6).

7.6 Demonstrate that Algorithm 2 (Section 7.3) will not correctly compute the local rank when the inputs values V are not necessarily in sorted order. Modify it so that it does.

7.7 Demonstrate that Algorithm 3 (Section 7.3) will not correctly compute fan-out when the inputs values x are not necessarily in sorted order. Modify it so that it does.

7.8 Show that Algorithm 4 (Section 7.3) can be simulated on the cube-connected cycles interconnection pattern without asymptotic time-loss, even though it is not strictly simple-ascend.

7.9 (Preparata and Vuillemin [104]) Give a composite algorithm for multiplying two $n \times n$ matrices in time $O(\log n)$ on n^3 processors. Express your algorithm using our high-level programming language.

8 The AKS Sorting Network

For over a decade it was thought that the $O(\log^2 n)$ depth, $O(n \log^2 n)$ size sorting network of Batcher (see Sections 2.1 and 2.2) may be the best possible. It was not until fairly recently that an asymptotically optimal $O(\log n)$ depth, $O(n \log n)$ size network was found by Ajtai, Komlós and Szemerédi [5,6]. This chapter is devoted to an elegant version of their algorithm due to M. S. Paterson. Until recently, Paterson's result existed only in oral tradition, with only sketchy notes (for example, Leighton [72]) in circulation. The material in this chapter is based on [72], with the emphasis placed on clarity and simplicity, rather than the pursuit of the smallest constant multiple. A definitive version of the algorithm, in which a more sophisticated analysis gives a superior constant multiple, has been recently published by Paterson [100]. The first section of this chapter examines the basic building-blocks of the algorithm, called ϵ-nearsorters, which are constructed using a special family of graphs known as expander graphs. The second section contains the abstract algorithm, with the third section is devoted to a correctness proof and the details of implementing the algorithm as a sorting network.

8.1. Halvers and Nearsorters

Suppose G is a bipartite graph, that is, $G = (V_1, V_2, E)$, $V_1 \cap V_2 = \emptyset$, $E \subseteq V_1 \times V_2$. If $A \subseteq V_1$, write $\Gamma(A)$ for the set of neighbours of vertices in A, $\{v \in V_2 \mid \exists\, u \in A\ (u,v) \in E\}$. Similarly, if $A \subseteq V_2$, write $\Gamma(A)$ for $\{u \in V_1 \mid \exists\, v \in A\ (u,v) \in E\}$. G is said to be *d-regular* if every vertex has degree d, that is, for all $v \in V_1 \cup V_2$, $|\Gamma(\{v\})| = d$. A d-regular bipartite graph must have $|V_1| = |V_2|$.

Definition. Suppose $\beta \geq 1$, $\alpha \leq 1$, $d \in \mathbb{N}$, with $\alpha\beta \leq 1$. An (α,β,d)-*expander* is a d-regular bipartite graph $G = (V_1, V_2, E)$ with $|V_1| = |V_2| = n$, such that for every $A \subseteq V_i$ with $|A| \leq \alpha n$, $|\Gamma(A)| \geq \beta |A|$, for $i = 1,2$.

Theorem 8.1.1 (Hall [49]). A bipartite graph $G = (V_1, V_2, E)$ has a perfect matching iff for all $A \subseteq V_1$, $|\Gamma(A)| \geq |A|$.

Proof. See, for example, Even [27]. $\square$

Corollary 8.1.2 Every d-regular bipartite graph can be edge-coloured using d colours so that every pair of edges with a common vertex have different colours.

Proof. The result follows by induction on d. The hypothesis is clearly true for 1-regular graphs. Suppose the hypothesis holds for (d–1)-regular graphs, and that $G = (V_1, V_2, E)$ is d-regular. Note that every d-regular bipartite graph $G = (V_1, V_2, E)$ is a (1,1,d)-expander. (For a contradiction, suppose there exists $A \subseteq V_1$ such that $|\Gamma(A)| < |A|$. Let E_1 be the set of edges incident with A, and E_2 the set of edges incident with $\Gamma(A)$. Clearly by the definition of $\Gamma(A)$, $|E_1| \leq |E_2|$. But $|E_1| = d|A|$ and $|E_2| = d|\Gamma(A)| < d|A|$, which implies that $|E_2| < |E_1|$.) Thus by Theorem 8.1.1, G has a perfect matching. This perfect matching can be coloured monochromatically, and upon its removal leaves a (d–1)-regular graph, which by the induction hypothesis can be coloured with d–1 colours. $\square$

Theorem 8.1.3 For all $\beta > 1$, $\alpha > 0$ with $\alpha\beta < 1$ there exists a constant $d(\alpha,\beta)$ such that arbitrarily large $(\alpha,\beta,d(\alpha,\beta))$-expanders exist.

Proof. The proof of this result is beyond the scope of this book. A simple but tedious counting argument shows that, for sufficiently large n, most regular bipartite graphs of large degree are expander graphs. Some explicit constructions of expander graphs are known, but these have degree far larger than those shown to exist by the counting argument. The interested reader can consult Alon [7], Gabber and Galil [35], Jimbo and Maruoka [58], Klawe [63], Lubotzsky, Phillips and Sarnak [77], Margulis [80] and Pippenger [101]. $\square$

Definition. Let $X = \langle x_1, x_2, \ldots, x_n \rangle$ be a sequence of n distinct numbers, and $X(i,j)$ denote $\{x_i, x_{i+1}, \ldots, x_j\}$. For $1 \leq k \leq n/2$ let S_k be the set of k smallest numbers in X (that is, $|S_k| = k$ and for all $x_i \in S_k$ and $x_j \notin S_k$, $x_i < x_j$) and L_k be the set of k largest numbers in X. Then X is said to be γ-*halved* if for all $k \leq n/2$, $|S_k \cap X(\lfloor n/2 \rfloor + 1, n)| \leq \gamma k$ and $|L_k \cap X(1, \lfloor n/2 \rfloor)| \leq \gamma k$. A γ-*halver* is a comparator network which γ-halves its inputs.

114

Lemma 8.1.4 For every $0 < \gamma < 1$ and $n > 0$ there exist n-input γ-halvers of depth $d(\frac{\gamma}{2}, \frac{2}{\gamma} - 1)$, for the function d mentioned in Theorem 8.1.3.

Proof. If n is so small that n-vertex expander graphs cannot be found, then a Batcher sorting network will suffice (see Section 2.2). This will have constant depth. Because of the large constant multiples involved in the construction of expander graphs, we will assume that the depth is dominated by $d(\frac{\gamma}{2}, \frac{2}{\gamma} - 1)$. Suppose that n is sufficiently large, and that n is even. Take an (α, β, d)-expander $G = (V_1, V_2, E)$ with $V_1 = \{1, 2, ..., \lfloor n/2 \rfloor\}$, $V_2 = \{\lfloor n/2 \rfloor + 1, ..., n\}$, $\alpha = \gamma$, $\beta = \frac{1-\alpha}{\alpha}$ and $d = d(\gamma, \frac{1-\gamma}{\gamma})$. This expander graph is guaranteed to exist (for large enough n) by Theorem 8.1.3. Colour its edges with colours drawn from the set $\{1, 2, ..., d\}$ (this is possible by Corollary 8.1.2), and construct an n-input comparison network with a comparator between channels i and j at level k precisely when there is an edge coloured k between vertices i and j in G. Clearly the network has depth:

$$d = d(\gamma, \frac{1-\gamma}{\gamma}) \leq d(\frac{\gamma}{2}, \frac{2}{\gamma} - 1).$$

(We assume that $d(\alpha, \beta)$ is monotone nondecreasing as $\beta \to \infty$.)

Claim 1. All comparators cross the centre-line, that is, $i \leq n/2$ and $j > n/2$.
Proof. This is obvious by construction, whether n is even or odd. $\square$

Suppose that the inputs to the network are $x_1, ..., x_n$ and the outputs are $y_1, ..., y_n$. Let S_k be the set of k smallest numbers in $x_1, ..., x_n$, and $Y(i,j) = \{y_i, y_{i+1}, ..., y_j\}$. We will show that for all $k \leq n/2$, $|S_k \cap Y(n/2+1, n)| \leq \gamma k$; the corresponding result for L_k follows in a similar manner.

Claim 2. If there is a comparator between channels i and j on any level, then $y_i < y_j$.
Proof. To see this, note that at the level containing the comparator, the value on channel i is less than the value on channel j, and that by Claim 1, $i \leq n/2$ and $j > n/2$, hence (again by Claim 1) the value on channel i cannot be increased by subsequent comparisons and the value on channel j cannot be decreased by subsequent comparisons. $\square$

Let $B \subseteq \{n/2+1, ..., n\}$ be the set of channels which wrongly contain members of S_k at the final level, that is, $S_k \cap Y(n/2+1, n) = \{y_i \mid i \in B\}$, and $\overline{B}$ be the set of channels that are compared to channels in B at any level.

Claim 3. Each channel in B carries a member of S_k at every level.

Proof. The result follows by induction on the distance from the final level. □

Claim 4. Each channel in $\overline{B}$ carries a member of S_k at the outputs.

Proof. By Claims 2 and 3. □

We are required to prove that $|B| \leq \gamma k$. For a contradiction, suppose $|B| > \gamma k$. By the expander property, $|\overline{B}| > \beta|B| > \beta\gamma k$. Since (by Claim 1) $B \cap \overline{B} = \emptyset$, this means that $|B \cup \overline{B}| > (\beta+1)\gamma k$. Since, by Claims 3 and 4, every channel in $B \cup \overline{B}$ carries a different member of S_k at the output level, this implies that $|S_k| > (\beta+1)\gamma k$. However, since we chose $\beta = (1-\gamma)/\gamma$, this says that $|S_k| > k$, which contradicts the definition of S_k.

Now suppose that n is odd. It is possible, using an argument similar to the above, with $\alpha = \gamma/2$, to produce a γ-halver of the appropriate depth (see Exercise 8.2). □

Definition. Let $X = <x_1,x_2,...,x_n>$ be a sequence of n distinct numbers, and $X(i,j)$ denote $\{x_i,x_{i+1},...,x_j\}$. For $1 \leq k \leq n$ let S_k be the set of k smallest numbers in X (that is, $|S_k| = k$ and for all $x_i \in S_k$, $x_j \notin S_k$, $s_i < s_j$) and L_k be the set of k largest numbers in X. Then X is said to be ϵ-*nearsorted* if for all $1 \leq k \leq n$, $|S_k \cap X(k+\epsilon n,n)| \leq \epsilon k$ and $|L_k \cap X(1,n-k-\epsilon n)| \leq \epsilon k$. An ϵ-*nearsorter* is a ϵ-halver which ϵ-nearsorts its inputs.

Lemma 8.1.5 For every $0 < \epsilon < 1$ there exist ϵ-nearsorters of depth $\xi.d(\frac{\epsilon}{2\xi},\frac{2\xi}{\epsilon}-1)$, where $\xi = \lceil -\log \epsilon \rceil$ and d is the function from Theorem 8.1.3.

Proof. Suppose n is a power of 2, and $s \leq \log n$. Define an (n,s,γ)-network, where $\gamma < 1$, as follows. An $(n,0,\gamma)$-network is empty. For $s \geq 1$, an (n,s,γ)-network is constructed from an n-input γ-halver and two $(n/2,s-1,\gamma)$-networks as in Figure 8.1.1.

Suppose that the inputs to the network are $x_1,...,x_n$ and the outputs are $y_1,...,y_n$. Let S_k be the set of k smallest numbers in $X = \{x_1,...,x_n\}$, L_k be the set of k largest numbers in X and $Y(i,j) = \{y_i,...,y_j\}$. Suppose we call the recursive $(n/2,s-1,\gamma)$-network whose outputs are $Y(1,n/2)$ the *smaller* sub-network, and the other the *larger* sub-network.

We claim that for $1 \leq k \leq n$, $|S_k \cap Y(k+n/2^s,n)| \leq \gamma ks$, that is, only a small proportion of small values find themselves far from the "smaller" end of

116

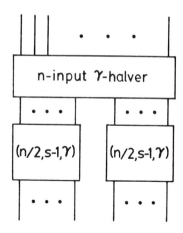

Figure 8.1.1 Recursive construction of an (n, s, γ)–network.

the outputs. (The corresponding result for L_k will follow in a similar manner). The proof is by induction on s. The hypothesis is true for $s = 0$, since $n/2^s = n$, and hence for all k, $Y(k+n/2^s, n) = \emptyset$. Now suppose $s \geq 1$.

Case 1. $k \leq n/2$.

The γ–halver may cause at most γk members of S_k to enter the larger sub-network, resulting (in the worst case) in them arriving at $Y(k+n/2^s, n)$. Furthermore, out of the k smallest values that enter the smaller sub-network, at most $\gamma k(s-1)$ of them will end up in $Y(k+\dfrac{n/2}{2^{s-1}}, n/2)$ (by the induction hypothesis). Thus, out of the members of S_k that are sent to the smaller sub-network, at most $\gamma k(s-1)$ of them will end up in $Y(k+\dfrac{n}{2^s}, n/2)$.

Therefore:

$$| S_k \cap Y(k+n/2^s, n) | \leq \gamma k + \gamma k(s-1) = \gamma ks$$

Case 2. $k > n/2$.

At most $\gamma(n-k)$ members of L_{n-k} will be forced into the smaller sub-network by the first γ–halver. This displaces at most $\gamma(n-k) \leq \gamma k$ members of S_k from $Y(1, n/2)$, which (in the worst case) arrive at $Y(k+n/2^s, n)$. By the induction hypothesis, at most $\gamma(k-n/2)(s-1) \leq \gamma k(s-1)$ of the $k-n/2$ smallest values entering the larger sub-network are displaced from

$Y(n/2+1, k-\frac{n}{2}+\frac{n/2}{2^{s-1}}-1)$. These k–n/2 smallest values must all be from S_k.

Therefore:

$$| S_k \cap Y(k+n/2^s, n) | \le \gamma k + \gamma k(s-1) - \gamma ks$$

Let $\xi = \lceil -\log \epsilon \rceil$. Consider an $(n, \xi, \frac{\epsilon}{\xi})$-network. For all $1 \le k \le n$, $| S_k \cap Y(k+\epsilon n, n) | \le \epsilon k$ and symmetrically $| L_k \cap Y(1, n-k-\epsilon n) | \le \epsilon k$. That is, it is an ϵ–nearsorter. It has $s = \xi$ layers of γ–halvers, (where $\gamma = \frac{\epsilon}{\xi}$), each of which has depth $d(\frac{\epsilon}{2\xi}, \frac{2\xi}{\epsilon}-1)$ by Lemma 8.1.4. Thus the total depth is $\xi \, d(\frac{\epsilon}{2\xi}, \frac{2\xi}{\epsilon}-1)$. A similar argument for arbitrary n will give the same depth (see Exercise 8.2). $\square$

8.2. An Abstract Sorting Algorithm

The parallel machine model that we shall use is slightly unorthodox. We will see later how to transform an algorithm for this model into a sorting network. Assume that n, the number of values to be sorted, is a power of 2. We also assume, without loss of generality, that the values to be sorted are distinct. We will use 2n–1 *bags*, each of which is capable of holding many input values. These bags are arranged in the shape of a complete binary tree. The root bag is defined to be at level 1, and all children of level-k bags are defined to be at level k+1, for $k \ge 1$.

Suppose that each of the bags has the power to halve its inputs, that is, to separate the values in its possession into two equal-size sets S_1, S_2 such that for all $s_1 \in S_1, s_2 \in S_2$, $s_1 < s_2$. Then we could sort n values as follows. Initially place all of them in the root bag. Halve them, and send the set of smaller values to the left child and the set of larger values to the right child. Each child in parallel halves its values and sends the smaller set to its left child, etc. Continuing in this fashion, the input values each follow a direct path from the root to the appropriate leaf, and thus sorting is achieved in only log n halving and routing steps.

Unfortunately, this will not lead to an O(log n) depth sorting network, since the process of halving n inputs requires a comparison network of depth $\Omega(\log n)$

(see Exercise 8.1). However, we can substitute a γ-halver (for some small constant γ), which by the results of the previous section has constant depth. After the first γ-halving step, a small fraction of the values in the smaller half (symmetrically, the larger half) have been put into the wrong set, and thus will be passed to the wrong child. Such values which have strayed from a direct path from the root to the appropriate leaf are termed *strangers*.

Our aim, then, is to ensure that these strangers get back on track. Note that strangers are either smaller or larger than the values which legitimately belong in the bag to which they have been erroneously routed. If we ϵ-nearsort, instead of γ-halve, the values in each bag (for some small constant ϵ), then all but a small fraction of the strangers will find themselves either at the far left-hand (the "smallest") or the far right-hand (the "largest") end of the bag respectively. These strangers can be passed back up the tree in an effort to get them back on track, whilst the legitimate values in the centre of the bag can be sent further down the tree, carrying with them a small fraction of the old strangers plus a hopefully small number of new strangers.

We must ensure that the number of strangers is small, so that only a small number of values in each bag need be passed up the tree. If the fraction of values passed up the tree is too large, then the algorithm will not terminate in $O(\log n)$ nearsorting and routing steps, in which case all hope of obtaining an $O(\log n)$ depth sorting network is lost. We also need to ensure that the algorithm terminates with exactly one of the values in each leaf bag, in sorted order, that is, with no strangers.

Suppose $A,\epsilon,\lambda,\mu,\nu,\delta \in R$, with $A \geq 1$, $0 < \epsilon < \dfrac{1}{2}$ and $0 < \lambda,\mu,\nu,\delta < 1$. In particular, let:

$$\begin{aligned} A &= 4.959 & \nu &= 0.7728 \\ \epsilon &= 0.0171 & \lambda &= 0.0586 \\ \mu &= 0.0061 & \delta &= 0.0051 \end{aligned}$$

Lemma 8.2.1 The following inequalities hold:

$$\frac{1}{2A} + 2\lambda A + 3\mu A \leq \nu \tag{1}$$

$$A\nu \geq 1 \tag{2}$$

$$2\mu + \epsilon \leq \frac{\lambda}{2} \tag{3}$$

$$2\delta^2 A^2 + \epsilon \leq \delta A\nu \tag{4}$$

$$2\delta A < 1 \tag{5}$$

$$2\mu\delta A + \frac{1}{2A(4A^2-1)} + \frac{2A\mu\delta}{1-2A\delta} + \frac{\mu}{A} + \frac{\epsilon}{2A} \leq \mu\nu \tag{6}$$

Proof. By inspection. $\square$

Definition. For $k \geq 1$, $t \geq 0$, the *capacity* of a level-k bag at time t is defined to be $C(k,t) = A^{k-1}\nu^t n$.

Let us say "at time t" to denote the period immediately after t steps of the algorithm have been executed. Each step consists of four separate parts, which we will call *phases*. The tth step of the algorithm, $t \geq 1$, is the following for a bag at level $k \geq 1$. Each bag B synchronously performs the same sequence of operations.

1. Collect any values which arrived during the $(t-1)^{th}$ step. If there are an odd number of values, select an arbitrary one and call it *special*; ϵ–nearsort the non-special values in either case.

2. If $k > 1$ and $\mu C(k,t-1) \geq 1$, then pass the $\left\lfloor \frac{\lambda}{2}C(k,t-1) \right\rfloor$ "smallest" (that is, the smallest values as determined by the nearsorting process), and $\left\lfloor \frac{\lambda}{2}C(k,t-1) \right\rfloor$ "largest" values to the parent of B. If there are not enough non-special values in the current bag, then pass up whatever is available. Note that this leaves an even number of non-special values in B. We will later show that the number of strangers in a level k bag after t–1 steps of the algorithm is at most $\mu C(k,t-1)$. Thus this phase achieves the following: if B can possibly contain strangers, then pass up a fraction of its contents.

3. If $k > 1$, $\mu C(k,t-1) \geq 1$ and B contains an odd number of values, then pass the special value to its parent. Thus if there is a possibility of B containing strangers, and it has an odd number of values, then an extra value is passed

120

up. If there are no strangers, then there is no harm in keeping the extra value.

4. Split the remaining non-special values evenly into a "smaller" half and a "larger" half, as determined by the nearsorting process in Phase 1. Send the "smaller" values to the left child and the "larger" values to the right child of B. If the special value was retained in Phase 3, then retain it to the next step.

At time $t = 0$ the algorithm is started with all n values in the root, and all other bags empty. We claim that it terminates with one value in each of the leaf bags, in ascending order from left to right.

Lemma 8.2.2 The root bag contains an even number of values at all times.

Proof. We will prove that all bags at level k contain the same number of values at time $t \geq 0$. This implies that there is an even number of values in the tree below the root; therefore (since n is even) the root must also contain an even number of values.

The proof of this claim follows by induction on t. It is certainly true at time $t = 0$ since all bags at level $k \geq 2$ are empty at that time. Now suppose that the hypothesis is true at time t–1. By the induction hypothesis all bags at level k–1 contain the same number of values at time t–1. Thus, by the symmetry of the algorithm, every bag at level k receives the same number of values from its parent in Phase 4 of the tth step. By the induction hypothesis all bags at level k+1 contain the same number of values at time t–1. Thus, by the symmetry of the algorithm, every bag at level k receives the same number of values from its children in Phases 2 and 3 of the tth step. Therefore, since all bags at level k act symmetrically, it follows that they all receive the same number of values during the tth step. $\square$

Lemma 8.2.3 For $k \geq 1$, $t \geq 0$ the number of values in any bag at level k, time t is at most $\max(C(k,t),1)$.

Proof. The proof is by induction on t. The hypothesis is certainly true for $t = 0$, since $C(1,0) = n$ and the root holds all n values at that time. Now suppose $t \geq 1$. Consider a bag B at level k. By the induction hypothesis, B receives at most $\frac{1}{2}C(k–1,t–1)$ values from its parent (and is at risk of receiving this many if its parent is the root bag or is no longer passing values up in Phases 2 and 3). It can also receive at most $2\left\lfloor \frac{\lambda}{2}C(k+1,t–1) \right\rfloor +1$ values from each child. It may also inherit the special value from itself in Phase 4 of the tth step. There are two cases to consider, depending on whether B can be given anything by its children.

Case 1. $\mu C(k+1,t-1) \geq 1$.

B receives at most $2 \left\lfloor \dfrac{\lambda}{2} C(k+1,t-1) \right\rfloor + 1$ values from each child, and may also inherit a single item from itself during the tth step. Thus the total number received is at most:

$$C(k-1,t-1)/2 + 4 \left\lfloor \frac{\lambda}{2} C(k+1,t-1) \right\rfloor + 3$$

$$\leq A^{k-2}\nu^{t-1}n/2 + 2\lambda A^k \nu^{t-1}n + 3$$

$$\leq A^{k-2}\nu^{t-1}n/2 + 2\lambda A^k \nu^{t-1}n + 3\mu A^k \nu^{t-1}n$$

Thus it is sufficient to prove that:

$$A^{k-2}\nu^{t-1}n/2 + 2\lambda A^k \nu^{t-1}n + 3\mu A^k \nu^{t-1}n \leq A^{k-1}\nu^t n$$

That is,

$$\frac{1}{2A} + 2\lambda A + 3\mu A \leq \nu$$

This inequality holds by Lemma 8.2.1 (1).

Case 2. $\mu C(k+1,t-1) < 1$.
B receives no values from its children in the tth step of the algorithm. There are two sub-cases to consider, depending on whether B receives any values from its parent.

Case 2.1 $C(k-1,t-1) < 2$.
The parent of B can pass down no values in Phase 4, since it has at most one value. Thus B receives no values from above or below, and retains only its special value, if it has one.

Case 2.2 $C(k-1,t-1) \geq 2$.
By the induction hypothesis, B receives at most $\dfrac{C(k-1,t-1)}{2}$ values from its parent, and may also retain its special value, if it has one. Thus the number of values received by B is at most:

$$\frac{C(k-1,t-1)}{2} + 1 \leq C(k-1,t-1)$$

This is bounded above by $C(k,t)$ provided $A^{k-2}\nu^{t-1}n \leq A^{k-1}\nu^t n$, that is, $A\nu \geq 1$, which holds by Lemma 8.2.1 (2). $\square$

Lemma 8.2.4 After $O(\log n)$ steps, the n values are distributed one-per-bag in the leaf bags.

Proof. As time proceeds, the capacity of the root will eventually drop below one. By Lemma 8.2.3, this implies that the number of values contained in the root bag will eventually drop to at most one and will not increase thereafter. But by Lemma 8.2.2 the number of values in the root bag is always even, therefore when the capacity of the root bag drops below one, the number of values in the root bag must be zero. Eventually the capacity of the level-2 bags drops below one, implying by a similar argument that they contain no values at that time. The same can be said of levels 3,4,...,log n in turn (since n is a power of 2). Finally, the capacity of the leaf bags drops below one, at which point they are each in possession of at most one value, while all bags which are above them in the tree are empty. The symmetry of the algorithm ensures that each leaf bag contains exactly one value. A steady-state is reached at that point.

Thus the algorithm reaches a steady-state at or before time τ, when $C(\log n + 1, \tau) < 1$. Let us say that the algorithm *terminates* at time τ. Then at termination, $A^{\log n}\nu^\tau n < 1$; therefore (taking logs of both sides) the algorithm has certainly terminated when:

$$\tau > \frac{1 + \log A}{\log \dfrac{1}{\nu}} \log n$$

Thus, for our choice of constants, termination is achieved at or before time $9 \log n$. $\square$

8.3. The Correctness Proof

It remains to show that when the algorithm reaches the steady-state, the values in the leaves are in ascending order from left to right. Consider an input value v. We say that a bag B is at *distance* 0 for v if v is the ith input value in sorted order, $1 \leq i \leq n$, and the ith leaf of the tree (numbering leaves consecutively from left to right, starting with 1) is a descendant of B, that is, B is on a strictly descending path from the root bag to the correct leaf bag for v. A bag is at *distance* d for v, where d > 0, if its parent is at distance d–1 for v. We say that v has *strangeness* r at time t if it is contained in a bag at distance r for v at that time. Intuitively, the strangeness of a value is the number of upward moves that it must make before it rejoins the path from the root to the correct leaf. A value which has non-zero strangeness will be termed a *stranger*.

Definition. $S_r(k,t)$ is the maximum number of values of strangeness at least r contained in any bag at level k, at time t.

Lemma 8.3.1 For r > 0, t ≥ 0, k ≥ 1, $S_r(k,t) < \mu\delta^{r-1}C(k,t)$.

Proof. The result follows by induction on t. The hypothesis is certainly true for t = 0 since at that time all values are held in the root bag, and hence there are no strangers.

Now suppose that t > 0. Firstly, we claim that the fraction of values passed up from each bag B at level k during the Phase 2 of the tth step is large enough to hold most of the strangers at time t–1. By Lemma 8.2.3, after the ϵ-nearsort we know that at most $\epsilon S_1(k,t-1)$ small strangers are erroneously displaced a distance of more than $\epsilon C(k,t-1)$ from the $S_1(k,t-1)$ "smallest" places (symmetrically for the large strangers). Therefore we require that the fraction of values passed up be large enough to hold the $S_1(k,t-1) + \epsilon C(k,t-1)$ "smallest" values, which must include all but an ϵ-fraction of the small strangers (symmetrically for the large strangers). That is, for all k ≥ 0,

$$S_1(k,t-1) + \epsilon C(k,t-1) \leq \left\lfloor \frac{\lambda}{2} C(k,t-1) \right\rfloor$$

Thus it is sufficient to prove that:

$$S_1(k,t-1) + \epsilon C(k,t-1) \leq \frac{\lambda}{2} C(k,t-1) - 1$$

Equivalently,

$$S_1(k,t-1) + \epsilon A^{k-1}\nu^{t-1}n + 1 \leq \frac{\lambda}{2} A^{k-1}\nu^{t-1}n$$

By the induction hypothesis it is sufficient to prove that:

$$\mu A^{k-1}\nu^{t-1}n + \epsilon A^{k-1}\nu^{t-1}n + 1 \leq \frac{\lambda}{2} A^{k-1}\nu^{t-1}n$$

Now, if B is passing up values, it follows that $\mu A^{k-1}\nu^{t-1}n \geq 1$. Thus it is sufficient to prove that:

$$\mu A^{k-1} \nu^{t-1} n + \epsilon A^{k-1} \nu^{t-1} n + \mu A^{k-1} \nu^{t-1} n \leq \frac{\lambda}{2} A^{k-1} \nu^{t-1} n$$

Thus it is sufficient to require that $2\mu + \epsilon \leq \frac{\lambda}{2}$. This inequality holds by Lemma 8.2.1 (3).

Our claim allows us to easily place an upper-bound on the number of values of strangeness $r \geq 2$ or more received by a bag at level k during the tth step of the algorithm. At worst, it can receive all of the strangers held by its children (at most $S_{r+1}(k+1,t-1)$ from each child). All of its parent's strangers get passed up except for at most an ϵ-fraction of them dropped in the nearsorting process (that is, it inherits at most $\epsilon S_{r-1}(k-1,t-1)$ values from its parent), by the above claim. If it inherits a single value from itself in Phase 4, then by the induction hypothesis it held no strangers in the previous time-step, and hence that single value is not strange. Thus:

$$S_r(k,t) \leq 2S_{r+1}(k+1,t-1) + \epsilon S_{r-1}(k-1,t-1)$$

$$\leq 2\mu \delta^r A^k \nu^{t-1} n + \epsilon \mu \delta^{r-2} A^{k-2} \nu^{t-1} n \qquad \text{(by the induction hypothesis)}$$

Thus it is sufficient to show that:

$$2\mu \delta^r A^k \nu^{t-1} n + \epsilon \mu \delta^{r-2} A^{k-2} \nu^{t-1} n \leq \mu \delta^{r-1} A^{k-1} \nu^t n$$

Dividing through by $\mu \delta^{r-2} A^{k-2} \nu^{t-1} n$ tells us that we require:

$$2\delta^2 A^2 + \epsilon \leq \delta A \nu$$

which holds by Lemma 8.2.1 (4).

Now suppose $r = 1$. A bag at level k can receive strangers during the tth step of the algorithm from as many as three sources.

1. By having values of strangeness 2 or more passed up from its children. As in the case $r \geq 2$, it can receive at most $2S_2(k+1,t-1) \leq 2\mu \delta A^k \nu^{t-1} n$ from this source.

2. By having strange items passed down to it from its parent.

3. By having non-strange values erroneously passed down to it from its parent (that is, values which should have been passed to its sibling).

Note that if it inherits a value from itself, then by the induction hypothesis it had no strangers at time t−1, and so the inherited value cannot be strange. It remains to provide an upper-bound on the number of strangers from the second and third sources.

Consider a bag B at level k-1, time t-1. We are interested in the number of strangers that it passes down to its children during the tth step of the algorithm, in order to get an upper-bound on $S_1(k,t)$. There are three factors which could cause it to pass strangers to one of its children.

1. Non-strangers becoming strangers because of unbalanced non-strangers. Ideally B should contain as many *left-seeking values* (that is, values which are bound for leaves which are descendants of its left child) as right-seeking. If this balance is disturbed then Phase 4 of the tth step risks sending non-strangers to the wrong child, where they become strangers.

2. Non-strangers becoming strangers because of unbalanced strangers. Similarly, if B contains more *left-seeking strangers* (that is, values which are bound for leaf bags which are to the left of the leaves below B) than right-seeking (or vice-versa), the balance will be disturbed even more. At time t-1, B can contain at most $S_1(k-1,t-1)$ strangers. By the induction hypothesis, $S_1(k-1,t-1) \le \mu A^{k-2}\nu^{t-1}n$. In the worst case, these can be all left-seeking strangers (say). These displace an equal number of non-strange left-seeking values into the wrong half during Phase 4 of the tth step, causing them to erroneously be sent to the right child where they become strangers. In general there will be s_l left-seeking strangers and s_r right-seeking strangers. Suppose $s_l > s_r$. Suppose that the ϵ–nearsorter erroneously puts e_l of the left-seeking strangers into the right half, and e_r of the right-seeking strangers into the left half, where $e_l < s_l$ and $e_r < s_r$. The right child will receive $(s_l-e_l)-(s_r-e_r)$ left-seeking non-strangers (which thus become strange) due to the displacement. Thus the number of strangers received by the right child (and symmetrically by the left child) from this source is at most:

$$(s_l-e_l)-(s_r-e_r) \le s_l \le S_1(k-1,t-1) \le \mu A^{k-2}\nu^{t-1}n$$

3. Strangers and non-strangers becoming strangers because of an error in nearsorting. In Phase 1 of the tth step, the nearsort process may cause an ϵ-fraction of the smallest (and symmetrically the largest) half of the values contained in B to be sent to the wrong child. By Lemma 8.2.3 this contributes at most $\frac{\epsilon}{2}A^{k-2}\nu^{t-1}n$ strangers to that child.

Thus the total number of strangers received by a bag at level k during the tth step is at most $2\mu\delta A^k\nu^{t-1}n$ from its children, plus:

$$\Delta + \mu A^{k-2} \nu^{t-1} n + \frac{\epsilon}{2} A^{k-2} \nu^{t-1} n$$

from its parent, where Δ is the displacement due to the presence of an unbalanced number of left-seeking and right-seeking non-strangers in its parent. We must now derive an upper-bound for Δ.

Consider the following idealized version of our algorithm. Each value is considered not as an atomic item, but rather as a divisible entity. More formally, assign each value v a *size* $w(v) \in R$, initially equal to one. We allow multiple copies of each value to appear in the tree, so long as the sum of their respective sizes is equal to one. We modify the algorithm as follows.

1. Collect any values which arrived during the $(t-1)^{th}$ step and sort them.
2. For each value v of size $w(v)$:
   (i) Modify its size to $(1-\lambda)w(v)$, and
   (ii) Pass a copy of v with size $\lambda w(v)$ to the parent bag.
3. Null.
4. Split the remaining values evenly into the smaller half and the larger half, as determined by the sorting process in Phase 1. Send the smaller values to the left child, and the larger values to the right child.

Note that changes have been made to all four phases. There are no strangers when this new algorithm is run, since both sources of strangeness (faulty near-sorters in Phase 1 and unbalanced left and right-seeking values in Phase 4) have been eliminated. Let us say that the "number of values" in each bag is the sum of the sizes of those values. In analogy to Lemma 8.2.3, it is easy to show that the number of values in a level-k bag at time t is at most $C(k,t)$ (see Exercise 8.5). Let D be a bag at level k. Suppose we call a value *important* for D if it is bound for one of its descendants. Note that since there are no strangers in this new algorithm, at all times the values which are important to D are (possibly fragmented) either on the path from the root to D or in a proper descendant of D. The bags alternate between being empty and (possibly) non-empty.

Suppose bag D is empty at time $t-1$. By the symmetry of the algorithm, the parent of D must contain exactly the same number of important and unimportant values, and thus must contain at most $\frac{1}{2}C(k-1,t-1)$ important values. The grand-parent is empty due to the alternating structure of the algorithm. The great-grandparent of D has exactly one-eighth of its values important for D, and hence contains at most $\frac{1}{8}C(k-3,t-1)$ important values. Thus the number of important values above B is at most:

$$\frac{1}{2}C(k-1,t-1) + \frac{1}{8}C(k-3,t-1) + \frac{1}{32}C(k-5,t-1) + \cdots$$

and the number of important values above the parent of D is at most:

$$\frac{1}{8}C(k-3,t-1) + \frac{1}{32}C(k-5,t-1) + \frac{1}{128}C(k-7,t-1) + \cdots$$

$$\leq \frac{1}{8}\sum_{i=0}^{\infty}\frac{C(k-3-2i,t-1)}{4^i}$$

$$= \frac{1}{8}\sum_{i=0}^{\infty}\frac{1}{4^i}A^{k-2i-4}\nu^{t-1}n$$

$$= \frac{1}{8}\nu^{t-1}A^{k-4}n\sum_{i=0}^{\infty}\left(\frac{1}{4A^2}\right)^i$$

$$\leq \frac{\nu^{t-1}A^{k-2}n}{2(4A^2-1)}$$

The values in the tree below D are important since there are no strangers.

Now suppose we treat the values as atomic units again, returning Phases 2, 3 and 4 to their original form. This may change the distribution of the important values on the path from the root to D. In the worst case, all of the important values above D will find themselves in D's parent. That is, the parent of D can receive at most

$$\frac{\nu^{t-1}A^{k-2}n}{2(4A^2-1)}$$

excess important values from above. Note that the number of values in the tree below D cannot decrease since the number of values passed up from each bag during each time-step does not increase.

Finally, suppose that we return Phase 1 to its original state (replacing sorting by nearsorting). This does not affect the distribution of values in the tree, but will almost certainly affect their strangeness. Since there are now strangers, it follows that some of the important values below D may have strayed, and may in the worst case find themselves in the parent of D. However, these will have been replaced by unimportant values, which will hence be strange. By the induction hypothesis, we have an upper-bound on the possible number of strangers below D, and hence on the number of stray important values. The number of unimportant values below D is at most:

$$2S_2(k+1,t-1) + 4S_3(k+2,t-1) + 8S_4(k+3,t-1) + \cdots$$

$$\leq \sum_{i=1}^{\infty} 2^i S_{i+1}(k+i,t-1)$$

$$\leq \sum_{i=1}^{\infty} 2^i \mu \delta^i A^{k+i-1} \nu^{t-1} n \qquad \text{(by the induction hypothesis)}$$

$$= \mu A^{k-1} \nu^{t-1} n \sum_{i=1}^{\infty} (2\delta A)^i$$

$$\leq \frac{2\mu \delta A^k \nu^{t-1} n}{1-2\delta A}$$

since $2\delta A < 1$ by Lemma 8.2.1 (5). Thus the parent of D can contain at most:

$$\frac{2\mu \delta A^k \nu^{t-1} n}{1-2\delta A}$$

excess important values from below, which tells us that:

$$\Delta \leq \frac{\nu^{t-1} A^{k-2} n}{2(4A^2-1)} + \frac{2\mu \delta A^k \nu^{t-1} n}{1-2\delta A}$$

Thus the number of strangers received by a bag at level k, time t is at most:

$$2\mu \delta A^k \nu^{t-1} n + \frac{\nu^{t-1} A^{k-2} n}{2(4A^2-1)} + \frac{2\mu \delta A^k \nu^{t-1} n}{1-2\delta A} + \mu A^{k-2} \nu^{t-1} n + \frac{\epsilon}{2} \nu^{t-1} A^{k-2} n$$

To prove the induction hypothesis, it remains to prove that this value is at most $\mu \nu^t A^{k-1} n$. That is,

$$2\mu \delta A + \frac{1}{2A(4A^2-1)} + \frac{2A\mu \delta}{1-2A\delta} + \frac{\mu}{A} + \frac{\epsilon}{2A} \leq \nu \mu$$

This inequality holds by Lemma 8.2.1 (6). $\square$

Theorem 8.3.2 There is a sorting network of depth $O(\log n)$.

Proof. Lemma 8.3.1 ensures that at all times $S_1(k,t) \leq \mu C(k,t)$. The algorithm terminates at time τ, where $C(\log n,\tau) < 1$. Therefore $S_1(\log n,\tau) < 1$. That is, when the algorithm terminates there are no strangers. Thus the values in the leaves are in ascending order from left to right.

It is straightforward to construct an $O(\log n)$ depth sorting network from this algorithm. The network is divided up into layers, each of which corresponds to a snapshot of the tree of bags at some point in time. Each bag is then represented by a subset of the channels. The contents of each bag can be near-sorted by placing an ϵ-nearsorter on the appropriate channels. The depth of the network is thus equal to the depth of the nearsorters times the running-time of the abstract algorithm. Thus by Lemma 8.1.5 and Lemma 8.2.4, the depth is at most:

$$d(\frac{\epsilon}{2\xi},\frac{2\xi}{\epsilon} - 1)\, \xi \left\lceil (1 + \log A)/\log \frac{1}{\nu} \right\rceil \log n$$

where $\xi = \lceil -\log \epsilon \rceil$ and d is the function relating to the degree of expander graphs in Theorem 8.1.3. For our choice of constants, the constant multiple is bounded above by $54\, d(\frac{1}{702},701)$. $\square$

Our construction is based on constant-depth γ-halvers with $\gamma = \epsilon/\xi = 0.00285$. Paterson [100] has proved by a direct counting argument that there exist γ-halvers of depth at most 711 for our choice of γ. Therefore our algorithm gives rise to a sorting network of depth 38,394 log n. Paterson manages by a more sophisticated analysis to reduce the constant multiple to around 6100.

8.4. Exercises

8.1 A *halver* is a γ-halver with $\gamma = 0$ (see Section 8.1). Show that an n-input halver must have depth $\Omega(\log n)$.

8.2 Complete the proof of Lemma 8.1.4 when n is odd. Hence complete the proof of Lemma 8.1.5.

8.3 What is the role of the constant A in the AKS sorting algorithm? Which inequality (or inequalities) becomes unsatisfiable if it is removed?

8.4 All bags alternate between being empty (more accurately, holding either zero or one value) and holding many values. Thus at any one time up to half of the bags that could have been useful are lying idle. How can the algorithm be modified to make use of these bags? Is there any advantage to the modified algorithm?

8.5 Show that in the modified version of the abstract algorithm used in the proof of Lemma 8.3.1, the number of values in a bag at level k, time t is at most C(k,t).

8.6 When analyzing the number of values of strangeness 1, we used the fact that an ϵ-nearsorter is an ϵ-halver. Our ϵ-nearsorters are actually $\frac{\epsilon}{2\xi}$-halvers, where $\xi = \lceil -\log \epsilon \rceil$. Use this fact to modify the inequalities of Lemma 8.2.1 and derive a superior set of constants. What is the depth of this new sorting network?

9 Simultaneous Resource Bounds

This chapter is centred around a simulation of our general network model on a more practical model, with particular attention paid to the resources of hardware and parallel time. The first section contains a general theorem which characterizes the computational power needed to simulate a resource-bounded network. Many specific instances of this theorem (for particular machine models) have already appeared in the literature [10,16,38,74,86,128,126]. In the second section we construct our universal feasible network. This feasible network is, as has already been mentioned, to be universal for the general network model. The result follows as a fairly straightforward corollary to the general theorem of the first section, by application of the techniques developed in Chapter 7.

In the third section we propose a hardware measure for general networks. This hardware measure is compared to popular definitions of hardware which have appeared in the literature (including size and width of uniform circuits), using simulations based on the result of Section 9.1. We examine the extended parallel computation thesis [24,25], which is an attempt to characterize "reasonable" time and hardware bounded parallel computers. This states that time and hardware on any reasonable parallel machine model are simultaneously polynomially related to space and reversals on a deterministic Turing machine. The fourth and final section is devoted to obtaining improved simulations of space and reversal-bounded deterministic Turing machines by width and depth-bounded uniform circuits.

Most of the material in this chapter is from Parberry [92,97,98].

9.1. A General Simulation Theorem

The central result of this section is a theorem which describes the computational power needed to simulate a resource-bounded network. As a fairly easy corollary, we will in Section 9.2 be able to construct a feasible network which is universal for the general model of Section 3.1. In order to keep the proof as manageable as possible, the simulation will be functional rather than machine-based.

If $n > 0$, define an n-*tuple* X over some set S to be a sequence of n elements $<X_0,X_1, \ldots , X_{n-1}>$, such that $X_i \in S$, $0 \leq i < n$. Let S^n denote the set of all n-tuples over S, $S^* = \bigcup_{n \geq 0} S^n$ and $S \times T = \{<s,t> \mid s \in S, t \in T\}$, for arbitrary sets S and T. Ordering of n-tuples is lexicographic (first-field-first). For example, if $X,Y \in Z^n$, then $X < Y$ iff there exists j with $0 \leq j < n$ such that $X_j < Y_j$ and for $0 \leq i < j$, $X_i = Y_i$.

Let M be a $P(n)$ processor, $S(n)$ space bounded network. To simplify the presentation we will assume that:

(i) All local instructions operate only on registers r_0,r_1,r_2. Register r_i be read from or written to only when $i \geq 3$.

(ii) Read instructions have the form "extract values p,a from r_0,r_1 respectively, read register r_a of processor p and place the value obtained into r_0".

(iii) Write instructions have the form "extract values p,a,w from registers r_0,r_1,r_2 respectively and write w into register r_a of processor p".

(iv) Multiple reads are allowed, and in the case of write conflicts, the smallest value being written into a register is the one which succeeds.

Note that (i), (ii) and (iii) are sufficient for the example instruction-set of Section 3.1, since a processor can address its own registers by the use of reads and writes. The general case follows in a similar manner.

For convenience we define a special null element *null* and adopt the conventions that for all X and n, *null* is always a member of X^n, and that for all $i \geq 0$, $null_i = S(n)$. Define the *configuration* of M to be a member of $C_M = (Z^3 \times N)^{P(n)} \times (N^2 \times Z)^{S(n)}$. For example, we take

$$<<x_0,x_1, \cdots ,x_{P(n)-1}>,<y_0,y_1, \cdots ,y_{S(n)-1}>>$$

to indicate the following. If $x_i = <a_i,b_i,c_i,d_i>$ then processor i has values a_i,b_i,c_i in its registers r_0,r_1,r_2 respectively, and it is to execute the d_i^{th} instruction of the program of M next (with d_i out of range indicating that the processor has halted). If $null \neq y_i = <p_i,a_i,v_i>$, $a_i \geq 3$, then register r_{a_i} of processor p_i contains v_i. In particular, where the latter is concerned we insist that:

(i) Only registers with non-zero contents are listed. These are listed left-justified in lexicographic order.

(ii) The remaining entries are filled, if necessary, with the value *null*.

Definitions. We now define some useful functions. Let $sorted((Z^n)^m) \subseteq (Z^n)^m$ be the set of m-sequences X such that $X_0 \leq X_1 \leq \cdots \leq X_{m-1}$. For convenience, if $X \in (Z^n)^m$, let $(X_{-1})_0 \doteq (X_m)_0 = -1$. Then

(1) sort:$(\mathbf{Z}^3)^n \to (\mathbf{Z}^3)^n$ maps unsorted sequences of distinct ordered pairs into sorted ones. More precisely,

$$\text{sort}(X)_i = \begin{cases} X_j & \text{if } i = |\{k \mid 0 \leq k < n, X_k < X_j\}| \\ null & \text{otherwise} \end{cases}$$

(2) merge:$\text{sorted}((\mathbf{Z}^3)^n) \times \text{sorted}((\mathbf{Z}^3)^m) \to (\mathbf{Z}^4)^{n+m}$ merges two sorted sequences of distinct ordered pairs.

$$\text{merge}(X,Y)_i = \begin{cases} <(X_j)_0,(X_j)_1,(X_j)_2,1> & \text{if } X_j \neq null,\ i = |\{k \mid X_k < X_j\}| + \\ & |\{k \mid <(Y_k)_0,(Y_k)_1> \leq <(X_j)_0,(X_j)_1>\}| \\ <(Y_j)_0,(Y_j)_1,(Y_j)_2,0> & \text{if } Y_j \neq null,\ i = |\{k \mid Y_k < Y_j\}| + \\ & |\{k \mid <(X_k)_0,(X_k)_1> < <(Y_j)_0,(Y_j)_1>\}| \\ null & \text{otherwise} \end{cases}$$

(3) fanout:$\text{sorted}((\mathbf{Z}^4)^n) \to (\mathbf{Z}^2)^n$ achieves the fan-out of data values to multiple read requests. Define first(X,i) to be the index $j \leq i$ such that the jth tuple in X is numerically the first which agrees with the ith tuple of X in the first two places, that is, $<(X_j)_0,(X_j)_1> = <(X_i)_0,(X_i)_1>$, but either $(X_{j-1})_0 \neq (X_i)_0$ or $(X_{j-1})_1 \neq (X_i)_1$.

$$\text{fanout}(X)_i = \begin{cases} <(X_i)_2,(X_j)_2> & \text{if } (X_j)_3 = 0, \text{ where } j = \text{first}(X,i) < i \\ <(X_i)_2,0> & \text{if } (X_j)_3 = 1, \text{ where } j = \text{first}(X,i) \\ null & \text{otherwise} \end{cases}$$

(4) deliver:$(\mathbf{Z}^4)^n \to (\mathbf{Z}^3)^n$ performs the fan-in of multiple write requests.

$$\text{deliver}(X)_i = \begin{cases} <(X_i)_0,(X_i)_1,(X_i)_2> & \text{if } ((X_i)_3 = 0 \text{ and } X_{i+1} \neq <(X_i)_0,(X_i)_1,v,1> \\ & \text{for all } v \in \mathbf{Z}), \text{or } ((X_i)_3 = 1 \text{ and } (X_i)_2 \neq 0 \\ & \text{and } X_{i-1} \neq <(X_i)_0,(X_i)_1,v,1> \text{for all } v \in \mathbf{Z}). \\ null & \text{otherwise} \end{cases}$$

(5) concentrate:$(\mathbf{Z}^*)^n \to (\mathbf{Z}^*)^n$ moves all non-*null* entries to the left-hand end of the sequence.

$$\text{concentrate}(X)_i = \begin{cases} X_j & \text{if } X_j \neq null \text{ and } i = |\{X_k \mid X_k \neq null, 0 \leq k < j\}| \\ null & \text{otherwise} \end{cases}$$

Let $\delta_M : C_M \to C_M$ be the next-configuration function of M. That is, if $C \in C_M$ then $\delta_M(C)$ is the configuration which follows from C according to the program of M. Let $\hat{M}$ be the network obtained from M by changing all read and write instructions to NO-OPS (for example, add zero to a register), and define $\hat{\delta}_M = \delta_{\hat{M}}$.

Theorem 9.1.1 Suppose a machine can:

(i)   Merge a sequence of length n with a sequence of length m using resources $R_1(n,m)$.

(ii) Fanout, deliver and concentrate a sequence of length n using resources $R_2(n)$.

(iii) Sort a sequence of length n using resources $R_3(n)$.

(iv) Compute $\hat{\delta}_M$ for $P(n)$ processors using resources $R_4(P(n))$.

Then it can compute δ_M using resources proportional to

$$R_1(P(n),S(n))+R_2(P(n)+S(n))+R_3(P(n))+R_4(P(n)).$$

Proof. We make the assumption that the model is capable of storing configurations of M in such a manner that they can be dismantled and reassembled using negligible resources. For example, we assume that $\text{readrequest},\text{writerequest}:C_M\to(\mathbf{Z}^3)^{P(n)}$, $\text{data}:C_M\to(\mathbf{Z}^3)^{S(n)}$ defined by:

$$\text{readrequest}(X,Y)_i = \begin{cases} <(X_i)_0,(X_i)_1,i> & \text{if the } (X_i)_3{}^{\text{th}} \text{ instruction} \\ & \text{of M is a read} \\ null & \text{otherwise} \end{cases}$$

$$\text{writerequest}(X,Y)_i = \begin{cases} <(X_i)_0,(X_i)_1,(X_i)_2> & \text{if the } (X_i)_3{}^{\text{th}} \text{ instruction} \\ & \text{of M is a write} \\ null & \text{otherwise} \end{cases}$$

$$\text{data}(X,Y) = Y$$

can be computed easily. This is clearly the case when the processors of the simulating machine are (efficiently) universal for the processors of the simulated machine.

Let $C\in C_M$ be a configuration of M. The aim is to simulate a single step of M starting in configuration C. Internal computations can be handled directly by application of $\hat{\delta}_M$. Read requests are satisfied by computing:

$$x = \text{sort}(\text{readrequest}(C))$$

$$y = \text{merge}(x,\text{data}(C))$$

The new processor configurations can then be obtained from $\text{sort}(\text{concentrate}(\text{fanout}(y)))$. Write requests are simulated by computing:

$$x = \text{sort}(\text{writerequest}(C))$$

$$y = \text{merge}(x, \text{data}(C))$$

The new register contents can then be computed from concentrate(deliver(y)).

For example, suppose in a particular step, processors 0,1,2 and 3 wish to read register 4 of processor 3, register 6 of processor 0, register 7 of processor 1 and register 6 of processor 0 respectively. Further suppose that the only non-zero registers at that time are register 6 of processor 0, register 9 of processor 1 and register 4 of processor 3, which contain the values 99, 89 and 69 respectively. Then:

$$\text{readrequest}(C) = <<3,4,0>,<0,6,1>,<1,7,2>,<0,6,3>>$$

This is sorted to give:

$$x = <<0,6,1>,<0,6,3>,<1,7,2>,<3,4,0>>$$

Also:

$$\text{data}(C) = <<0,6,99>,<1,9,89>,<3,4,69>>$$

This is merged with x to give:

$$y = <<0,6,99,0>,<0,6,1,1>,<0,6,3,1>,<1,9,89,0>,$$

$$<1,7,2,1>,<3,4,69,0>,<3,4,0,1>>$$

Fanout is performed, resulting in:

$$<null,<1,99>,<3,99>,null,<2,0>,null,<0,69>>$$

This is concentrated:

$$<<1,99>,<3,99>,<2,0>,<0,69>,null,null,null>$$

And finally sorted, to give the requested values in the correct order:

$$<<0,69><1,99>,<2,0>,<3,99>,>$$

Suppose processors 0, 1, 2 and 3 wish to write values 0, 77, 50 and 28 to register 4 of processor 3, register 6 of processor 0, register 7 of processor 1 and register 6 of processor 0 respectively. Further suppose that the current register-contents are exactly the same as in the read-request example above. Then:

$$\text{writerequest}(C) = <<3,4,0>,<0,6,77>,<1,7,50>,<0,6,28>>$$

This is sorted to give:

$$x = <<0{,}6{,}28>{,}<0{,}6{,}77>{,}<1{,}7{,}50>{,}<3{,}4{,}0>>$$

Also:

$$\text{data}(C) = <<0{,}6{,}99>{,}<1{,}9{,}89>{,}<3{,}4{,}69>>$$

This is merged with x to give:

$$y = <<0{,}6{,}99{,}0>{,}<0{,}6{,}28{,}1>{,}<0{,}6{,}77{,}1>{,}<1{,}7{,}50{,}1>{,}$$

$$<1{,}9{,}89{,}0>{,}<3{,}4{,}69{,}0>{,}<3{,}4{,}0{,}1>>$$

Deliver is performed:

$$<null{,}<0{,}6{,}28>{,}null<1{,}7{,}50>{,}<1{,}9{,}89>{,}null{,}null>$$

This is concentrated:

$$<<0{,}6{,}28>{,}<1{,}7{,}50>{,}<1{,}9{,}89>{,}null{,}null{,}null{,}null>$$

This results in the new sequence of register contents, in the same format as data(C) above:

$$<<0{,}6{,}28>{,}<1{,}7{,}50>{,}<1{,}9{,}89>>$$

□

9.2. A Universal Parallel Machine

Specific instances of Theorem 9.1.1 (the simulation of networks or shared-memory machines on other parallel machine models) have appeared many times in the current literature. It can be used to:

(1) Provide general communication between the processors of a feasible network (which is equivalent to simulating a network on a feasible network) [86].

(2) Simulate restricted-access networks on a universal network with constant degree and easy-to-compute interconnections [38].

(3) Simulate shared-memory machines on a network with constant degree and easy-to-compute interconnections. This has been observed in the case where no memory access conflicts are allowed [74], or $P(n) = S(n)$ [16].

(4) Remove memory access conflicts from shared-memory machines [126].

(5) Simulate shared-memory machines on a variant of the feasible network which uses a small number of "large" processors (with a large amount of local memory and "powerful" instruction set) and a larger number of

"small" processors (with a constant amount of local memory and minimal instruction-set) [128].

(6) Construct a multi-access memory [10] to provide a practical implementation of a shared-memory machine as a physical device.

(7) Simulate space and reversal bounded Turing machines by width and depth bounded uniform circuits (and vice-versa) [102].

Application (7) will be explored further in the next two sections. In this section we will concentrate on the application (1).

Corollary 9.2.1 There is a feasible network which can simulate any network of $P(n)$ processors and space $S(n)$, using $S(n)$ processors, the same word-size as the simulated machine, set-up time $O(\log S(n))$ and delay $O(\log^2 P(n) + \log S(n))$.

Proof. A $P(n)+S(n)$ processor feasible network can be used as follows. Note that $S(n) \geq n$, so initially every processor has at most one input symbol. The first $P(n)$ processors are to simulate the processes (keeping only registers r_0, r_1, r_2 of their respective process); the remaining $S(n)$ are to hold the remaining register contents. The set-up time comes from the need to first concentrate the input values (to get rid of any zeros), and route them out to the register-holders using procedures Rank and Concentrate from [86,88]. An additional $O(\log P(n))$ steps are required to broadcast the program of the simulated network to the first $P(n)$ processors using Algorithm 1 of Section 7.3. The result then follows from Theorems 9.1.1 and 7.4.1, noting that a $P(n)+S(n)$ processor feasible network based on either the shuffle-exchange, cube-connected-cycles or cub-connected lines can:

(1) Sort $P(n)$ items in time $O(\log^2 P(n))$ using one of Batcher's sorting algorithms (see Theorem 7.1.5).

(2) Merge $P(n)+S(n)$ items in time $O(\log S(n))$ by using odd-even merge (see Theorem 7.1.5).

(3) Fan-out $P(n)+S(n)$ items in time $O(\log S(n))$ by using Algorithm 3 of Section 7.3. Alternatively, procedures Rank, Concentrate and Generalize from [86] can be utilized, as in that reference.

(4) Deliver $P(n)+S(n)$ items in time $O(\log S(n))$ by using procedure Concentrate from [86,88].

(5) Concentrate $P(n)+S(n)$ items in time $O(\log S(n))$ using procedures Rank and Concentrate from [86,88]. □

The time complexity of Theorem 9.2.1 is dominated by the cost of sorting the read and write requests. This can be reduced by substituting the sorting algorithm of Ajtai, Komlós and Szemerédi (see Chapter 8) for (1). Although this results in a better asymptotic time-bound, the constant multiple is too large to be of any practical use. The algorithm as presented in [5] has a constant multiple of several million, although this has more recently been reduced by M. S. Paterson (using the method sketched in Chapter 8). For our purposes, Corollary 9.2.1 is to be regarded as superior. If the number of processors is increased to $S(n)^{1+\epsilon}$ for any real number $\epsilon > 0$ then a more practical $O(\log n)$ delay can be obtained using the sorting algorithm of Nassimi and Sahni [88]. The reduction to sorting can be avoided entirely by allowing the number of processors to increase by a polynomial (see Exercise 9.1).

Leighton [73] has discovered an elegant method for sorting $P(n)$ items in time $O(\log P(n))$, using only $P(n)$ processors, based upon the AKS sorting network (see Chapter 8). Thus we have:

Corollary 9.2.2 There is a feasible network which can simulate any $S(n)$ space bounded network using $O(S(n))$ processors, the same word-size and delay $O(\log S(n))$.

What if the processors of the universal network are allowed to have more than a constant amount of memory? Then:

(1) $O(\log S(n))$ delay, with a more reasonable constant multiple, can be achieved on a probabilistic network (with overwhelming probability) on $S(n)$ processors by using the sorting algorithm of [107].

(2) The processor bound in (1) can be reduced to $P(n)$ for the simulation of shared-memory machines, with a delay of $O(\log^2 P(n))$ [8]. The delay can be reduced to $O(\log P(n))$ on a probabilistic universal network [60].

(3) A delay of $O(\log^2 P(n))$ with $P(n)$ processors can easily be achieved on a deterministic network for the simulation of restricted-access networks [86]. (The delay can also be reduced by the use of the technique of Corollary 9.2.2).

Note that the universal network conserves many of the notions of "reasonableness" mentioned in Section 4.3. For example:

(1) If the network being simulated satisfies the parallel computation thesis, then so does the universal network.

(2) If the simulated network is small and fast (provided $T(n) = \Omega(\log P(n))$) the universal network is small and fast.

(3) Bounds upon word-size are maintained.

9.3. A Hardware Measure

In this section we attempt to formulate a hardware measure for our network model. The amount of hardware needed to build a universal feasible network is governed by the amount of memory needed and the complexity of the instruction-set. To simplify matters, we will concentrate on networks with the minimal instruction-set. We claim that space $\times$ wordsize is a good hardware measure for such a network (or indeed, any machine where memory-costs dominate the cost of a processing-unit). In order to justify this claim, we can relate this to the measures of hardware on other popularly-accepted models, whilst maintaining time to within a polynomial.

A *uniform circuit* is an infinite family $C = (C_0, C_1, ...)$ of combinational circuits, one for each input-size (see, for example [15,21,102,108]). Without loss of generality we assume that the circuits are built using gates which realize functions drawn from the class B_2 of two-input Boolean functions. An input of size n is presented, in some suitably encoded form, to the inputs of C_n. The output of C_n is then taken as the output of C. C is said to have *depth* D(n) if the length of the longest path from an input to an output in C_n is at most D(n), for $n \geq 0$. It has *size* Z(n) if C_n has Z(n) gates. Suppose we draw a circuit as a sequence of levels, numbered consecutively from 0 to D(n). Level 0 consists of the inputs. Gates at level i, i > 0, have inputs from the outputs of gates at level $<$ i. The *thickness* [102] of a circuit at level i is the number of gates at levels $<$ i upon which one or more gates at level i depend. A circuit has *width* W(n) if C_n has maximum thickness at most W(n). We assume $D(n) = \Omega(\log W(n))$; a circuit with D(n) $<$ log W(n) would have redundant gates.

The function $f:N^2 \times \{left,right\} \rightarrow N$ where for $n \geq 0$ the j-input of gate $i \geq n$ is connected to the output of gate f(i,n,j), is called the *interconnection function* of C. We assume that gates 0,1,...,n-1 are distinguished gates representing the inputs. The function $g:N^2 \rightarrow B_2$, where for $n \geq 0$ gate $i \geq n$ of C_n is a g(i,n)-gate, is called the *gate function* of C. We insist that the interconnection and gate functions be computable in linear space (that is, space O(log Z(n))) by a deterministic Turing machine.

140

Corollary 9.3.1 Every network with P(n) processors, space S(n), time T(n) and word-size W(n) can be simulated by a uniform circuit of width $O(S(n)W(n))$ and depth either:

    (i) $O(T(n)(W(n) + \log S(n)))$, or

    (ii) $O(T(n)(\log W(n))(\log S(n)))$.

Proof. (Sketch). The circuit consists of T(n) levels, one for each simulated time-step. Each level has P(n) sub-circuits corresponding to a single step of a processor, and a further S(n) sub-circuits carrying register values. Between each level is a circuit for carrying out inter-processor communication, built out of a sorter, merger, concentrator etc. as in Corollary 9.2.2. Each processor unit takes as input the program-counter, current values of registers r_0, r_1 and r_2, and incoming values from read requests. It produces outgoing read and write requests, and updated values for the aforementioned program-counter and registers (see Figure 9.3.1). These units fit together as in Figure 9.3.2.

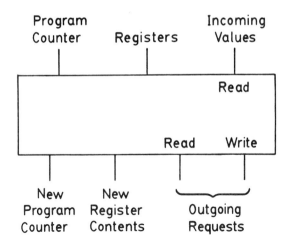

Figure 9.3.1 Block diagram representation of a circuit to compute a single step of a processor.

Each processor-unit has circuitry which:

(1) Deals with incoming data which has arrived in response to a read request in the last step.

(2) Performs a single instruction, issuing a read or write request as necessary.

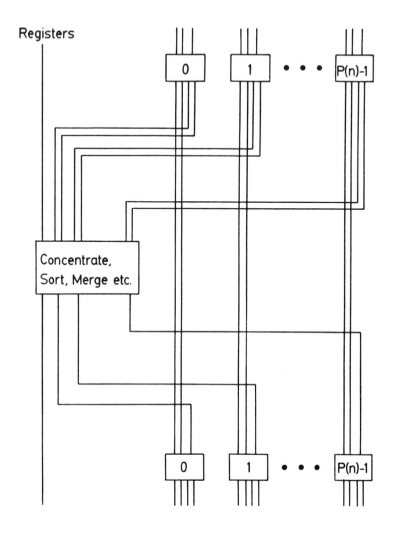

Figure 9.3.2 Block diagram of a circuit to compute a single step of a network.

The processor units have width $O(W(n))$ and depth $O(\log W(n))$. Circuits for sort, merge, concentrate etc. can be constructed with width $O(S(n)W(n))$ and depth either $O((\log S(n))(\log W(n)))$ or $O(W(n)+\log S(n))$ (see Exercise 9.2). The register contents have width $O(S(n)W(n))$. Thus the complete circuit has the required width and depth. $\square$

Note that in the general case, if the internal instructions can be computed by a uniform circuit of depth $d_I(n)$ and width $w_I(n)$, then $d_I(n)T(n)$ must be added to the depth, and $w_I(n)P(n)$ must be added to the width.

In Section 4.3 we saw a number of different ways of characterizing a "reasonable" parallel machine model. For example, the parallel computation thesis states that a parallel machine model is reasonable if time on that model is polynomially related to sequential space. Dymond [24,25] gives an extended version of the parallel computation thesis which takes into account both the time and the amount of hardware used. This can be loosely summed up as follows: time and hardware on any reasonable parallel machine model are simultaneously polynomially related to Turing machine reversals and space respectively (a *reversal* is said to occur when any tape-head changes direction).

This raises an obvious question: when are our network machines a "reasonable" parallel machine model according to the extended parallel computation thesis, given that space$\times$wordsize is taken as a measure of hardware? By Corollary 9.3.1 (i), we find that a $T(n)$ time, $P(n)$ processor bounded network which uses space $S(n)$ and has word-size $W(n)$ satisfies the extended parallel computation thesis provided:

(i)   Local instructions can be computed by a deterministic Turing machine using space $(W(n)S(n))^{O(1)}$ and $T(n)^{O(1)}$ reversals.

(ii) $P(n) = 2^{T(n)^{O(1)}}$. (Note that this implies that $S(n) = 2^{T(n)^{O(1)}}$.)

(iii) $W(n) = 2^{T(n)^{O(1)}}$.

Part (i) provides more evidence for the unit-cost hypothesis. Note that the Turing machine is to be given the value of $P(n)$ in binary along with any input of size n; if $P(n)$ is to be computed, then the necessary resources must be taken into account. Many useful functions, such as polynomials and poly-logs, can be computed within the required amount of resources.

In particular, for a machine with the minimal instruction-set:

Corollary 9.3.2 Every $P(n)$ processor network with the minimal instruction-set which runs in time $T(n)$, space $S(n)$ and word-size $W(n)$ can be simulated by a deterministic Turing machine using space $O(S(n)W(n))$ and reversals $O(T(n)(\log^2 P(n) + \log S(n)))$.

Proof. (Sketch). This result follows from Theorem 9.1.1 much in the same manner as Corollary 9.2.1. The composite sub-algorithms used thus have simple modules whose upper dimension is easy to compute.

Consider a simple-ascend class sub-algorithm which ascends to the full value of k, and uses the minimal instruction-set. Suppose the n inputs are initially encoded as binary strings on tape 1 of the Turing machine, each separated by a special blank symbol. The Turing machine computes in k phases (one for each dimension), each of which consists of a constant number of passes over two tapes. The first phase does the following. First, copy every alternate string on to tape 2. In a constant number of left-to-right scans over the tapes, perform the necessary data transfers in dimension 1, and the internal computations. Copy the (updated) strings from tape 2 back to tape 1. The word-size can increase by only a constant, so the overflow from each string can be stored temporarily by using a large tape alphabet, and the tape contents can be moved along as part of the copying process by making extra use of the second tape. (Extra tapes may be necessary for more powerful instruction-sets which increase the word-size more rapidly). This is the end of the first phase. Phase i, $2 \leq i \leq k$ achieves data transfers in dimension i by similarly copying alternate blocks of 2^{i-1} strings from tape 1 to tape 2, performing the transfers in a constant number of left-to-right scans, and copying the strings back to tape 1. $\square$

We will consider the converse of this result, the simulation of a Turing machine by a network, in the next section.

9.4. Circuits and Turing Machines

In order to justify his extended parallel computation thesis, Dymond [24,25] appeals to a seminal paper by Pippenger [102] which relates depth and size of uniform circuits to Turing machine reversals and time. Dymond prefers to use Turing machine space instead of time, and circuit width as a measure of hardware (rather than size) since it is a measure of the amount of hardware which comes into play at any given instant in time. We can use the results of this chapter to obtain simulations of space and reversal bounded Turing machines by uniform circuits.

We follow the general structure of the proof appearing in [102]. Pippenger simulates a Turing machine on an oblivious Turing machine, and then simulates this on a uniform circuit. We will simulate a Turing machine on a network. We can then build a uniform circuit by application of Corollary 9.3.1.

Theorem 9.4.1 An $S(n)$ space, $R(n)$ reversal bounded k-tape deterministic Turing machine can be simulated on a network with the minimal instruction-set, using processors and space $O(S(n)^k/\log S(n))$, time $O(R(n)\log S(n))$ and word-size $O(\log S(n))$.

Proof. Let M be a k-tape deterministic Turing machine which runs in space $S(n)$ and reversals $R(n)$. Following [102] define a *pass* to be all the steps of M from one reversal to the next (the first move is counted as a reversal for this purpose), and a *situation* to be the control state and head positions of M. It may be assumed that all transition rules of M which write a new value onto a tape cell also move the head away from that cell. This implies that symbols written during one pass cannot be read until the next. Let $d(n) = 2^{\lceil \log \log S(n) \rceil}$ and call a situation *special* if it has at least one head on the $(i\,d(n))^{th}$ cell of its tape, for some $i \in N$. Note that there are at most $O(S(n)^k/\log S(n))$ different special situations, and that at most $O(\log S(n))$ steps of M can occur between one special situation and the next.

In order to make the proof more readable, we will present the algorithm on a shared-memory machine. The simulation proceeds roughly as follows. The tape contents at the start of the current pass, the head directions and the initial situation for the current phase are stored in the shared memory. This is easy to do at the start of the initial pass; the algorithm will maintain this information from pass to pass. We reserve one processor (and two shared memory locations) for each special situation. The aim is to have these processors confer, via the shared memory, and decide which special situations are involved in the current pass. The processors corresponding to these special situations then simultaneously update the tape cell contents in shared memory; the final situation (which is detected by an attempted reversal) determines the head directions and the initial situation for the next pass. This proceeds for a total of $R(n)$ passes.

The simulation of a pass is achieved as follows. Processor i handles the ith special situation. Firstly, in parallel, each processor i computes the special situation which follows from special situation i, by doing a step-by-step read-only simulation of M on the tape contents in shared memory (by "read-only simulation" we mean that the tape-contents are not updated). This value is stored into array element s[i] in shared memory. If an illegal situation occurs during this process, or a reversal is detected (determined by examining the head directions for the current pass, which are stored in shared memory) then s[i] is set to i. All processors i execute the following code synchronously in parallel. Upon termination, shared array element active[i] will be set to true iff special situation i occurs in the current pass. Each processor can determine whether its special situation is the first special situation to occur in the current pass by using a step-wise read-only simulation of M starting at the initial situation of the pass.

> active[PID]:=(PID encodes the first special situation in this pass)
> **for** b:=1 **to** $\lceil \log S(n) \rceil$ **do**
> **if** active[PID] **then** active[s[PID]]:=true
> s[PID]:=s[s[PID]]

Those processors i with active[i] = true can then update the tape contents; the last special situation is readily available (in all entries of s), from which the final situation of the current pass can be determined.

The running time is dominated by $O(\log S(n))$ for each pass. This comes from:

(1) Decoding of PIDs (each of $O(\log S(n))$ bits) into special situations.

(2) Determining the first special situation from the initial situation and the final situation from the last special situation by simulating at most $O(\log S(n))$ steps of M.

(3) Computing the · special-situation transition function by simulating $O(\log S(n))$ steps of M.

(4) Computing the active array in $O(\log S(n))$ steps.

(5) Updating the tape contents by simulating $O(\log S(n))$ steps of M.

Repeating this for R(n) pass gives us the required result. □

Corollary 9.4.2 An $S(n)$ space, $R(n)$ reversal bounded deterministic k-tape Turing machine can be simulated by a uniform circuit of depth $O(R(n)\log^2 S(n))$ and width $O(S(n)^k)$.

Proof. The result follows immediately from Theorem 9.4.1 and Corollary 9.3.1 (i). □

Corollary 9.4.3 A $T(n)$ time, $R(n)$ reversal bounded deterministic k-tape Turing machine can be simulated by a uniform circuit of depth $O(R(n)\log^2 T(n))$ and size $O(R(n)T(n)^k\log^2 T(n))$.

This is a small improvement over the results of Pippenger [102] who obtains depth $O(R(n)\log^4 T(n))$ and size $O(R(n)T(n)^k\log^4 T(n))$.

Pippenger focusses on the class of languages recognizable in polynomial size and poly-log depth by a uniform circuit family (equivalently, polynomial space and poly-log reversals by a deterministic Turing machine). This class is called NC ("Nick's Class") by Cook [19,22], a nomenclature which has been adopted by the research community. Whilst Pippenger was the first to consider the resources of uniform circuit size and depth simultaneously, simulations of single-resource bounded uniform circuits were earlier studied by Borodin [15]. Ruzzo [108] has demonstrated that NC is fairly robust under different definitions of uniformity.

One interpretation of the extended parallel computation thesis is that NC is the class of languages recognizable by polynomial hardware (small), poly-log running-time (fast) parallel computers. NC is contained in POLYLOGSPACE, and NSPACE(log n) is contained in NC (see Exercise 9.4). We have already seen (Section 5.3 and Corollary 9.3.2) that GAP∈NC. Since NC⊆POLYLOGSPACE it is unlikely that P⊆NC, that is, there are probably problems which are feasibly-computable on a sequential machine, but cannot be solved by small, fast parallel computers. For example, the circuit-value problem (see Section 5.3) is probably not a member of NC by virtue of its being log-space complete for P. However, although small networks do not appear to provide an exponential speedup of members of P, a speedup of a factor of log n is possible, by Corollary 6.2.6.

NC is one of the more popular topics of research in parallel complexity theory. Indeed, there is probably sufficient material to warrant a monograph devoted entirely to the subject. For some of the more recent results, the reader can consult Aggarwal et al [2], Ben-Or et al [12], Klein and Reif [64], Kozen and Yap [66], Lovasz [76], and Mulmuley [85]. Adding randomness to small, fast parallel computers appears to increase their computing power. The class of languages recognizable by small, fast probabilistic parallel computers is called RNC ("random NC"). A result of Adleman [1] on sampling can be used to show that RNC is contained in the non-uniform analogue of NC. Some of the recent results on RNC include Anderson [9], Galil and Pan [36], Gazit [40], Karp, Upfal and Wigderson [62], Luks and McKenzie [78], Miller and Reif [83], and Vazirani and Vazirani [125].

9.5. Exercises

9.1 Re-prove Corollary 9.2.1 (the universal feasible network) on $S(n)^2$ processors without recourse to a reduction to sorting.

9.2 Show that n values of b bits can be sorted by a uniform circuit of width O(bn) and depth:
 (i) $O((\log n)(\log b))$.
 (ii) $O(b + \log n)$.

Show that any simple algorithm (see Chapter 7) which uses the minimal instruction-set with word-size W(n) on P(n) processors can be simulated by a uniform circuit of width $O(P(n)W(n))$ and depth:
 (i) $O((\log P(n))(\log W(n)))$.
 (ii) $O(W(n) + \log P(n))$.

9.3 Complete the proof of Corollary 9.3.2, that is, show that every P(n) processor network which runs in time T(n), space S(n) and word-size W(n) can be simulated by a deterministic Turing machine using space $O(S(n)W(n))$ and reversals $O\big(T(n)(\log^2 P(n) + \log S(n))\big)$.

9.4 Show that $NC \subseteq POLYLOGSPACE$ and $NSPACE(\log n) \subseteq NC$.

9.5 Show that the tree circuit-value problem (see Section 5.3) is a member of NC by presenting a poly-log running-time, polynomial processor, logarithmic word-size shared-memory machine algorithm.

9.6 (Brent and Goldschlager [46]). Show that the context-free membership problem (see Exercises 5.6 and 5.7) can be recognized in $O(\log n)$ time by a polynomial-processor shared-memory machine provided no ϵ–productions are allowed, and hence deduce that it is a member of NC. (Hint: consider the technique used in Exercise 5.6). What can be said about the context-free membership problem if ϵ–productions are allowed?

148

10 More on Universal Machines

In this chapter we investigate universal networks in more detail. The first section examines in some detail a parallel machine which is (strongly-literal) universal for restricted-access, fixed-structure networks. The second section is devoted to lower-bounds on literal simulations. The delay of Corollary 9.2.3 is easily seen to be asymptotically optimal for a literal simulation. However, no such elementary lower-bound can be found for a simulation which is not literal, as is demonstrated by the existence of a nondeterministic universal network which has constant average delay. We also find that the delay of the universal network described in the first section is asymptotically optimal for a strongly-literal simulation of degree-3 networks, which is a fairly strong result since it uses asymptotically the same amount of time when the degree is any constant.

In the second section we find that the latter lower-bound can be beaten by the non-literal simulation of Meyer auf der Heide [54]. The third section considers oblivious universal networks. A literal simulation is said to be *oblivious* (after Borodin and Hopcroft [16]) if the routes taken by data packets sent in response to read or write requests depend only upon their respective sources and destinations. By extending the work of Borodin and Hopcroft [16] and Lang [71] we obtain asymptotically matching upper and lower-bounds of $\Theta(\frac{P_1(n)}{\sqrt{P_2(n)}} + \log P_1(n))$ for the delay required for an oblivious simulation of a $P_1(n)$ processor network on a $P_2(n)$ processor, constant-degree universal network.

10.1. A Restricted Universal Machine

In this section we will consider a fixed-structure model with restricted access (see Section 4.3). Each dedicated processor will be initialized with the processor-identities of the neighbours of its processes. We shall see that slightly more efficient simulations are made possible by the presence of this extra information (which cannot be provided in a model with modifiable structure). In a fixed-structure model, it is quite reasonable to expect the user to provide this information (perhaps in the form of an easy-to-compute interconnection function, in which case its resource requirements should be added to the set-up time for the universal network), since it forms part of the specification which would be required by a fabrication device, should the network be realized in hardware.

One problem with the universal network of Section 9.2 is that the number of processors is (asymptotically) dominated by the space requirements of the machine being simulated. Thus the number of processors used by the universal network may be significantly larger than the number used by the simulated machine. This condition is forced upon the universal network by our requirement that it be a feasible network. Suppose that we weaken condition (i) of a feasible network by allowing the processors of the universal network to have more than a constant number of registers, while requiring it to be a restricted-access network (recall from Section 4.3 that once the number of registers is restricted to a constant, then the network can without loss of generality be assumed to be restricted-access). More formally, define an *elemental network* to be a restricted-access, fixed-structure network with interconnection scheme (P,D,G), such that:

(i)   The degree, $D(n)$, is a constant.

(ii) The interconnection function G can be computed in time $O(\log P(n))$ by a deterministic Turing machine.

Consider the universal network of Section 9.2. It is not *per se* possible to reduce the number of processors from $S(n)$ to $P(n)$ by allowing the universal network to be elemental instead of feasible, since some processor may have a significant fraction of its registers accessed simultaneously by its neighbours. These accesses can only occur singly through the narrow window posed by the communication register; in consequence the delay would increase by, in the worst case, $S(n)/P(n)$.

In contrast, suppose that the network being simulated is itself a restricted-access, fixed-structure network. If its degree is fairly small, then an $O(\log P(n))$-delay simulation can be achieved without recourse to the reduction to sorting used in Chapter 9, with its attendant high constant-multiples due to the use of the sorting network of Ajtai, Komlós and Szemerédi (see Chapter 8). Further, we can even allow the restricted-access network being simulated to access all of its neighbours simultaneously. We call the number of accessible neighbours the *arity* of the network. Note that arity is bounded above by degree.

Theorem 10.1.1 There is a P(n)D(n) processor universal network which can simulate any P(n) processor, restricted-access, fixed-structure network of arity and degree D(n), with delay $O(\log P(n) + D(n))$ and set-up time $O(\log^4 P(n) + D(n))$.

Proof. (Outline). Suppose $\alpha = \lceil \log P(n) \rceil$ and $\beta = \lceil \log D(n) \rceil$. We describe our algorithm on an $(\alpha + \beta)$-cube. Let M be a P(n) processor network with degree and arity D(n). Processor i, $0 \le i < P(n)$ of the universal network will simulate processor i of M. Let i[d] denote the dth neighbour of processor i of M, in order of ascending PID. For $0 \le i < P(n)$ let W_i be the β-cube consisting of processors $2^\alpha k + i$, for $0 \le k < 2^\beta$, of the universal network.

As part of the initialization, each processor i $0 \le i < P(n)$ will receive D(n) identification numbers I(i[d],i) for $0 \le d < D(n)$ such that:

(1) $0 \le I(i[d],i) < D(n)$ for all $0 \le i < P(n)$, $0 \le d < D(n)$, and

(2) For all $0 \le i_1,i_2,j < P(n)$, if $I(j,i_1)$ and $I(j,i_2)$ are both defined, and $I(j,i_1) = I(j,i_2)$ then $i_1 = i_2$.

Thus processor i is the $I(i[d],i)^{th}$ neighbour of processor i[d], in ascending order of PID. This is achieved as follows. Processor i $0 \le i < P(n)$ prepares D(n) packets (i[d],i), $0 \le d < D(n)$, and scatters them around the $2^\beta \ge D(n)$ processors of W_i, at most one packet per processor, using Algorithm 4 of Section 7.3. These packets are then sorted within the $(\alpha + \beta)$-cube in lexicographic (first-field-first) order. Each processor j, $0 \le j < 2^{\alpha + \beta}$ thus receives some packet $(i_j[d],i_j)$. It then sets variable v to $i_j[d]$. Running Algorithm 2 of Section 7.3 on the $(\alpha + \beta)$-cube computes the local rank of each processor, which in this case is $I(i_j[d],i_j)$. Armed with this information, for $0 \le i < P(n)$ the processor in charge of packet (i[d],i) transforms it into (i,i[d],I(i[d],i)). These packets are sorted back to their respective W_i's, and then gathered back into processor i by reversing the scattering algorithm.

After the initialization phase, each step of the simulation proceeds as follows. First, requests to read communication registers are fulfilled. Processor i $0 \le i < P(n)$ prepares D(n) request packets (i[d],I(i[d],i),i), $0 \le d < D(n)$. These are scattered at most one-per-processor around the processors of W_i, using Algorithm 4. Once this has been carried out, let Π be the permutation which carries packet (i[d],I(i[d],i),i) to processor $2^\alpha I(i[d],i) + i[d]$, for $0 \le i < P(n)$. Once Π has been applied, W_i contains the D(n) requests from the neighbours of processor i of M, $0 \le i < P(n)$. Processor i can then fulfill the D(n) requests by broadcasting the contents of the communication register of processor i of M around the processors of W_i using Algorithm 1. The fulfilled requests are routed back to their originating processors by reversing the above process. Processor i of the universal network can then simulate the internal computation of processor i of M, $0 \leq i < P(n)$. Finally, requests to write to communication registers are handled in a similar manner.

Repeating this t times enables us to simulate t steps of M. Note that Π is the same for each step. A fixed permutation can be carried out in time $O(\log P(n))$ by simulating one of Waksman's permutation networks (see Theorem 7.1.3). This requires $O(\log^4 P(n))$ set-up time, however (see Theorem 7.1.4). The total set-up time is thus comprised of:

(1) $O(\log^2 P(n) + D(n))$ to compute the identification numbers $I(i[d],i)$. The $\log^2$ term comes from sorting using Theorem 7.1.5. The $D(n)$ term comes from the use of Algorithm 4 of Section 7.3 to scatter $D(n)$ values.
(2) $O(\log^4 P(n))$ to set up Π.

The delay is comprised of:

(1) $O(D(n))$ to prepare and broadcast the request packets,
(2) $O(\log P(n))$ to compute Π,
(3) $O(\log D(n))$ to fulfill the request packets,
(4) $O(D(n))$ to gather in the fulfilled request packets.

All of the algorithms used in this simulation can be implemented on either the shuffle-exchange, cube-connected cycles or cube-connected lines interconnection patterns (see Chapter 7) without asymptotic time-loss. $\square$

There are many obvious variants of the above Theorem, taking into account different possible relationships between degree and arity. For example, for a network with low arity we have:

Corollary 10.1.2 There is a $P(n).D(n)$ processor universal network which can simulate any $P(n)$ processor, restricted-access, fixed-structure network of degree $D(n)$ and arity $O(\log P(n))$, with delay $O(\log P(n))$ and set-up time $O(\log^4 P(n) + D(n))$.

In particular, by taking $D(n) = O(1)$ (and using the processor-saving theorems of Section 7.4) we have:

Corollary 10.1.3 (Galil and Paul [38]) There is a $P(n)$ processor universal network which can simulate any $P(n)$ processor, restricted-access, fixed-structure network of constant degree with delay $O(\log P(n))$ and set-up time $O(\log^4 P(n))$.

152

10.2. Some Lower-Bounds

In Section 9.2 we saw several examples of an $S(n)$-processor feasible network which can perform an $O(\log S(n))$ delay literal simulation of any $S(n)$ space-bounded network (see Section 4.4 for definitions). It is easy to see that this delay is optimal for a literal simulation, by considering the following argument. Suppose $T:N \to N$ is such that $T(n) \leq n$. Consider the n-processor network with the following program, where x of processor i is initially the ith input symbol, $0 \leq i < n$.

$$y:=x$$
$$\textbf{for } i:=0 \textbf{ to } T(n)\text{--}1 \textbf{ do}$$
$$y:=y + (x \textbf{ of processor } i)$$

M runs in time $O(T(n))$, yet every constant-degree universal network must take time $\Omega(T(n) \log n)$ to perform a literal simulation of M (no matter how many processors are available), even if the universal network is allowed to have more than a constant number of registers per processor. For if there are $O(n/\log n)$ dedicated processors then one processor must be looking after $\Omega(\log n)$ registers of M, which requires time $\Omega(\log n)$ to keep up-to-date. Otherwise, since the simulation is literal, the contents of the requisite register must be broadcast to the $\Omega(n/\log n)$ other dedicated processors during each iteration, which takes time $\Omega(\log n)$ on a constant-degree network.

Note that this lower-bound is based upon two important properties: the limited data-carrying capacity of constant-degree networks, and the large amount of traffic created by a literal simulation. If we relax the requirement that the simulation be literal, then no such simple lower-bound technique is available. For example a nondeterministic universal network can achieve a constant average delay, literal simulation of a $P(n)$ processor, $T(n)$ running-time restricted-access network with $T(n) = \Omega(\log P(n))$.

We define a nondeterministic network similarly to the deterministic model of Section 3.1, with the following modifications:

(1) Two extra instructions are allowed.

(a) $r_i \leftarrow random\ (r_j)$, and

(b) fail.

The former assigns to register r_i a value between 0 and the contents of r_j, and is called a *guess*. The latter is a special kind of halt instruction. A processor which has executed it is said to have *failed*.

(2) A computation is said to *succeed* if no processor has failed. A nondeterministic network M is said to *compute* a relation $R \subseteq N^* \times N^*$ if for every input x, $<x,y> \in R$ iff there is a sequence of guessed values such that M succeeds and produces output y. Nondeterministic resources are defined, in the usual manner, to be the maximum over all inputs x of size n, of the minimum over all successful computations on input x, of the resources used on that computation. By convention, the resources are taken to be zero when no successful computation exists.

Theorem 10.2.1 There is a $P(n) \log P(n)$ processor, constant-degree nondeterministic universal network which can simulate any $T(n)$ time, $P(n)$ processor bounded nondeterministic restricted-access network in time $O(T(n) + \log P(n))$.

Proof. Suppose M is a $T(n)$ time, $P(n)$ processor bounded restricted-access network. For the present, assume $T(n) = \Omega(\log P(n))$. Fix n, and let $\alpha = \lceil \log P(n) \rceil$, $\beta = \lceil \log \alpha \rceil$. We will describe our algorithm on an $(\alpha+\beta+2)$-cube. Processor i of the universal network will simulate process i, $0 \leq i < P(n)$. The algorithm consists of $\lceil T(n)/\alpha \rceil$ phases, each of which corresponds to α steps of M.

The first phase proceeds as follows. Suppose at the tth step of M, $1 \leq t \leq \alpha$, process i wishes to read the communication register of process $\Gamma(i,t)$. Instead of obtaining the correct value from processor $\Gamma(i,t)$, it nondeterministically guesses some value d_t which it uses instead, having recorded it, along with the value $\Gamma(i,t)$, for later verification. The α values c_t, $1 \leq t \leq \alpha$, where c_t denotes the contents of the communication register of processor i at time t, are also recorded. The effects of possible write-attempts are also guessed and recorded in a similar manner

For each i such that $0 \leq i < P(n)$ let W_i be the (beta+2)-cube consisting of processors $2^\alpha j + i$, $0 \leq j < 2^{\beta+2}$. Having simulated α steps with guessed data values, the verification procedure is as follows. Processor i, $0 \leq i < P(n)$ prepares α read-request packets $(\Gamma(i,t),t)$, each being a request for the contents of the communication register of process $\Gamma(i,t)$ at time t. It also prepares α data packets (i,t,c_t), and similarly α write-request packets. These are scattered around the $2^{\beta+2} \geq 4\alpha$ processors of W_i, at most one packet per processor, using Algorithm 4 of Section 7.3. The request packets are fulfilled using the techniques of Theorem 9.1.1. The guessed data values are then compared to the fulfilled requests, and any processor which detects a discrepancy fails immediately.

Thus α steps of M can be simulated in time $O(\log P(n)+\alpha) = O(\alpha)$. Note that $O(P(n)\log P(n))$ items can be sorted in time $O(\log P(n))$ using $O(P(n)\log P(n))$ processors by guessing a set of switch positions of the Waksman permutation network (see Theorem 7.1.3), and verifying afterwards that the permuted values are in sorted order. By repeating this for $\lceil T(n)/\alpha \rceil$ phases we are able to simulate $T(n)$ steps of M in time $O(T(n))$ as required. A set-up time of $O(\log P(n))$ is required to broadcast the program of the simulated network, using Algorithm 1 of Section 7.3. □

In Section 10.1 we saw a very special kind of literal simulation of a $P(n)$ processor, constant-degree, restricted-access network M on a universal network U. This had the property that:

(1) Each *processor* i of M has a dedicated processor d_i in U.
(2) This dedicated processor looks after *all* registers of processor i of M.
(3) $d_i \neq d_j$ for $i \neq j$.
(4) The initial dedicated processor assignment is the same for all simulated networks.
(5) The dedicated processor assignment does not change with time.

Under these very strict conditions, a delay of $O(\log P(n))$ was achieved using only $P(n)$ processors (Corollary 10.1.3). We will call simulations with property (5) *strongly-literal*. Meyer auf der Heide [52] has shown that the above delay is optimal for a strongly-literal simulation of a constant-degree, restricted-access network. It is relatively easy to strengthen this to show that the delay is optimal even for the simulation of networks with degree 3.

Theorem 10.2.2 (Parberry [91]) A strongly-literal universal network with $P(n)^{\alpha P(n)}$ processors, where $\alpha < 1/2$, and degree $D(n)$ must have delay $\Omega(\log P(n)/\log D(n))$ when simulating a $P(n)$ processor, degree-3 network.

Proof. Suppose we have an m-processor, degree-d universal network which can carry out a strongly-literal simulation of any degree-3, p-processor network with delay k. We will show that $k = \Omega(\log p/\log d)$ when simulating a special kind of network whose interconnection pattern is a degree-3 graph called a *matched-cycle*. A p-vertex matched-cycle has vertex-set $\{0,1, \cdots ,p-1\}$ and:

(1) Vertex v is joined to vertices $(v\pm1) \bmod p$ (cycle edges).
(2) The remaining edges form a graph of degree 1 (that is, they constitute part of a matching).

Let M be a network with one register per processor, whose interconnection pattern is a matched cycle. Each processor i of M, $0 \leq i < p$ is assigned a dedicated processor d_i in the universal network. Without loss of generality we will assume that each processor of the universal network is to be assigned to at most one processor of M (each multiply-assigned dedicated processor of U can be replaced by a ring of distinct dedicated processors without disturbing the time or processor bounds in the statement of the Theorem). Let N be the number of matched-cycle graphs, N_1 be the number of dedicated processor assignments which work for at least one matched-cycle graph, and N_2 be the maximum number of matched-cycles for which any given assignment can be used.

Claim 1. $N \geq p!/(2^{3p/2}(p/2)!)$

Proof. Without loss of generality suppose p is even. Then there are $p!/(2^{p/2}(p/2)!)$ matchings on p vertices (see Exercise 10.1). At most 2^p of these matchings can give rise to the same matched-cycle (by filling in the missing cycle edges), so there are at least $p!/(2^{3p/2}(p/2)!)$ matched-cycles. $\square$

Claim 2. $N_1 \leq md^{k(p-1)}$.

Proof. If a particular processor assignment is to work for a matched-cycle, then processor d_i must be at distance at most k from $d_{(i+1) \bmod n}$ in the interconnection pattern of the universal network, $0 \leq i < p$. Thus there are m choices for d_0, but at most d^k choices for d_1, and similarly d^k choices for each of $d_2, d_3, \ldots, d_{p-1}$. $\square$

Claim 3. $N_2 \leq d^{kp}$.

Proof. Fix a processor assignment. Consider the networks M for which that processor assignment works. Each processor i of M can be adjacent to the (at most) d^k processors j such that d_i and d_j are at distance at most k in the interconnection pattern of the universal network. Thus each vertex in the interconnection pattern of M can be adjacent to at most d^k other vertices via a matching edge. $\square$

If the universal network is to simulate all matched-cycles within the stated resource-bounds, then (by the Claims) we must have $N_1 N_2 \geq N$. Thus:

$$p!/(2^{3p/2}(p/2)!) \leq md^{k(2p-1)}$$

That is,

$$\frac{p}{2}\log p < k(2p-1)\log d + \log m + O(p)$$

Hence if $m < p^{\alpha p}$ for all $\alpha < 1/2$, we see that $k = \Omega(\log p/\log d)$. $\square$

156

Thus a constant-degree universal network must have delay $\Omega(\log P(n))$. Here is yet another interpretation of the unit-cost hypothesis. It is valid to charge one time-step for an internal computation which takes time $O(\log P(n))$ on the instruction-set of the universal network.

10.3. A Non-Literal Simulation

In Section 10.2 we saw an $\Omega(\log P(n))$ lower-bound on the delay of a strongly-literal simulation of a $P(n)$ processor, constant-degree restricted-access network. Here we will see that relaxing the literalness condition allows a more efficient simulation of fixed-structure networks. In a literal simulation there is ample opportunity during the simulation of a single step for the data to be routed from the dedicated processors in response to read or write requests. In a non-literal (but step-wise) simulation, this information may start out from the dedicated processors at an earlier point in time, being kept up-to-date along the way by auxiliary processors. Using this technique, we have:

Theorem 10.3.1 (Meyer auf der Heide [54]) There is a constant-degree universal network with $P(n)^{1+\epsilon}$ processors for any $\epsilon > 0$ which can simulate any $P(n)$ processor, constant-degree, fixed-structure, restricted-access network with constant delay and set-up time $O(\log^4 P(n))$.

Proof. (Sketch). Suppose the network to be simulated has degree d. Without loss of generality we can assume that it communicates by reads alone. The universal network has $P(n)$ dedicated processors, one for each process. Each dedicated processor is the root of a complete binary tree of depth $t \lceil \log d \rceil$, where $t > 0$ is some value to be determined later. Vertices at depth $i \lceil \log d \rceil$, $0 \leq i \leq t$ are said to be on the ith *level*. The dedicated processors are thus on the 0th level.

The simulation will proceed in $\lceil T(n)/t \rceil$ phases, each corresponding to t steps of the simulated machine. The trees will be initialized so that each processor on the ith level will be attempting to simulate one of the processes which are adjacent to the process of its ancestor on the $(i-1)^{\text{st}}$ level. Each process thus has many processors attempting to simulate it. A request from a process in a processor on the ith level, $0 \leq i < t$, to read the communication register of one of its neighbours is passed on to whichever $(i+1)^{\text{st}}$-level successor of that processor is attempting to simulate that neighbour. A request by a process in a processor on the tth level to read the communication register of one of its neighbours is ignored.

Thus after i steps have been simulated, the processors on level t–i+1 have probably been led astray in their simulation of a process by being misinformed by processors on the next level. All other processors have simulated correctly. After t steps, only the dedicated processors can be guaranteed to have not deviated. This part of the simulation takes O(t) steps.

Meanwhile, the dedicated processors save the communication register contents of their processes at each of the t simulated time-steps. These t values are to be routed to the processors on all levels which are attempting to simulate the same process. Armed with this information, these processors can re-compute the last t steps internally, and get back to a correct state. The trees are then ready to simulate another t steps without further initialization.

Suppose all processors of the trees are at the head of a distinct sub-cube of $2^{\lceil \log t \rceil}$ processors, and that further edges are added to make the whole structure into a multidimensional cube (with embedded trees) of $O(t\, P(n)d^t)$ processors. The correction stage can be carried out by having each level-i processor, $1 \leq i < t$, prepare t requests for the correct communication register contents at each of the t steps of the phase. The dedicated processors prepare t packets which provide this information. We then:

(1) Scatter them around the sub-cubes in time O(t) using Algorithm 4 of Section 7.3.

(2) Permute the requests and data into sorted order. Note that the permutation is the same for each phase, so Theorem 7.1.3 can be applied to give time $O(t+\log P(n))$.

(3) The techniques of Corollary 9.2.1 are then used to satisfy these requests in time $O(t+\log P(n))$.

(4) The satisfied requests are gathered back by reversing (1) and (2).

This gives a time-bound of $O(t+\log P(n))$ to simulate t steps. A total of $O(t\, P(n)d^t)$ processors are needed. Choosing $t = \epsilon\log_d P(n) - \log_d\log_d P(n)$ for some $\epsilon > 0$ gives constant average delay using $O(P(n)^{1+\epsilon})$ processors. The set-up time consists of:

(a) Time to assign processes to processors at each level of the trees.

(b) Initialization of the permutation used to sort the requests in part (2) above.

(c) Distribution of inputs, outputs and the program of the simulated machine.

158

The assignment in (a) can be achieved level-by-level starting at the dedicated processors. This cost (and the cost of (c)) is dominated by the $O(\log^4 P(n))$ required in Theorem 7.1.4 for (b) (see Exercise 10.2).

All algorithms which use the cube-part of the interconnection pattern are composite, and thus the algorithm can be implemented on a shuffle-exchange, cube-connected-cycles or cube-connected lines, with embedded trees, of degree 6. It is also possible to dispense with the trees (see Exercise 10.3). □

10.4. Oblivious Simulations

We complete this chapter by considering a very strict form of a strongly-literal simulation of a restricted-access network, which we shall call *oblivious*. Consider a single step of a strongly-literal simulation with dedicated processors d_i. If process i wishes to read the contents of the communication register of process j, then during this simulated time-step the required value can be provided by dedicated processor d_j and routed to d_i. (Similarly, if process i wishes to write into the communication register of process j, the value can be routed from d_i to d_j). If the routes taken by these data items depend solely on the source d_j and the destination d_i (respectively d_i and d_j in the case of a write), then the strongly-literal simulation is said to be *oblivious*. If in addition the next step in the route depends solely on the current location of the data packet and the eventual destination, then it is said to be *source-oblivious*.

The following lower-bound is a simple extension of Theorem 1 of Borodin and Hopcroft [16].

Theorem 10.4.1 An oblivious simulation of a $P_1(n)$ processor network on a constant-degree, $P_2(n)$ processor universal network must have delay $\Omega(\frac{P_1(n)}{\sqrt{P_2(n)}} + \log P_1(n))$.

Proof. Fix n, and let $p_1 = P_1(n)$, $p_2 = P_2(n)$. Suppose the universal network has degree d, dedicated processors d_i, $0 \le i < p_1$, and interconnection graph G.

For $0 \le i,j < p_1$ let $R_{j,i}$ be the path in G corresponding to the route taken by a data packet sent from processor d_j to processor d_i of the universal network in response to a request by process i to read the communication register of process j. Since the simulation is to be oblivious, these paths are invariant with time. Note that a path may consist of a single vertex (in the case where $d_i = d_j$), and that two paths may coincide along part, or even all, of their length. For $0 \leq i < p_1$ let G_i be the graph obtained from G by removing all edges which do not lie on some route $R_{j,i}$, for $0 \leq j < p_1$.

Suppose $k \geq 0$. For each i, $0 \leq i < p_1$ construct a set of vertices V_i from the vertices of G_i as follows. Initially V_i consists solely of vertex d_i (the destination of the routes which comprise G_i). Repeat the following until no new vertices are added: if v lies on at least k routes in G_i (that is, $| \{j \mid v \text{ lies on } R_{j,i}\} | \geq k$), and v is adjacent in G_i to some vertex in V_i, then add v to V_i. Then V_i consists of the largest set of vertices of G_i, clustered around the destination d_i, which are on k or more routes.

Let $T_i = | V_i |$, and $\overline{V}_i$ denote the set of vertices of G not in V_i. Let q be the maximum number of processes to be simulated by any dedicated processor, that is, $q = \max\limits_{0 \leq i < p_1} | \{j \mid 0 \leq j < p_1 \text{ and } d_i = d_j\} |$. Then at most T_iq routes of G_i start from vertices in V_i, so at least p_1-T_iq start from $\overline{V}_i$. In order to get from the vertices of $\overline{V}_i$ to vertex i, these must pass through the vertices of $\overline{V}_i$ which are adjacent to vertices of V_i in G_i. By the definition of V_i, each of these can carry at most k–1 routes of G_i. Hence there must be at least $\dfrac{p_1-T_iq}{k-1}$ such vertices. Furthermore, since G has degree d, there can be at most $T_i(d-1)$ vertices of $\overline{V}_i$ which are adjacent to vertices if V_i in G. Therefore it must be the case that:

$$T_i(d-1) \geq \frac{p_1-T_iq}{k-1}$$

That is,

$$T_i \geq \frac{p_1}{(d-1)(k-1)+q}.$$

Let $T = \min\limits_{0 \leq i < p_1} T_i$, and for each vertex j of G, $0 \leq j < p_2$, let $C_j = | \{i \mid 0 \leq i < p_1 \text{ and } j \in V_i\} |$. Now $\sum\limits_{j=0}^{p_2-1} C_j \geq p_1 T$, so there must be (by the pigeonhole principle) a vertex v with:

$$C_v \geq \frac{p_1 T}{p_2} \geq \frac{p_1^2}{p_2((d-1)(k-1)+q)}$$

Choose $k = \dfrac{p_1}{\sqrt{p_2(d-1)}} - \dfrac{q}{d-1}+1$. If $k < 2$ then the result follows: if

$q > p_1\sqrt{d-1}/(2\sqrt{p_2})$ then a lower-bound of $\Omega(p_1/\sqrt{p_2})$ follows immediately, otherwise $p_1/\sqrt{p_2} = O(1)$, and so a lower-bound of $\Omega(p_1/\sqrt{p_2})$ is trivial. Now suppose $k \geq 2$. Then $C_v \geq p_1/\sqrt{p_2(d-1)}$. If $q > p_1\sqrt{d-1}/(2\sqrt{p_2})$ then a lower-bound of $\Omega(p_1/\sqrt{p_2})$ follows immediately. Otherwise $k > p_1/(2\sqrt{p_2(d-1)})$ and so v lies on at least $k > p_1/(2\sqrt{p_2(d-1)})$ routes to vertex i for $C_v \geq p_1/\sqrt{p_2(d-1)}$ choices of destination i. Thus there is a combination of requests which results in $p_1/(2\sqrt{p_2(d-1)})$ packets being routed through vertex v; furthermore, each packet contains a different data item, which precludes the amalgamation of packets (assuming the universal network has the same word-size as the machine being simulated). Vertex v thus forms a bottleneck, giving us a time-loss of $\Omega(p_1/\sqrt{p_2})$ for each step of the simulation. This gives us a delay of $\Omega(P_1(n)/\sqrt{P_2(n)})$ for an oblivious simulation. This lower-bound very quickly becomes trivial, in fact when $P_2(n) = \Omega(P_1(n)^2)$ it gives us no information at all. In this case, Theorem 10.2.2 gives us a lower-bound of $\Omega(\log P_1(n))$. □

Borodin and Hopcroft [16] restricted their result to the special case in which $P_1(n) = P_2(n)$ and all dedicated processors are distinct. Lang [71] gives a matching upper-bound for the case where $P_1(n) = P_2(n)$ and the data-transfers form a permutation (which, in particular, means that there can be no read or write conflicts in the network to be simulated). However, it is fairly easy to extend his result to derive a general upper-bound which asymptotically matches the lower-bound of Theorem 10.4.1.

Theorem 10.4.2 Suppose $P_1(n) \leq P_2(n)$. There is a $P_2(n)$ processor universal network based on the shuffle-exchange which can carry out a source-oblivious simulation of a $P_1(n)$ processor network with delay $O(\dfrac{P_1(n)}{\sqrt{P_2(n)}} + \log P_1(n))$.

Proof. Fix n, and let $\alpha = \left\lceil \log P_1(n) \right\rceil$, $\beta = \left\lceil \log P_2(n) \right\rceil - \alpha$. We will describe our algorithm on an $(\alpha+\beta)$-cube. Processor $i2^\beta$ will simulate process i, $0 \leq i < P_1(n)$. The simulation of a single step proceeds as follows. Suppose process i, $0 \leq i < P_1(n)$ wishes to read the communication register of some process j_i, $0 \leq j_i < P_1(n)$. Then each processor $i2^\beta$, $0 \leq i < P_1(n)$ makes up a request packet (j_i, i). These packets are routed to the respective processors $j_i 2^\beta$, with multiple requests being combined as necessary. The requests are fulfilled and routed back to their sources along the same paths. Once read-requests have been dealt with in this manner, write-requests are handled analogously with a single routing.

The routing of read-requests is broken up into three parts. In each part we assume that the packets (j_i,i) are held in variables (j,i) of the requisite processor. Processors not in possession of a packet are deemed to hold the null packet (null,null). A *collision* is said to occur if two packets are resident in the same processor.

(a) Route the packets from $i2^\beta$ to $i2^\beta+(j_i \bmod 2^\beta)$.

This can be achieved easily using the following algorithm.

> **for** b:=1 **to** β **do**
>   **if** $PID_b = (j$ **of processor** $PID^{(b)})_b$
>   **then** (j,i):=(j,i) **of processor** $PID^{(b)}$
>   **else** (j,i):=(null,null)

There can be no collisions during this stage of the routing, since a packet from processor i remains in processors $i2^\beta+x$ for some $0 \le x < 2^\beta$.

(b) Route the packets from $i2^\beta+(j_i \bmod 2^\beta)$ to $\left\lfloor i/2^{\alpha-\beta} \right\rfloor 2^\alpha+j_i$.

This involves changing bits $\beta+1$ through α of the current location of each packet, which were previously the low-order bits (bits 1 through $\alpha-\beta$) of i, into the high-order bits (bits $\beta+1$ through α) of j.

To simplify our presentation, let us assume at first that there are no read-conflicts, so $j_{i_1} \ne j_{i_2}$ provided $i_1 \ne i_2$. We will return to the problem of read-conflicts later. Each processor has a queue, with unit-cost operations enqueue(x,y) (which places packet (x,y) at the tail of the queue), and dequeue (which removes the packet from head of the queue, and returns its value). An attempt to dequeue an empty queue returns the null packet.

This stage of the algorithm consists of $\alpha-\beta$ phases. During the kth phase, $1 \le k \le \alpha-\beta$, we move each packet (j_i,i) so that bit $\beta+k$ of its current location is the same as bit $\beta+k$ of $\left\lfloor i/2^{\alpha-\beta} \right\rfloor 2^\alpha+j_i$. This is sufficient to move packet (j_i,i) from $i2^\beta+(j_i \bmod 2^\beta)$ to $\left\lfloor i/2^{\alpha-\beta} \right\rfloor 2^\alpha+j_i$. Many collisions will occur; this is why each processor has a queue. In order to move every packet in the system in this manner, we must completely flush the queues during each phase. Let m_k be the maximum number of items in each queue at the start of phase k, $1 \le k < \alpha-\beta$, to be determined later.

```
initialize queue to be empty
for k:=1 to α–β do
    for t:=1 to m_k do
        if (j ≠ null) and (j_{β+k} = PID_{β+k})
            then enqueue(j,i)
        if (j of processor PID^{(β+k)} ≠ null) and
            (PID_{β+k} = (j of processor PID^{(β+k)})_{β+k})
            then enqueue((j,i) of processor PID^{(β+k)})
    (j,i):=dequeue
```

To make our analysis easier, we will include the packet (j,i) as part of the queue, since we have used variables (j,i) as a dummy head-of-queue item in the algorithm. At the beginning of Phase 1, the queues are empty, so $m_1 = 1$. After Phase k has terminated, a request from process i to process j will find itself in the queue of processor $\left\lfloor i/2^k \right\rfloor 2^{β+k} + (j \bmod 2^{β+k})$. Each request comes from a different source, and is bound for a different destination. Thus if two different requests, one from process i_1 to process j_1, and another from process i_2 to j_2 end up in the same queue at the end of the kth phase, then $i_1 \neq i_2$, $j_1 \neq j_2$ and

$$\left\lfloor i_1/2^k \right\rfloor 2^{β+k} + (j_1 \bmod 2^{β+k}) = \left\lfloor i_2/2^k \right\rfloor 2^{β+k} + (j_2 \bmod 2^{β+k}).$$

How many different choices of i_1 and i_2 are there? Since $i_1 \neq i_2$ and yet $\left\lfloor i_1/2^k \right\rfloor = \left\lfloor i_2/2^k \right\rfloor$, we are forced to assume that i_1 and i_2 differ only in the last k bits. Thus there are at most 2^k choices for the source, and so $m_k \leq 2^k$. Similarly, since $j_1 \neq j_2$ and yet $j_1 \bmod 2^{β+k} = j_2 \bmod 2^{β+k}$ we are forced to conclude that j_1 and j_2 differ only in the leading $α–β+k$ bits. Thus there are at most $2^{α–β–k}$ choices for the destination, and so $m_k \leq 2^{α–β–k}$. Putting both of these together, we conclude that $m_k \leq \min(2^k, 2^{α–β–k})$. Thus the algorithm will work if we set $m_k = \min(2^k, 2^{α–β–k})$. The delay is proportional to:

$$\sum_{k=0}^{α–β–1} m_k = \sum_{k=0}^{α–β–1} \min(2^k, 2^{α–β–k}).$$

If $α–β$ is even the latter is equal to $2^{(α–β+3)/2}-3$, and if it is odd it is equal to $3(2^{(α–β)/2}-1)$. Thus the delay is $O(\sqrt{2^{α–β}})$.

The case where read-conflicts are allowed is a little more complicated. As well as a queue, arm each processor with a stack, and the usual stack operations. Instead of enqueuing a packet, first check to see whether the queue already contains a packet bound for the same destination. The check can be carried out in constant time using an array acting as a bit-vector implementation of a set. If so, the newly arrived packet is relegated to the stack. This ensures that only packets with different destinations are put in any individual queue, which preserves the invariants necessary for the above timing analysis.

When, much later, the fulfilled request is routed back along the same path, the stack is checked before it is entered on the queue, and any requests for the same data item are fulfilled. By also stacking the time at which a duplicated request was received, the processor can tell when to unstack and despatch each fulfilled request in the return routing.

(c)   Route the packets from processor $\left\lfloor i/2^{\alpha-\beta} \right\rfloor 2^{\alpha}+j_i$ to $2^{\beta}j_i$.

This is done in two parts. First route it from $\left\lfloor i/2^{\alpha-\beta} \right\rfloor 2^{\alpha}+j_i$ to $j_i 2^{\beta}+(j_i \bmod 2^{\beta})$, and then from there to $j_i 2^{\beta}$. These two parts correspond to the two for-loops below.

> **for** b:$=\alpha+\beta$ **downto** $\beta+1$ **do**
>   **if** $\text{PID}_b = (\text{j of processor } \text{PID}^{(b)})_b$
>   **then** (j,i):=(j,i) **of processor** $\text{PID}^{(b)}$
> **for** b:$=\beta$ **downto** 1 **do**
>   **if** $\text{PID}_b = 0$
>   **then** (j,i):=(j,i) **of processor** $\text{PID}^{(b)}$

Since at all times there are at least α bits of j present in the location of each packet (j,i), and at the end of stage (b) above there are no two distinct packets bound for the same destination, there are no collisions.

Thus by applying the algorithms of parts (a), (b) and (c) consecutively, we can route the request packets in time:

$$O(\sqrt{2^{\alpha-\beta}}+\beta+\alpha) = O(\frac{P_1(n)}{\sqrt{P_2(n)}} + \log P_1(n))$$

on an $(\alpha+\beta)$–cube. Part (a) is a simple-ascend class algorithm, and part (c) is simple-descend. Thus by the use of Theorems 7.1.1 and 7.1.2 they can be realized on the cube-connected-cycles, cube-connected lines or shuffle-exchange interconnection patterns without asymptotic time-loss, using $P_2(n)$ processors.

The implementation of (b) needs special care however. It would be simple-ascend class except for the fact that m_k data transfers occur along dimensions

$\beta+k$, instead of the usual one. A careful analysis of the proof of Theorem 7.1.1 shows that this is easy to handle in the shuffle-exchange case. This does not appear to be the case with Theorem 7.1.2 however, due to the pipelining technique used. In the implementation of part (b) on the shuffle-exchange, processes must be moved around at the end of each phase. It takes time proportional to m^k to move the queue at the start of the kth phase, giving asymptotically the same delay as above.

We have not yet described how the fulfilled requests are to be routed back to their sources along the same paths. We simply reverse the above algorithm, by making each ascending loop descend, and vice-versa. In the case where conflicts are allowed, the stacks need not be moved from processor to processor in the simulation of Theorem 7.1.1. They are simply implemented as an array at each processor, and elements to be stacked are stored in the processor in which the process is currently resident. Since the algorithm returns the fulfilled requests in a mirror-image of the original routing, each process will be back in the correct place when it wishes to remove a particular item from its stack. □

10.5. Exercises

10.1 Prove that if n is even, then there are $n!/(2^{n/2}(n/2)!)$ perfect matchings on n vertices.

10.2 Give a detailed analysis of the set-up time in Theorem 10.3.1.

10.3 Show how to implement the algorithm of Theorem 10.3.1 on the shuffle-exchange or cube-connected cycles interconnection pattern without asymptotic increase in resources.

11   Unbounded Fan-in Parallelism

We saw in Section 6.2 that networks with large word-size and large number of processors are extremely powerful. Let us consider networks with polynomial word-size, which we will call *massively parallel computers* since they can have an exponential number of processors. Our interest in such networks in Chapter 6 stemmed, not from a belief that an exponential number of processors is practical, but from the observation that it is possible to derive efficient algorithms for more reasonable models by using them as sub-routines on a small number of inputs. Thus, with our interest aroused, we now turn to the more general question of characterizing the computational power of massively parallel computers. In particular, we wish to characterize the languages which can be accepted in constant time.

It is clear that neither the parallel computation thesis nor the extended parallel computation thesis holds for massively parallel computers, in particular both theses run into trouble when sub-logarithmic running-time is involved. We saw in Section 6.2 that much can be achieved in sub-logarithmic running-time by a massively parallel computer (including recognition of every language in NP). This was noted by Blum [13], who interpreted this as saying that the parallel computation thesis is "wrong", a sentiment opposed by this author [91,94]. The central aim of this chapter is to derive a parallel computation thesis which does hold for massively parallel computers, even for constant running-time. The material comes from Parberry and Schnitger [99].

In the first section we meet an unbounded fan-in circuit model and see that it is equivalent to a shared-memory machine. The second section introduces the final parallel machine model of this Monograph, the alternating Turing machine. Section three contains simulations between alternating Turing machines and shared-memory machines and derives a new parallel computation thesis from the evidence that they provide.

11.1. Unbounded Fan-in Circuits

We define a *uniform unbounded fan-in circuit* analogously to the uniform circuit of Section 9.3, with the following exceptions.

1. The gates are unbounded fan-in ANDs, ORs and unary negations.
2. We require that the connection and gate languages be recognizable by a linear-time deterministic Turing machine (that is, a deterministic Turing machine which runs in time $O(\log Z(n))$, where $Z(n)$ is the size of the circuit).

In the current literature, the size $Z(n)$ is usually defined to be the number of wires, instead of the number of gates. Note that these two measures are equivalent to within a polynomial provided $Z(n) = \Omega(n)$ (which is the case for all but the most degenerate circuits). Unbounded fan-in circuits can easily be modified to compute functions (rather than just act as acceptors) in the usual manner.

Clearly the negations can be pushed back to the level immediately before the inputs by application of De Morgan's laws, as follows. Suppose we have a circuit built from unbounded fan-in ANDs, ORs and unary negations. We will build an equivalent circuit from only AND and OR gates, using the inputs and their negation, whilst increasing the size by a factor of two and conserving the depth. Suppose the circuit has input $x_0,...,x_{n-1}$. Let $\overline{x}_0,...,\overline{x}_{n-1}$ denote the negations of these inputs. Define $\nu(x_i) = x_i$ and $\overline{\nu}(x_i) = \overline{x}_i$, for $0 \leq i < n$. The new circuit is constructed level-by-level from the inputs as follows. For each gate g in the original circuit, with inputs from gates $g_1,...,g_m$ for some $m > 0$, there are two gates $\nu(g)$ and $\overline{\nu}(g)$ in the new circuit. There are three cases to consider:

1. g is an OR gate. In this case, $\nu(g)$ is an OR gate with inputs from gates $\nu(g_1),...,\nu(g_m)$ and $\overline{\nu}(g)$ is an AND gate with inputs from gates $\overline{\nu}(g_1),...,\overline{\nu}(g_m)$.
2. g is an AND gate. In this case, $\nu(g)$ is an AND gate with inputs from gates $\nu(g_1),...,\nu(g_m)$ and $\overline{\nu}(g)$ is an OR gate with inputs from gates $\overline{\nu}(g_1),...,\overline{\nu}(g_m)$.
3. g is a unary negation ($m = 1$). Then $\nu(g)$ is simply a wire from $\overline{\nu}(g_1)$ and $\overline{\nu}(g)$ is a wire from $\nu(g_1)$.

It is easy to prove by induction on the level that for every gate g in the original circuit, gate $\nu(g)$ in the new circuit outputs the same value as g, and $\overline{\nu}(g)$ its negation. This is a classical technique in circuit design known as *double-rail logic.* It has been used extensively in other machine models for much the same purpose (see, for example, [18,42,48]).

Shared-memory machines and unbounded fan-in circuits are very closely related.

Theorem 11.1.1 (Stockmeyer and Vishkin [119]) A uniform unbounded fan-in circuit of depth $D(n)$ and size $Z(n)$ can be simulated by a shared-memory machine with the minimal instruction-set, $Z(n)^{O(1)}$ processors and time $O(D(n))$.

Proof. (Sketch) Without loss of generality, assume that the circuit is built from unbounded fan-in OR gates and unary negation gates. We will use $Z(n)^{2+c}$ processors, where c is a constant which depends on the constants associated with the Turing machine in the uniformity condition. We reserve a shared-memory location for the value of each gate (initially set to zero except for the inputs, which are counted as gates for this purpose). Suppose $S[j]$ is the location reserved for gate j, $0 \leq j < n$.

Processor $<i,j>$, $0 \leq i,j < Z(n)$ determines whether the output from gate i goes into gate j, and the type of gate j. It does this by using a team of $2^{O(\log Z(n))} = Z(n)^{O(1)}$ processors to simulate the deterministic Turing machines for the connection and gate languages in constant time (see Lemma 6.2.1). If processor $<i,j>$ finds that the link does exist, then it does the following:

(i)   If gate j is an OR and $S[i] = 1$, then it attempts to write a 1 into $S[j]$.

(ii) If gate j is a unary negation, then it sets $S[j]$ to the negation of the value in $S[i]$.

The running time is thus proportional to the depth of the circuit, whilst the number of processors is polynomial in the size. The output can be collected from the appropriate shared-memory locations according to the output convention of the circuit, and dealt with according to the output convention of the shared-memory machine. The details of the book-keeping computation necessary to manage the team-work have been omitted; the techniques of Chapter 6 suffice. $\square$

Theorem 11.1.2 (Stockmeyer and Vishkin [119]) A shared-memory machine with the minimal instruction-set, word-size $W(n)$, processors $P(n)$ and time $T(n)$ can be simulated by a uniform unbounded fan-in circuit of depth $O(T(n))$ and size $T(n)W(n)^{O(1)}P(n)^{O(1)}$.

Proof. See Exercise 11.1. $\square$

Thus size and depth of a uniform unbounded fan-in circuit is equivalent to processors and time of a shared-memory machine (provided that, for the latter, the running-time is at most a polynomial in the number of processors), the first pair of resources by a constant multiple, and the second pair by a polynomial. Suppose we define the *address complexity* of a parallel machine to be the number of bits necessary to describe a single unit of hardware, for example, the word-size of a shared-memory machine or network, and log of the size of a uniform unbounded fan-in circuit. Then, even if we modify the uniformity condition of an unbounded fan-in circuit to include acceptance of the gate and connection languages by a polynomial-time deterministic Turing machine, we see that depth and address complexity of a uniform unbounded fan-in circuit is equivalent to time and address complexity of a shared-memory machine (provided that, for the latter, the running-time is at most a polynomial in the number of processors), the first pair of resources by a constant multiple, and the second pair by a polynomial.

There are many interesting functions which can be computed in constant depth and polynomial size by an unbounded fan-in circuit, for example, the addition of two integers (see Exercise 11.2). However, many apparently simple functions require superpolynomial size in order to obtain constant depth. One such problem is the *parity function,* which takes n bits as input, and outputs 1 if there are an odd number of ones in the input, and 0 otherwise. Independently, Furst, Saxe and Sipser [34] and Ajtai [4] proved that a superpolynomial number of processors is required to compute the parity of n bits in constant time on a non-uniform model. Subsequently, Andrew Yao [134] has shown that $2^{n^{1-\lambda}}$ processors are necessary, for some real number $\lambda > 0$. A slightly tighter result was obtained by Hastad [51]. The latter results imply an $\Omega(\log n/\log \log n)$ lower-bound on depth for polynomial size. Both of these results can be matched by upper-bounds using Lemma 6.1.5, Theorem 6.1.10 and Theorem 11.1.2 (see Exercise 11.2).

11.2. Alternating Turing Machines

A k-tape *alternating Turing machine* [18] is similar to the standard Turing machine, but has the extra ability to make existential and universal guesses. It has k read-write *work-tapes,* a finite-state control, and random-access to its input via a write-only *index-tape.* The latter device is necessary if we are to discuss sublinear running-time (otherwise, as with the standard deterministic Turing machine, at least linear time is required to scan the input tape). It also has a read-only *guess-tape*. All tapes are infinite in one direction, and have cells numbered 1,2,..., each of which can hold a single symbol. Each tape has a single head, which scans a single tape cell. For technical reasons we will use a slightly non-standard alternating Turing machine model. Formally, a k-tape alternating Turing machine is a 10-tuple $(Q,\Gamma,\Sigma,\delta,q_0,q_a,q_r,q_e,q_u)$, where:

Σ is a finite *input alphabet*. Without loss of generality, we will take $\Sigma = \{0,1\}$.

Γ is a finite *tape alphabet*, $\Sigma \subset \Gamma$. Without loss of generality, we will take $\Gamma = \{0,1,b\}$, where b is the distinguished blank symbol.

Q is a finite set of states, including five distinct distinguished states, as follows.

q_0 is the *initial state*, q_a the *accept state*, q_r the *reject state*, q_e the *existential state* and q_u the *universal state*.

δ is the transition function. If $\Delta = \{left,stay,right\}$ is the set of directions in which a tape-head may move, then

$$\delta:\Sigma\times(Q-\{q_a,q_r,q_e,q_u\})\times\Gamma^{k+1}\rightarrow Q\times(\Gamma\times\Delta)^k\times(\Sigma\times\Delta)\times\Delta.$$

We define a *configuration* of an alternating Turing machine in the same manner as a deterministic Turing machine (see, for example, Aho, Hopcroft and Ullman [3], where it is called an *instantaneous description*); that is, it is a snapshot of the machine at some instant in time. A configuration with state q_e or q_u is called a *branching* configuration, all others are called *non-branching*. A configuration with state q_a or q_r is called a *halting* configuration. An alternating Turing machine is started with all heads in the first cell of their respective tapes, and all tape cells blank except for the first cell on the index tape, which contains the symbol '1'. The finite-state control is in state q_0. This is called the *initial configuration*. Consider an arbitrary configuration of an alternating Turing machine. The action of the machine on input $x_1,x_2,...,x_n$ is similar to that of a deterministic Turing machine, except where branching configurations are concerned. The contents of the index tape are interpreted as the binary representation of some non-negative integer i (with its least-significant bit in the first tape-cell).

(i)   Suppose the finite-state control is in state $q\in Q-\{q_a,q_r,q_e,q_u\}$, symbol $s_0\in\Gamma$ is under the guess-head, symbols $s_1,s_2,...,s_k$ are under the k work-tape heads, and:

$$\delta(x_i,q,s_0,s_1,...,s_k) = \big(r,(t_1,d_1),...,(t_k,d_k),(t_{k+1},d_{k+1}),d_{k+2}\big).$$

Then t_j is written in the cell under the head on the jth work-tape and the head is moved one cell in direction d_j, $1 \le j \le k$, t_{k+1} is written in the cell under the head on the index-tape and the index-head is moved one cell in direction d_{k+1}, the guess-head is moved one cell in direction d_{k+2}, and the finite-state control moves into state r. The new configuration thus obtained is called the *successor* of the original. A configuration is called *accepting* if its successor is accepting. The *time requirement* of the original configuration is defined to be one plus the time requirement of its successor. The *alternation requirement* of the original configuration is defined to be equal to the alternation requirement of its successor.

(ii)   If the finite-state control is in state $q \in \{q_a, q_r\}$ then the alternating Turing machine halts. If $q = q_a$ then the configuration is called *accepting*. The *time requirement* and *alternation requirement* is defined to be zero in both cases.

(iii)   Suppose the finite-state control is in state q_u or q_e and the guess-head is on cell g of the guess-tape. The alternating Turing machine is restarted in state q_0, with its work-tapes and index-tape unaltered, a random string of symbols from Σ written on cells one through g of the guess-tape (the remaining cells left blank), and the guess-head returned to the first cell. Each of these 2^g possible new configurations are called *successors* of the original configuration. The configuration is said to be *accepting* if either:

(a)   The finite-state control was in state q_e and at least one of its successors is accepting (existential branching), or

(b)   The finite-state control was in state q_u and all of its successors are accepting (universal branching).

The *time requirement* of the original configuration is defined to be one plus the longest time requirement of its successors. The *alternation requirement* is defined to be one plus the smallest alternation requirement of its accepting successors in the case of existential branching, and one plus the largest alternation requirement of its successors in the case of universal branching (and is taken to be zero if no accepting successors exist).

An alternating Turing machine is said to *accept* its input if its initial configuration is accepting. The language recognized by an alternating Turing machine is the set of accepted strings over alphabet Σ. An alternating Turing machine is said to run in *time* T(n) if, for all input strings of length n, the initial configuration has time requirement bounded above by T(n). It is said to use A(n) *alternations* if, for all input strings of length n, the initial configuration has alternation requirement bounded above by A(n).

Note that we can constrain polynomial-time alternating Turing machines to alternate between existential and universal branching (separated by deterministic computation); hence the nomenclature "alternations" (see Exercise 11.4). One standard result on alternating Turing machines that we will need is the following:

Theorem 11.2.1 (Chandra, Kozen and Stockmeyer [18]) Alternating Turing machines which run in polynomial time and constant alternations recognize exactly the polynomial-time hierarchy.

The reader unfamiliar with the polynomial-time hierarchy should consult Stockmeyer [120] or Garey and Johnson [39].

11.3. A New Parallel Computation Thesis

For the purposes of this section, we call a shared-memory machine *reasonable* provided it has the general instruction-set (see Section 3.1) and has $T(n) = W(n)^{O(1)}$. First we consider the simulation of a T(n) time-bounded, W(n) word-size bounded shared-memory machine on an alternating Turing machine. We say that $W(n) = \Omega(\log n)$ is *time-constructible* if a k-tape deterministic Turing machine can, when given the binary representation of n, compute the binary representation of W(n) in time O(W(n)). Most useful functions are time-constructible, for example, polynomials and poly-logs.

Theorem 11.3.1 Suppose W(n) is time-constructible. An alternating Turing machine can simulate a T(n) time-bounded, W(n) word-size shared-memory machine with the minimal instruction-set using O(T(n)) alternations and time O(T(n)W(n)).

Proof. (Sketch). Let M be a shared-memory machine which runs in time T(n) and uses word-size W(n). Let $x_1, x_2, ..., x_n$ be an input to M. For the purposes of this proof, we will assume that each $x_i \in \{0,1\}$. In general, each x_i will be an integer of at most W(n) bits. In this case, the input to the alternating Turing machine will be a binary encoding of this sequence. We will demonstrate an alternating Turing machine which accepts this input string iff M does. On input $x_1, x_2, ..., x_n$, the alternating Turing machine first determines n in time O(log n) by successively checking whether input-tape cells 0,1,2,4,... contain the blank symbol (we assume without loss of generality that n is a power of 2), and then computes $w = W(n)$. During the simulation of M, the alternating Turing machine represents individual registers, memory locations and time-counts with a sequence of $O(w)$ contiguous work-tape cells. The program of M is stored in the finite-state control. We will write $I[l]$ for the lth instruction of this program, $l \geq 1$.

Each of the following mutually recursive Boolean procedures returns the value of the quantified Boolean formula given as its statement part. Quantified variables range over all possible values of length w.

procedure target(p,t,h)
    comment returns true if processor p changes register r_h at time t
    $\exists l \, (pc(p,t,l) \, \wedge$
    $(I[l]$ is of the form "$r_h \leftarrow x$" or "$r_{r_i} \leftarrow r_j$" with local(i,p,t-1,h)))

procedure write(p,t,h)
    comment returns true if processor p writes into shared-memory cell s_i at time t
    $\exists l \, (pc(p,t,l) \, \wedge \, (I[l]$ is "$s_{r_i} \leftarrow r_j$") $\wedge \, local(i,p,t-1,h))$

procedure result(p,t,v)
    comment returns true if processor p computes value v at time t
    $\exists l \, (pc(p,t,l) \, \wedge$
    (**case** $I[l]$ **of**
        "$r_i \leftarrow constant$": const $= v$
        "$r_i \leftarrow r_j \circ r_k$": $\exists v_1 \exists v_2 \, (local(j,p,t-1,v_1) \, \wedge \, local(k,p,t-1,v_2) \, \wedge \, (v = v_1 \circ v_2))$
        "$r_i \leftarrow r_{r_j}$": $\exists v_1 \, (local(j,p,t-1,v_1) \, \wedge \, local(v_1,p,t-1,v))$
        "$r_{r_i} \leftarrow r_j$": local(j,p,t-1,v)
        "$r_i \leftarrow PID$": $v = p$
        "$r_i \leftarrow s_{r_j}$": $\exists v_1 \, (local(j,p,t-1,v_1) \, \wedge \, shared(v_1,p,t-1,v))$
        "$s_{r_i} \leftarrow r_j$": local(j,p,t-1,v)
    ))

procedure pc(p,t,l)

    comment returns true if program-counter of processor p at time t is l

    $(t = 0 \ \wedge \ l = 1) \ \vee \ (pc(p,t-1,0) \ \wedge \ l = 0) \ \vee$

        $\exists k \ \big(pc(p,t-1,k) \ \wedge$

        (**case** I[k] **of**

            "**goto** m **if** $r_i \geq 0$": $\exists v$ local(i,p,t 1,v) $\wedge$

                                (**if** $v \geq 0$ **then** l = m **else** l = k+1)

            "halt": l = 0

            others: l = k+1

        ))

procedure local(i,p,t,v)

    comment returns true if register r_i of processor p gets value v at time t

    $(t = 0 \ \wedge \ v = 0) \ \vee$

    $(target(p,t,i) \ \wedge \ result(p,t,v)) \ \vee$

    $(\neg target(p,t,i) \ \wedge \ local(i,p,t-1,v))$

procedure shared(i,t,v)

    comment returns true if shared-memory cell s_i contains v at time t

    $(t = 0 \ \wedge \ 1 \leq i \leq n \ \wedge \ v = x_i) \ \vee$

    $(t = 0 \ \wedge \ i > n \ \wedge \ v = 0) \ \vee$

    $(\ \exists p \ (write(i,p,t) \ \wedge \ result(p,t,v) \ \wedge \ \neg \exists \ q < p \ write(i,q,t))) \ \vee$

    $((\neg \ \exists p \ write(p,t)) \ \wedge \ shared(i,t-1,v))$

    The Boolean operations $\wedge$ and $\vee$ are computed by branching universally and existentially respectively. Negations can be computed directly, or pushed back to the final states (see [18]). Quantifiers are computed by guessing quantified values. The simulation of individual instructions of M is carried out deterministically. The alternating Turing machine simulates M by computing $\exists t \ (\forall p \ (pc(p,t,0)) \ \wedge \ shared(0,t,1))$.

    We claim that any call to procedures result(p,t,v), target(p,t,h), write(i,p,t), pc(p,t,l), local(i,p,t,v) or shared(i,t,v) requires at most O(t) alternations. Let r (t), t (t), w (t), p (t), l (t) and s (t) denote the number of alternations required by these procedures respectively. Then:

$$r \ (0) = t \ (0) = w \ (0) = p \ (0) = l \ (0) = s \ (0) = 0$$

174

and:

$$r\,(t) \le \max\bigl(p\,(t){+}2, l\,(t{-}1){+}6, s\,(t{-}1){+}6\bigr)$$

$$t\,(t) \le \max\bigl(p\,(t){+}2, l\,(t{-}1){+}4\bigr)$$

$$w\,(t) \le \max\bigl(p\,(t){+}2, t\,(t){+}2\bigr)$$

$$p\,(t) \le \max\bigl(p\,(t{-}1){+}3, l\,(t{-}1){+}7\bigr)$$

$$l\,(t) \le \max\bigl(t\,(t){+}3, r\,(t){+}2, l\,(t{-}1){+}2\bigr)$$

$$s\,(t) \le \max\bigl(w\,(t){+}6, r\,(t){+}5, s\,(t{-}1){+}3\bigr)$$

Thus, in particular, $s\,(t) \le 28t{+}21$, and so the simulation of a T(n) time-bounded shared-memory machine uses O(T(n)) alternations. If M has the minimal instruction-set, then the computation between each alternation takes time O(W(n)) (since it only involves guessing register contents, and simulating local instructions of M). This gives the required result. □

Note that if the shared-memory machine has the general instruction-set, then the running-time of the alternating Turing machine increases by only a polynomial.

Corollary 11.3.2 Suppose W(n) is time-constructible. An alternating Turing machine can simulate a reasonable T(n) time-bounded, W(n) word-size shared-memory machine using O(T(n)) alternations and time $W(n)^{O(1)}$.

Next we consider the converse: simulation of an alternating Turing machine on a shared-memory machine.

Theorem 11.3.3 Suppose T(n) is time-constructible. A shared-memory machine with the minimal instruction-set can simulate a T(n) time-bounded, A(n) alternation-bounded k-tape alternating Turing machine in time O(A(n)) and word-size O(T(n)A(n)).

Proof. (Sketch). The shared-memory machine first evaluates T(n) in constant time and word-size O(T(n)) (by use of Lemma 6.1.1), and constructs a look-up table showing, for every non-branching configuration, the configuration which follows by the rules of δ in t steps of the alternating Turing machine, $1 \le t \le$ T(n), (with the convention that once the alternating Turing machine enters a halting or branching configuration, then it remains there). The table can be constructed in constant time by utilizing the technique used in the proof of Lemma 6.2.1. A slight modification is necessary to determine the input pointer. The position of the head on the index-tape can easily be computed from the rule sequence in the same manner that the work-tape head positions are computed in Lemma 6.2.1.

The input pointers can be computed in constant time using word-size $T(n)^{1-\lambda}$ for any real number $\lambda > 0$, by using a technique similar to Lemma 6.1.5.

The simulation then proceeds as follows. The alternating Turing machine is simulated up to the point when a branching or halting configuration is entered for the first time (using the look-up table and Lemma 6.1.6). Call this new configuration C. If the accept state has been entered, then the computation is accepting, and this can be reported in the appropriate way (similarly if the reject state has been entered). Otherwise C is a branching configuration. The processors divide themselves into as many as $2^{O(T(n))}$ teams, one for each possible guess of the appropriate size (gleaned from the position of the guess-tape head in C), each of which continues the computation from the new configuration. When the teams have (recursively) completed their simulation, they report back as follows. In the case of existential branching, teams which find that their configurations are accepting attempt to write a one into a reserved shared-memory location which has been preset to zero. In the case of universal branching, teams which find that their configurations are rejecting attempt to write a zero into a reserved shared-memory location which has been preset to one.

Since the computation between branchings takes constant time, the entire simulation takes time $O(A(n))$. The word-size is dominated by $O(T(n)A(n))$ for the recursive branching. $\square$

Corollary 11.3.4 A reasonable shared-memory machine can simulate a $T(n)$ time-bounded, $A(n)$ alternation-bounded k-tape alternating Turing machine in time $O(A(n))$ and word-size $O(T(n)^2)$.

Proof. The shared-memory machine of Theorem 11.3.3 is reasonable since the number of alternations that an alternating Turing machine can perform is bounded above by its running time. $\square$

Results similar to Theorems 11.3.1 and 11.3.3 using alternating Turing machine space instead of time were attributed to Ruzzo and Tompa by Stockmeyer and Vishkin [119], and appear in that reference.

Thus we see that time and word-size on a reasonable shared-memory machine are simultaneously equivalent to alternations and time on an alternating Turing machine. The first equivalence holds to within a constant multiple, and the second to within a polynomial. This, together with the results of Section 11.1, provides evidence for a parallel computation thesis for unbounded fan-in parallelism: "In a parallel machine with unbounded fan-in communication, time and address complexity are simultaneously equivalent to alternations and time on an alternating Turing machine, the former to within a constant, and the latter a polynomial''. Our results also show that, for constant parallel time, address complexity is equivalent *to within a constant multiple* to time on a constant-alternation alternating Turing machine. Thus, for example, (by Theorem 11.2.1) constant-time massively parallel computers recognize exactly the languages in the polynomial-time hierarchy, and constant-time polynomial-size parallel computers recognize exactly the languages in Sipser's logarithmic-time hierarchy [117].

This new parallel computation thesis sheds some light on a dilemma raised by Cook [22]: It is popular to take alternating time as a measure of "parallel time" since (by Corollaries 11.3.2, 11.3.4 and Theorems 5.4.1 and 5.4.3) alternating time is polynomially related to sequential space, which implies that alternating Turing machines satisfy the parallel computation thesis (see Chapter 5). Unfortunately, as Cook points out, the alternating Turing machine has no resource corresponding to "hardware". This led Dymond to his formulation of the extended parallel computation thesis (see Section 9.4). Our results suggest that the reason why the alternating Turing machine appeared to have no resource corresponding to "hardware" was that the wrong resource had been chosen for "parallel time". Instead, *number of alternations* corresponds to "parallel time", and alternating time is related to, not hardware, but "address complexity", that is, the number of bits necessary to describe an individual unit of hardware.

This gives us our final justification for the unit-cost hypothesis. As far as our new parallel computation thesis is concerned, it is reasonable to charge a single unit of time for instructions which can be computed by a deterministic Turing machine in polynomial time. Given this condition, shared-memory machines (or networks) satisfy the new parallel computation thesis provided $T(n) = W(n)^{O(1)}$. This latter condition is in contrast with the original parallel computation thesis, which requires that $W(n) = T(n)^{O(1)}$ (see Section 5.4).

11.4. Exercises

11.1 Prove Theorem 11.1.2. That is, show that a shared-memory machine with the minimal instruction-set, word-size $W(n)$, processors $P(n)$ and time $T(n)$ can be simulated by a uniform unbounded fan-in circuit of depth $O(T(n))$ and size $T(n)W(n)^{O(1)}P(n)^{O(1)}$ (Hint: consider the technique used in Exercise

9.1).

11.2 Show that a uniform unbounded fan-in circuit can perform the addition of two non-negative integers in constant depth and polynomial size.

11.3 Give a uniform unbounded fan-in circuit for the parity function:

(i)   With size $O(2^n)$ and depth 5.

(ii) With size $2^{n^{1-\lambda}}$ for any $0 < \lambda < 1$ and constant depth. (Hint: such a circuit certainly exists, by Lemma 6.1.5 and Theorem 11.1.2. An explicit circuit can be constructed by applying the technique of Lemma 6.1.5 directly in the circuit model).

(iii) With polynomial size and depth $O(\log n/\log \log n)$. Try to make your circuit as small as possible. (Hint: such a circuit certainly exists, by Theorems 6.1.10 and 11.1.2. An explicit circuit can be constructed by applying the technique of Theorem 6.1.10 directly in the circuit model).

11.4 Show that a polynomial-time alternating Turing machine can be constrained to alternate between existential and universal branching (see Section 11.2).

12   Conclusion

We have presented a complexity theory of parallel computation based on a network model, and have argued that this model is good from both a practical and a theoretical point of view. The concept of a universal network is central to our arguments. We have found a practical universal network which can efficiently simulate the more general model. Thus the user of a practical universal network is free to program in a high-level language whose virtual architecture corresponds to (and the theoretician is provided with a motive for studying) the more abstract models.

We have seen various kinds of universal network. A literal simulation is often more efficient than a strongly-literal one in the sense that slightly fewer processors are needed (this is tied in strongly with our non-standard definition of parallel space). On the other hand, the number of processors can be reduced even further and the simulation made strongly-literal if the machines being simulated are restricted-access networks. Upper-bounds on the time required for these simulations can be asymptotically matched by lower-bounds. The situation is quite the opposite, however, in the non-literal case.

We have seen that networks with a large word-size (and large number of processors) are very powerful, even when those processors have a modest instruction-set. In particular, any computable function can be computed in constant time if sufficiently many processors are present. Furthermore, an arbitrary polynomial speed-up of a sequential machine is possible on a network which satisfies the parallel computation thesis (although an exponential speed-up is probably not).

The choice of a unit-cost measure of time, although controversial in sequential models, can be defended in the parallel case. We have seen a diversely-motivated assemblage of evidence for belief in the unit-cost hypothesis.

(a)   (Section 5.3). Networks with a unit-cost measure of time are "reasonable" in the sense that they satisfy the parallel computation thesis provided a $T(n)$ time-bounded network has instructions which can be simulated by a Turing machine using space $T(n)^{O(1)}$ (with the addition of the extra requirement that $W(n) = T(n)^{O(1)}$).

(b) (Section 5.3). To ensure that individual processors behave like log-cost sequential machines, replace Turing machine space by deterministic Turing machine time in part (a) above.

(c) (Section 9.2). In practice, the average user would probably prefer to own a universal network, rather than go to the expense of fabricating special-purpose networks for each application. In this case, it is valid to use unit-cost charging for a $P(n)$ processor network whose instructions take time $O(\log P(n))$ on the universal machine.

(d) (Section 9.4). Networks with a unit-cost measure of time are "reasonable" in the sense that they satisfy the extended parallel computation thesis provided an $S(n)$ space-bounded network with word-size $W(n)$ has instructions which can be computed by a deterministic Turing machine using space $(W(n)S(n))^{O(1)}$ and $T(n)^{O(1)}$ reversals, provided that $P(n) = 2^{T(n)^{O(1)}}$ and $W(n) = 2^{T(n)^{O(1)}}$; note that it is sufficient to have $W(n) = T(n)^{O(1)}$ as in (a) above).

(e) (Section 9.4) As a special case of (d), networks with a unit-cost measure of time are "reasonable" in the sense that they are small and fast provided they have polynomial processors and word-size, poly-log running-time and instructions which can be computed by a deterministic Turing machine using polynomial space and poly-log reversals. These networks recognize exactly the languages in NC. NC is remarkably robust. For example, if we restrict the model to lazy-activation feasible networks with the minimal instruction-set, they still recognize exactly the languages in NC.

(f) (Section 11.3). Networks with a unit-cost measure of time are "reasonable" in the sense that they satisfy the new parallel computation thesis provided they have instructions which can be computed in polynomial time by a deterministic Turing machine (with the addition of the extra requirement that $T(n) = W(n)^{O(1)}$).

Thus the unit-cost hypothesis appears to hold for a wide range of instruction-sets far more powerful than the commonly-used arithmetic instruction-sets proposed in Section 3.1.

There is currently much argument amongst researchers in parallel complexity theory as to what constitutes a good model of a parallel computer. The general consensus is that the parallel computation thesis is too weak, since it characterizes only parallel time, and allows the number of processors to grow exponentially. The extended parallel computation thesis (in the form of NC) appears to be one of the most popular paradigms, although an equally large body of researchers insist on further restrictions based on current technological trends. We have attempted to impartially map out the limits of the unit-cost hypothesis within the most widely-used frameworks.

References

1. L. Adleman, "Two theorems on random polynomial time," *Proc. 19th Ann. IEEE Symp. on Foundations of Computer Science*, pp. 75-83, 1978.

2. A. Aggarwal, B. Chazelle, L. Guibas, C. O'Dunlaing, and C. Yap, "Parallel computational geometry," *Proc. 26th Ann. IEEE Symp. on Foundations of Computer Science*, pp. 468-477, Portland, Oregon, Oct. 1985.

3. A. V. Aho, J. E. Hopcroft, and J. D. Ullman, *The Design and Analysis of Computer Algorithms,* Addison-Wesley, 1974.

4. M. Ajtai, "Σ_1^1-formulae on finite structures," *Annals of Pure and Applied Logic*, vol. 24, pp. 1-48, 1983.

5. M. Ajtai, J. Komlós, and E. Szemerédi, "An O(n.log n) sorting network," *Proc. 15th Ann. ACM Symp. on Theory of Computing*, pp. 1-9, Boston Mass., Apr. 1983.

6. M. Ajtai, J. Komlós, and E. Szemerédi, "Sorting in c.log n parallel steps," *Combinatorica*, vol. 3, pp. 1-48, 1983.

7. N. Alon, "Expanders, sorting in rounds and superconcentrators of limited depth," *Proc. 17th Ann. ACM Symp. on Theory of Computing*, pp. 98-102, Providence, Rhode Island, May 1985.

8. H. Alt, T. Hagerup, K. Mehlhorn, and F. P. Preparata, "Simulation of idealized parallel computers on more realistic ones," Unpublished Manuscript, 1986.

9. R. Anderson, "A parallel algorithm for the maximal path problem," *Proc. 17th Ann. ACM Symp. on Theory of Computing*, pp. 33-37, Providence, Rhode Island, May 1985.

10. K. E. Batcher, "Sorting networks and their applications," *Proc. AFIPS Spring Joint Computer Conference*, vol. 32, pp. 307-314, Apr. 1968.

11. P. Beame, "Limits on the power of concurrent-write parallel machines," *Proc. 18th Ann. ACM Symp. on Theory of Computing*, pp. 169-176, Berkeley, CA, May 1986.

12. M. Ben-Or, E. Feig, D. Kozen, and P. Tiwari, "A fast parallel algorithm for determining all roots of a polynomial with real roots," *Proc. 18th Ann. ACM Symp. on Theory of Computing*, pp. 340-349, Berkeley, CA, May 1986.

13. N. Blum, "A note on the 'parallel computation thesis'," *Inf. Proc. Lett.*, vol. 17, pp. 203-205, 1983.

14. R. V. Book, "Translational lemmas, polynomial time and $(\log n)^j$ space," *Theor. Comput. Sci.*, vol. 1, pp. 215-226, 1976.

15. A. Borodin, "On relating time and space to size and depth," *SIAM J. Comp.*, vol. 6, no. 4, pp. 733-744, Dec. 1977.

16. A. Borodin and J. E. Hopcroft, "Routing, merging and sorting on parallel models of computation," *Proc. 14th Ann. ACM Symp. on Theory of Computing*, May 1982.

17. R. C. Bose and R. J. Nelson, "A sorting problem," *J. ACM*, vol. 9, pp. 282-296, 1962.

18. A. K. Chandra, D. C. Kozen, and L. J. Stockmeyer, "Alternation," *J. ACM*, vol. 28, no. 1, pp. 114-133, Jan. 1981.

19. S. Cook, "A taxonomy of problems with fast parallel algorithms," *Inf. Control*, vol. 64, pp. 2-22, 1985.

20. S. Cook, C. Dwork, and R. Reischuk, "Upper and lower time bounds for parallel random access machines without simultaneous writes," *SIAM J. Comp.*, vol. 15, no. 1, pp. 87-97, Feb. 1986.

21. S. A. Cook, "Deterministic CFL's are accepted simultaneously in polynomial time and log squared space," *Proc. 11th Ann. ACM Symp. on Theory of Computing*, pp. 338-345, Apr. 1979.

22. S. A. Cook, "Towards a complexity theory of synchronous parallel computation," *L'Enseignement Mathematique*, vol. 30, 1980.

23. S. A. Cook and R. A. Reckhow, "Time-bounded random access machines," *J. Comput. Sys. Sci.*, vol. 7, no. 4, pp. 354-375, 1973.

24. P. W. Dymond, "Simultaneous resource bounds and parallel computations," Ph. D. Thesis, Technical Report TR145/80, Dept. of Computer Science, Univ. of Toronto, Aug. 1980.

25. P. W. Dymond and S. A. Cook, "Hardware complexity and parallel computation," *Proc. 21st Ann. IEEE Symp. on Foundations of Computer Science*, pp. 360-372, Oct. 1980.

26. P. W. Dymond and M. Tompa, "Speedups of deterministic machines by synchronous parallel machines," *J. Comput. Sys. Sci.*, vol. 30, pp. 149-161, 1985.

27. S. Even, *Graph Algorithms,* Pitman, 1979.

28. F. Fich, P. Ragde, and A. Wigderson, "Relationships between concurrent-write models of parallel computation," *Proc. 3rd ACM Symp. on Principles*

of Distributed Computing, pp. 179-184, 1984.

29. F. E. Fich, F. Meyer auf der Heide, P. Ragde, and A. Wigderson, "One, two, three ... infinity: lower bounds for parallel computation," *Proc. 17th Ann. ACM Symp. on Theory of Computing*, pp. 48-58, Providence, Rhode Island, May 1985.

30. J. P. Fishburn and R. A. Finkel, "Quotient networks," *IEEE Trans. Comput.*, vol. C-31, no. 4, Apr. 1982.

31. R. W. Floyd and D. E. Knuth, "The Bose-Nelson sorting problem," in *A Survey of Combinatorial Theory*, ed. J. N. Srivastava, North-Holland, 1973.

32. M. Flynn, "Very high-speed computing systems," *Proc. IEEE*, vol. 54, pp. 1901-1909, Dec. 1966.

33. S. Fortune and J. Wyllie, "Parallelism in random access machines," *Proc. 10th Ann. ACM Symp. on Theory of Computing*, pp. 114-118, 1978.

34. M. Furst, J. B. Saxe, and M. Sipser, "Parity, circuits and the polynomial time hierarchy," *Math. Syst. Theory*, vol. 17, no. 1, pp. 13-27, 1984.

35. O. Gabber and Z. Galil, "Explicit constructions of linear size superconcentrators," *Proc. 20th Ann. IEEE Symp. on Foundations of Computer Science*, pp. 364-370, Oct. 1979.

36. Z. Galil and V. Pan, "Improved processor bounds for algebraic and combinatorial problems in RNC," *Proc. 26th Ann. IEEE Symp. on Foundations of Computer Science*, pp. 490-495, Portland, Oregon, Oct. 1985.

37. Z. Galil and W. J. Paul, "An efficient general purpose parallel computer," *Proc. 13th Ann. ACM Symp. on Theory of Computing*, pp. 247-262, 1981.

38. Z. Galil and W. J. Paul, "An efficient general purpose parallel computer," *J. ACM*, vol. 30, no. 2, pp. 360-387, Apr. 1983.

39. M. R. Garey and D. S. Johnson, *Computers and Intractability: a Guide to the Theory of NP-completeness,* W. H. Freeman, 1979.

40. H. Gazit, "An optimal randomized parallel algorithm for finding connected components in a graph," *Proc. 27th Ann. Symp. on Foundations of Computer Science*, pp. 492-501, October 1986.

41. L. M. Goldschlager, "Synchronous parallel computation," Ph. D. Thesis, Technical Report TR-114, Dept. of Computer Science, Univ. of Toronto, Dec. 1977.

42. L. M. Goldschlager, "The monotone and planar circuit value problems are log space complete for P," *SIGACT News*, vol. 9, no. 2, pp. 25-29, 1977.

43. L. M. Goldschlager, "A space efficient algorithm for the monotone planar circuit value problem," *Inf. Proc. Lett.*, vol. 10, no. 1, pp. 25-27, Feb. 1980.

44. L. M. Goldschlager, "ε-productions in context-free grammars," *Acta Inf.*, vol. 16, no. 3, pp. 303-308, 1981.

45. L. M. Goldschlager, "A universal interconnection pattern for parallel computers," *J. ACM*, vol. 29, no. 4, pp. 1073-1086, Oct. 1982.

46. L. M. Goldschlager and R. P. Brent, "A parallel algorithm for context free parsing," *Australian Computer Science Communications*, vol. 6, no. 1, 1984.

47. L. M. Goldschlager and A. M. Lister, *Computer science: a modern introduction,* Prentice-Hall, 1983.

48. L. M. Goldschlager and I. Parberry, "On the construction of parallel computers from various bases of Boolean functions," *Theor. Comput. Sci.*, vol. 43, no. 1, pp. 43-48, May 1986.

49. P. Hall, "On representations of subsets," *J. London Math. Soc.*, vol. 10, pp. 26-30, 1935.

50. J. Hartmanis and J. Simon, "On the power of multiplication in random access machines," *Proc. 15th Ann. IEEE Symp. on Switching and Automata Theory*, pp. 13-23, 1974.

51. J. Hastad, "Improved lower bounds for small depth circuits," *Proc. 18th Ann. ACM Symp. on Theory of Computing*, pp. 6-20, Berkeley, CA, May 1986.

52. F. Meyer auf der Heide, "Efficiency of universal parallel computers," *Acta Inf.*, vol. 19, pp. 269-296, 1983.

53. F. Meyer auf der Heide, "Infinite cube-connected cycles," *Inf. Proc. Lett.*, vol. 16, pp. 1-2, Jan. 1983.

54. F. Meyer auf der Heide, "Efficient simulations among several models of parallel computers," *SIAM J. Comp.*, vol. 15, no. 1, pp. 106-119, Feb. 1986.

55. F. Meyer auf der Heide and R. Reischuk, "On the limits to speed up parallel machines by large hardware and unbounded communication," *Proc. 25th Ann. IEEE Symp. on Foundations of Computer Science*, pp. 56-64, Singer Island, Florida, Oct. 1984.

56. F. Meyer auf der Heide and A. Wigderson, "The complexity of parallel sorting," *Proc. 26th Ann. IEEE Symp. on Foundations of Computer Science*, Portland, Oregon, Oct. 1985.

57. J. E. Hopcroft and J. D. Ullman, *Introduction to Automata Theory, Languages and Computation,* Addison-Wesley, 1979.

58. S. Jimbo and A. Maruoka, "Expanders obtained from affine transformations," *Proc. 17th Ann. ACM Symp. on Theory of Computing*, pp. 88-97, Providence, Rhode Island, May 1985.

59. N. Jones, "Space-bounded reducibility among combinatorial problems," *J. Comput. Sys. Sci.*, vol. 11, pp. 68-85, 1975.

60. A. R. Karlin and E. Upfal, "Parallel hashing - an efficient implementation of shared memory," *Proc. 18th Ann. ACM Symp. on Theory of Computing*, pp. 160-168, Berkeley, CA, May 1986.

61. R. M. Karp and R. J. Lipton, "Turing machines that take advice," *L'Enseignment Mathematique*, vol. 30, Feb. 1980.

62. R. M. Karp, E. Upfal, and A. Wigderson, "Constructing a perfect matching is in random NC," *Proc. 17th Ann. ACM Symp. on Theory of Computing*, pp. 23-32, Providence, Rhode Island, May 1985.

63. M. Klawe, "Limitations on explicit constructions of expanding graphs," *SIAM J. Comp.*, vol. 13, no. 1, pp. 46-56, Feb. 1984.

64. P. Klein and J. Reif, "An efficient parallel algorithm for planarity," *Proc. 27th Ann. Symp. on Foundations of Computer Science*, pp. 465-477, October 1986.

65. D. E. Knuth, "Sorting and Searching," *The Art of Computer Programming*, vol. 3, Addison-Wesley, 1973.

66. D. Kozen and C.-K. Yap, "Algebraic cell decomposition in NC," *Proc. 26th Ann. IEEE Symp. on Foundations of Computer Science*, pp. 515-521, Portland, Oregon, Oct. 1985.

67. C. P. Kruskal, "Upper and lower bounds on the performance of parallel algorithms," *Ph. D. Dissertation*, Courant Institute, New York Univ., 1981.

68. C. P. Kruskal and L. Rudolph, "Observations concerning multidimensional ultracomputers," Ultracomputer Note #6, Courant Institute, New York Univ., Jan. 1980.

69. R. E. Ladner, "The circuit value problem is log space complete for P," *SIGACT News*, vol. 7, no. 1, pp. 18-20, 1975.

70. R. E. Ladner and M. J. Fischer, "Parallel prefix computation," *J. ACM*, vol. 27, no. 4, pp. 831-838, Oct. 1980.

71. T. Lang, "Interconnections between processors and memory modules using the shuffle-exchange network," *IEEE Trans. Comput.*, vol. C-25, no. 5, May 1976.

72. F. T. Leighton, *Lecture Notes for 18.435, Theory of parallel computation and VLSI*, M.I.T., 1985.

73. F. T. Leighton, "Tight bounds on the complexity of parallel sorting," *IEEE Trans. Comput.*, vol. C-34, no. 4, Apr. 1985.

74. G. F. Lev, N. Pippenger, and L. G. Valiant, "A fast parallel algorithm for routing in permutation networks," *IEEE Trans. Comput.*, vol. C-30, no. 2, Feb. 1981.

75. M. Li and Y. Yesha, "New lower bounds for parallel computation," *Proc. 18th Ann. ACM Symp. on Theory of Computing*, pp. 177-187, Berkeley, CA, May 1986.

76. L. Lovasz, "Computing ears and branchings in parallel," *Proc. 26th Ann. IEEE Symp. on Foundations of Computer Science*, pp. 464-467, Portland, Oregon, Oct. 1985.

77. A. Lubotsky, R. Phillips, and P. Sarnak, "Explicit expanders and the Ramanujan conjecture," *Proc. 18th Ann. ACM Symp. on Theory of Computing*, pp. 240-246, Berkeley, CA, May 1986.

78. E. M. Luks and P. McKenzie, "Fast parallel computation with permutation groups," *Proc. 26th Ann. IEEE Symp. on Foundations of Computer Science*, pp. 505-514, Portland, Oregon, Oct. 1985.

79. N. Lynch, "Log space recognition and translation of parenthesis languages," *J. ACM*, vol. 24, no. 4, pp. 583-590, 1977.

80. G. Margulis, "Explicit constructions of superconcentrators," *Problemy Peredachi Informatsii*, vol. 9, no. 4, pp. 71-80, 1973.

81. W. F. McColl, "Planar crossovers," *IEEE Trans. Comput.*, vol. C-30, no. 3, 1981.

82. L. Meertens, "Recurrent ultracomputers are not log n - fast," Technical Report IW118/79, Dept. of Computer Science, Mathematisch Centrum, Sept. 1979.

83. G. L. Miller and J. Reif, "Parallel tree contraction and its application," *Proc. 26th Ann. IEEE Symp. on Foundations of Computer Science*, pp. 478-489, Portland, Oregon, Oct. 1985.

84. G. Miranker, L. Tang, and C. K. Wong, "A zero-time VLSI sorter," *IBM J. Res. Dev.*, vol. 27, no. 2, pp. 140-148, Mar. 1983.

85. K. Mulmuley, "A fast parallel algorithm to compute the rank of a matrix over an arbitrary field," *Proc. 18th Ann. ACM Symp. on Theory of Computing*, pp. 338-339, Berkeley, CA, May 1986.

86. D. Nassimi and S. Sahni, "Data broadcasting in SIMD computers," *IEEE Trans. Comput.*, vol. C-30, no. 2, pp. 101-106, Feb. 1981.

87. D. Nassimi and S. Sahni, "Parallel algorithms to set up the Benes permutation network," *IEEE Trans. Comput.*, vol. C-31, no. 2, Feb. 1982.

88. D. Nassimi and S. Sahni, "Parallel permutation and sorting algorithms and a new generalized connection network," *J. ACM*, vol. 29, no. 3, pp. 642-667, July 1982.

89. D. C. Opferman and N. T. Tsao-Wu, "On a class of rearrangeable switching networks," *Bell Syst. Tech. J.*, vol. 50, pp. 1579-1618, 1971.

90. J. Orenstein, T. H. Merrett, and L. Devroye, "Linear sorting with O(log n) processors," *BIT*, vol. 23, pp. 170-180, 1983.

91. I. Parberry, "A complexity theory of parallel computation," *Ph. D. Thesis*, Dept. of Computer Science, Univ. of Warwick, May 1984.

92. I. Parberry, "Some practical simulations of impractical parallel computers," in *VLSI: Algorithms and Architectures*, ed. P. Bertollazzi and F. Lucio, Proc. International Workshop on Parallel Computing and VLSI, pp. 27-37, North-Holland, 1985.

93. I. Parberry, "On the number of processors required to simulate Turing machines in constant parallel time," Technical Report CS-85-17, Dept. of Computer Science, Penn. State Univ., Aug. 1985.

94. I. Parberry, "Parallel speedup of sequential machines: a defense of the parallel computation thesis," *SIGACT News*, vol. 18, no. 1, pp. 54-67, 1986.

95. I. Parberry, "On recurrent and recursive interconnection patterns," *Inf. Proc. Lett.*, vol. 22, no. 6, pp. 285-289, May 1986.

96. I. Parberry, "On the time required to sum n semigroup elements on a parallel machine with simultaneous writes," in *Proc. 2nd International Workshop on Parallel Computing and VLSI*, Springer-Verlag Lecture Notes in Computer Science, vol. 227, pp. 296-304, Loutraki, Greece, July 1986.

97. I. Parberry, "Some practical simulations of impractical parallel computers," *Parallel Computing*, vol. 4, no. 1, pp. 93-101, Feb. 1987.

98. I. Parberry, "An improved simulation of space and reversal bounded deterministic Turing machines by width and depth bounded uniform circuits," *Inf. Proc. Lett.*, vol. 24, no. 6, April 1987.

99. I. Parberry and G. Schnitger, "Parallel computation with threshold functions (Preliminary Version)," in *Proc. Structure in Complexity Theory Conference*, Springer-Verlag Lecture Notes in Computer Science, vol. 223, pp. 272-290,

Berkeley, California, June 1986.

100. M. S. Paterson, "Improved sorting networks with O(log n) depth," Research Report 89, Dept. of Computer Science, Univ. of Warwick, Jan. 1987.

101. N. Pippenger, "Superconcentrators," *SIAM J. Comp.*, vol. 6, no. 2, June 1977.

102. N. Pippenger, "On simultaneous resource bounds," *Proc. 20th Ann. IEEE Symp. on Foundations of Computer Science*, pp. 307-311, Oct. 1979.

103. V. Pratt and L. J. Stockmeyer, "A characterization of the power of vector machines," *J. Comput. Sys. Sci.*, vol. 12, pp. 198-221, 1976.

104. F. P. Preparata and J. Vuillemin, "The cube-connected cycles: a versatile network for parallel computation," *Commun. ACM*, vol. 24, no. 5, pp. 300-309, May 1981.

105. M. J. Quinn and N. Deo, "Parallel algorithms and data structures in graph theory," Technical Report CS-82-098, Computer Science Dept., Washington State Univ., Oct. 1982, Revised June 1983.

106. J. Reif, "An optimal parallel bound for integer sorting," *Proc. 26th Ann. IEEE Symp. on Foundations of Computer Science*, pp. 496-504, Portland, Oregon, Oct. 1985.

107. J. Reif and L. Valiant, "Logarithmic time sort for linear size networks," *J. ACM*, vol. 34, no. 1, pp. 60-76, Jan. 1987.

108. W. L. Ruzzo, "On uniform circuit complexity," *J. Comput. Sys. Sci.*, vol. 22, no. 3, pp. 365-383, June 1981.

109. W. J. Savitch, "Relationships between nondeterministic and deterministic tape complexities," *J. Comput. Sys. Sci.*, vol. 4, no. 2, pp. 177-192, 1970.

110. W. J. Savitch, "Parallel random access machines with powerful instruction sets," *Math. Syst. Theory*, vol. 15, pp. 191-210, 1982.

111. A. Schorr, "Physical parallel devices are not much faster than sequential ones," *Inf. Proc. Lett.*, vol. 17, pp. 103-106, Aug. 1983.

112. J. T. Schwartz, "Ultracomputers," *ACM TOPLAS*, vol. 2, no. 4, pp. 484-521, Oct. 1980.

113. J. C. Sheperdson and H. E. Sturgis, "Computability of recursive functions," *J. ACM*, vol. 10, no. 2, pp. 217-255, 1963.

114. Y. Shiloach and U. Vishkin, "Finding the maximum, sorting and merging in a parallel computation model," *J. Algorithms*, vol. 2, pp. 88-102, 1981.

115. H. J. Siegal, "The theory underlying the partitioning of permutation networks," *IEEE Trans. Comput.*, vol. C-29, no. 9, Sept. 1980.

116. H. Simon, "A tight $\Omega(\log \log n)$-bound on the time for parallel RAM's to compute nondegenerated Boolean functions," *Inf. Control*, vol. 55, pp. 102-107, 1982.

117. M. Sipser, "Borel sets and circuit complexity," *Proc. 15th Ann. ACM Symp. on Theory of Computing*, pp. 61-69, Boston, Mass., Apr. 1983.

118. M. Snir, "On parallel searching," *SIAM J. Comp.*, vol. 14, no. 3, pp. 688-708, Aug. 1985.

119. L. Stockmeyer and U. Vishkin, "Simulation of parallel random access machines by circuits," *SIAM J. Comp.*, vol. 13, no. 2, pp. 409-422, May 1984.

120. L. J. Stockmeyer, "The polynomial time hierarchy," *Theor. Comput. Sci.*, vol. 3, pp. 1-22, 1977.

121. L. J. Stockmeyer and A. R. Meyer, "Word problems requiring exponential time: Preliminary Report," *Proc. 5th Ann. ACM Symp. on Theory of Computing*, pp. 1-9, Austin, Texas, 1973.

122. H. S. Stone, "Parallel processing with the perfect shuffle," *IEEE Trans. Comput.*, vol. C-20, no. 2, pp. 153-161, Feb. 1971.

123. S. S. Tseng and R. C. T. Lee, "A new parallel sorting algorithm based on min-mid-max operations," *BIT*, vol. 24, pp. 187-195, 1984.

124. E. Upfal, "A probabilistic relation between desireable and feasible models for parallel computation," *Proc. 16th Ann. ACM Symp. on Theory of Computing*, pp. 258-265, Washington, D.C., Apr.-May 1984.

125. U. Vazirani and V. Vazirani, "The two-processor scheduling problem is in R-NC," *Proc. 17th Ann. ACM Symp. on Theory of Computing*, pp. 11-21, Providence, Rhode Island, May 1985.

126. U. Vishkin, "Implementation of simultaneous memory address accesses in models that forbid it," *J. Algorithms*, vol. 4, no. 1, pp. 45-50, Mar. 1983.

127. U. Vishkin, "Synchronous parallel computation - a survey," Technical Report #71, Dept. of Computer Science, Courant Institute, New York Univ., Apr. 1983.

128. U. Vishkin, "A parallel-design space distributed implementation space (PDDI) general purpose computer," *Theor. Comput. Sci.*, vol. 32, no. 1,2, pp. 157-172, July 1984.

129. U. Vishkin and A. Wigderson, "Trade-offs between depth and width in parallel computation," *Proc. 24th Ann. IEEE Symp. on Foundations of Computer Science*, Tucson, Arizona, Nov. 1983.

130. D. C. Van Voorhis, "An improved lower bound for sorting networks," *IEEE Trans. Comput.*, vol. C-21, pp. 612-613, June 1972.

131. A. Waksman, "A permutation network," *J. ACM*, vol. 15, no. 1, pp. 159-163, Jan. 1968.

132. Y. Wallach, "Alternating sequential/parallel processing," *Springer-Verlag Lecture Notes in Computer Science*, vol. 127, 1982.

133. N. Wirth, *Algorithms+Data Structures=Programs,* Prentice-Hall, 1976.

134. A. C. Yao, "Separating the polynomial-time hierarchy by oracles," *Proc. 26th Ann. IEEE Symp. on Foundations of Computer Science*, Portland, Oregon, Oct. 1985.

Index

circuit-value problem, 50, 56-57, 59-61, 63, 79, 147

closed under polynomials, 55

collision, 162, 164

colour, 114-115

COM, *see* communication register

combinational circuit, 4, 17, 56, 60, 140

communication graph, 85-86

communication instruction, 23, 43, 46

communication line, 39, 41

communication register, 46, 150-151, 154, 157-159, 161

comparator, 4-11, 14-15, 19, 115-116

comparator network, 4, 6-10, 14-15, 19, 114, 116

compiler, 34

complement, 90

complete base, 56, 60

complete binary tree, 33, 80, 118, 157

completely-connected, 39-40, 46-47

composite algorithm, 89, 91-92, 94, 96, 100-101, 108, 111-112, 144, 159

computable, 24

computable function, 26

computation, 24, 41, 43

computation graph, 51-53

concentrate, 134-138, 141, 143

concurrent assignment, 27, 34

concurrent read, *see* simultaneous read

concurrent write, *see* simultaneous write

conditional assignment, 27

configuration, 51-53, 77-79, 109-111, 133-135, 170-172, 175-176

conglomerate, 46, 63

connection language, 167-169

constant-time constructible, 74-75

context-free grammar, 68-69

context-free membership problem, 69, 148

CRCW, 23

CREW, 23, 70

critical set, 86

critical string, 86

crossover, 60

cube, 89-91, 101-103, 105, 108, 151, 154, 158-159, 161, 164

cube-connected cycles, 89-90, 93-96, 100-101, 105, 107-112, 138, 152, 159, 164-165

cube-connected lines, 89, 96-101, 105, 107-109, 111-112, 138, 152, 159, 164

cube edge, 93, 98, 110-111

CVP, *see* circuit-value problem

cycle edge, 93, 96, 111, 155

De Morgan's Laws, 167

dedicated processor, 48-49, 149, 153, 155-161

degree, 21, 25, 30, 33, 39-40, 42-43, 46-47, 49, 86, 90-93, 95-96, 101, 113, 130, 137, 149-155, 157, 159-160

degree function, 41

DEGREE register, 40-41

delay, 48-49, 89, 92, 94, 107-109, 111, 138-139, 149-150, 152-153, 155, 157-159, 161, 163, 165

deliver, 134-138

depth, 4, 6, 8-9, 11-12, 14-15, 17-20,

145, 148-159, 161, 164, 166, 168-169, 177, 179-180

production, 68

program, 22, 40, 43

program-counter, 29-30, 35, 65, 82, 141, 174

quantifier, 53, 62

queue, 162-165

RAC, 2

RAM, 2, 22-23, 25-27, 29, 32, 34, 50

random NC, *see* NC, RNC

rank, 138

reachable set, 85

reachable symbol, 85-86

read, 2, 22-25, 40, 42-43, 45-46, 48-49, 70-72, 74, 80-83, 85, 133-135, 138, 141, 149, 151, 154, 157, 159, 161-163

read-only simulation, 146

reasonable encoding scheme, 52

recurrent interconnection pattern, template, 89, 94-101

recursive interconnection pattern, template, 95, 100

reduction to sorting, 139, 148, 150

register access conflict, *see* simultaneous read, simultaneous write

regular graph, 113-114

reject, 52, 65-66, 68

rejecting configuration, 176

reject state, 170, 176

restricted-access network, 46-47, 49, 85, 87, 137, 139, 149-150, 152-155, 157, 159, 179

restricted arithmetic instruction-set,

25, 29, 37, 42-43, 45, 49, 68, 70, 76, 79-80

reversal, 132, 138, 143-148, 180

right child, 34, 118, 121, 126-127

right-seeking, 126-127

right-shift, 25

RNC, 147

root bag, 118, 121, 123-124, 127-128

route, 17, 42, 48, 60, 91, 119, 138, 149, 152, 157-162, 164-165

Savitch's Theorem, 53, 64, 68

scatter, 105, 151-152, 154, 158

SE, *see* shuffle-exchange

selection, 26, 101

semigroup, 74-76, 87

sequencing, 26

sequential computation thesis, 28, 50

sequential space, 25, 28, 50-69, 132, 138, 140, 143-148, 177, 179-180

sequential time, 26, 47, 50, 52, 56-57, 59, 79-80, 144, 147, 150, 167, 169, 172, 180

set-up time, 48, 111, 138, 150, 152, 157-158

shared-memory machine, 2, 39, 43-45, 49, 62-63, 67, 70-84, 87, 137-139, 145-146, 148, 166, 168-169, 172, 175-177

shift, 25, 70-73

shuffle edge, 92, 109

shuffle-exchange, 89, 91-92, 95-96, 101, 105, 107-108, 138, 152, 159, 161, 164-165

SIMD, 21, 29-32, 38, 101

SIMDAG, 2, 28, 62-63

simple algorithm, 91, 144, 148